India on my Wheels

MY TRAVEL STORIES

GAYATRI VOHRA

BLUEROSE PUBLISHERS
India | U.K.

Copyright © Gayatri Vohra 2024

All rights reserved by author. No part of this publication may be reproduced, stored in a retrieval system or transmitted in any form or by any means, electronic, mechanical, photocopying, recording or otherwise, without the prior permission of the author. Although every precaution has been taken to verify the accuracy of the information contained herein, the publisher assumes no responsibility for any errors or omissions. No liability is assumed for damages that may result from the use of information contained within.

BlueRose Publishers takes no responsibility for any damages, losses, or liabilities that may arise from the use or misuse of the information, products, or services provided in this publication.

For permissions requests or inquiries regarding this publication, please contact:

BLUEROSE PUBLISHERS
www.BlueRoseONE.com
info@bluerosepublishers.com
+91 8882 898 898
+4407342408967

ISBN: 978-93-6261-093-5

Cover design: Rishav & Shivani
Typesetting: Sagar

First Edition: August 2024

This one is for you Arjun, with all my love.

Your spirit, love and light continue to inspire me every day.

Acknowledgement

This travel memoir is the culmination of countless journeys, not just across the geographical landscape of India, but also through the landscapes of my heart and mind. It would not have been possible without the support, inspiration, and guidance of many individuals, to whom I am deeply grateful.

Ajit, "*the Husband*" (as he is referred to in my stories), has been my unwavering pillar of support since the day I met him. He always encouraged my travels while never letting me doubt myself. We shared our responsibilities just as we shared our aspirations. My children, Gitanjali and Anirudh, have wholeheartedly supported my travels in every way. This book would not have been possible if not for the constant support of my family.

To all my co-travellers who have made my journeys so memorable - your companionship and our shared experiences have enriched my stories and you have contributed to my healing in your own unique ways. Thank you all from the bottom of my heart.

A huge shout out to Chief – as HV Kumar is fondly called. You have given me the confidence to step out and explore on my own. Without you, I doubt if I could have come this far.

Special thanks to Aman Channa, an ace photographer whom I follow on Instagram (@pixcellence_by_aman.channa). A lot of my travels in the recent times have been inspired by his stunning photographs.

I am deeply grateful to the countless strangers I encountered along the way. Their stories, their openness to share their world with me, and their generosity have truly left a mark on my heart. Some have even become friends for life. It is not just the places I visited but also the people I met that have made this journey unforgettable.

Lastly, to my readers, thank you for embarking on this journey with me. Your interest and enthusiasm for my stories will motivate me to continue exploring and sharing my adventures. While the journey is mine, it is also a reflection of the connections and relationships that have enriched my life and shaped my experiences. Thank you all for being a part of my journey.

Preface

"Life should not be a journey to the grave with the intention of arriving safely, in a pretty well-preserved body, but to skid in sideways in a cloud of smoke, chocolate in one hand, wine in the other, body totally used up, completely worn out, screaming - Now, THAT was a ride!"

Travel has been an integral part of my childhood, thanks to my father being in the Army. Moving to a new city every two years was a routine, sparking my curiosity to explore new places, make new friends, and create lasting memories. Many years later, as my thirst for adventure increased, off-roading seemed like a natural progression. Although I did not pursue it very seriously, I did have my fun. I and my constant companion for most of my adventures - my Scorpio car that I fondly called Rajjo, enjoyed every bit of it. The pure adrenaline rush one gets from driving on an off-the-road terrain creating your own path is incomparable. Knowing you can go anywhere irrespective of the kind of road you are travelling on is a very powerful feeling. You don't fear any terrain.

For me, life has been an off-the-road track. It has largely been beautiful but also sometimes unpredictable and unfair, taking me to places I was unprepared for. Childhood trauma and some unresolved issues led me into Depression. Despite having a very supportive family (my husband Ajit and our two wonderful kids, Gitanjali and Anirudh), I could sense that something was missing. While treatments provided temporary relief, I often found myself slipping back into the depressive phases. Travel was always a part of our lives, but these were really the touristy visits to regular touristy places. About 11 years ago, in the summer of 2013, I planned our first real road trip to Ladakh. This marked the beginning of many more exploratory travels. My love for driving made road trips a staple in my travels. As a natural progression to these journeys, I began writing my travel stories. Gradually, I realized that planning a road trip, embarking on one, and writing about it afterward was extremely cathartic. Slowly I began to heal. These experiences helped me evolve, teaching me humility and patience, and allowing me to shed a significant amount of emotional baggage that I had been carrying.

While many of my travels were with family and friends, I discovered the joy of solo travel. In fact, the most cathartic trips have been those I undertook alone. This book is a compilation of 11 journeys over the last 10 years, some solo, some with family and friends and even strangers too, covering the entire length of the country from Ladakh to Himachal Pradesh, Punjab, Rajasthan, Gujarat, Madhya Pradesh, Maharashtra, and all the way down to Karnataka and Tamil Nadu. My explorations were not just geographical but also culinary.

Each state has its own history, its own culinary nuances. The people I met along the way reinforced my belief in the goodness of humanity. Travel, indeed, has an extraordinary power to transform us. It broadens our horizons, enriches our understanding, and connects us to the myriad of experiences that make up the human tapestry. It is the unexpected friendships forged in the most unlikely places, the personal challenges overcome far away from home and the moments of sheer wonder that have made my journey thus far so worthwhile.

There is but one universal truth that lies in every travel tale that is told; the world is vast, beautiful and waiting to be discovered. I hope these stories ignite your wanderlust and remind you that, no matter how far we travel, the journey is always within. **It is the journey to the truth of who you are, the exploration of your deepest fears and desires, and the discovery of your authentic self.**

Bon voyage!

Contents

"Jan Mein Leh" - A Winter Himalayan Expedition
(January 2014) 1

The Golden Quadrilateral – The beginning of the journey called
'India On My wheels' (March 2016) 21

Beyond the Untamed Horizon -
Lahaul & Spiti (August 2016) 29

Mesmerising, Magical Rajasthan - A Solo Journey
(August 2017) 49

Kutch Nahin Dekha To Kuchh Nahi Dekha
(January - 2018) 79

Enchanting Shekhawati (March 2019) 105

The City Of Nawabs - Lucknow (April 2019) 117

The Sufi Trail ; Ajmer - Sarwar - Sambhar – Nagaur
(Nov 2019) 127

Punjab - The Land of Spirituality (November 2021) 137

Kuchh Din To Guzaro Gujarat Mein (January - 2022) 155

Meandering Through Peninsular India (June - 2022) 181

Echos and Reflections 237

"Jan Mein Leh" - A Winter Himalayan Expedition (January 2014)

Ladakh is one region which needs to be seen in all its seasons. I have childhood memories of Ladakh and even more recent ones from our family road trip in June 2013, but all of these were summer time visits. I had heard a lot about the winter landscape from my friends in the Army and it did intrigue me. The living conditions are so tough because of the extreme weather conditions that I always thought it was an impossibility to be able to travel within Ladakh in winters. And also, from memories of the childhood trips when my father was posted there, I was under the impression that Ladakh was closed to the civilians in winters. Of course, a lot has changed since then.

It all started in July 2013 when I joined a highway enthusiasts group called HVK - Fan, Forum and Message Board. That is when I got to know that travel within Ladakh was possible in winters. It was like a dream come true for me. I had to do this, and I had to do this soon. The excitement I felt was palpable. It had been far too long since I had done anything remotely crazy. This fitted the bill perfectly. It was time to push myself beyond my limits.

The target was fixed for end January 2014. The next thing to work on was who to go with. Taking a family member was never an option. For one, they had their own schedules and two, well, roughing out is not everyone's idea of fun. I asked 3 of my friends who were likely candidates but they refused. Ladakh in winters was incomprehensible. Just when I was giving up hope, a casual chat with a fellow HVKian brought me into a group of people who were planning on similar lines. A couple of days of discussions on WhatsApp and voila! Before I knew it the dates were fixed, the tickets were booked and an itinerary finalised. Hitesh, Rajesh, Shibu, Smitha, Chaitanya, Vineet, Bhaskar and me - Team 'Jan Mein Leh' was all set.

It was Aug - Sept 2013; five months to go and so much to prepare. Hotels, cabs, shoes, clothes and of course, most importantly exercise. Building up the stamina and preparing the body for temperatures upto -25° c and less with air that was extremely rarified. AMS (Acute Mountain Sickness) was a major concern. When one is driving into Ladakh, the ascent in terms of altitude is gradual which helps in the body getting well acclimatised. Here we were going to fly in. There would be a sudden change in oxygen levels in the atmosphere and not enough time for the body to acclimatise. Therefore, it was imperative that the lungs were strong enough.

Life is what it is and it will bring in its speed breakers. In the middle of all the excitement, there came in some health issues. And if my family had their way, they would have put a question mark on my going. In fact, there was a time when I was considering backing out. By the time all of that got sorted, it was one week through the month of December. With less than 6 weeks left, I had not started any preparations. Exercise had not even begun. Walking was not happening, so I started climbing the 10 floors to my apartment about 2-4 times every day. Steadily the lungs started supporting me and things seemed to be falling in place. Special jackets were ordered, shoes were done, quilted lowers, and gloves were bought and by the middle of January everything was in place. Well, exercise did become a bit erratic. Let's just say that I am just not cut out to exercise!

The first round of craziness came in when I sat down to pack my stuff. The list that got made out for 7 days was a long one. There were clothes - inner wear and outerwear (at any given point in time during the trip we were wearing about 6 layers on the upper body and 3 on the lower), food (cuppa noodles, dry fruits, chocolates, cheese slices – all high on calorie and protein quick eats), emergency medicines and oxygen cans. Packing all of this came with a few constraints -

1. we may have to carry our baggage on our own.
2. we were sharing the cabs - 4 people in 1, so we had to keep in mind the limited boot space.

The thing is medicines and essential emergency food couldn't be compromised upon. What got reduced were the clothes. For the kind of person I am, or rather was at that time, that was a task. A few discussions with the fellow travellers who are also bikers gave a very horrific solution; "Other than what you are wearing, just carry one more change." Only one change for SEVEN days?! That was an impossible thought. For me, not shampooing, bathing and changing everyday was unheard of. But there was no choice, and I did manage to pack just about that much. But in all my optimism I still did pack my shampoo and hair conditioner - just in case.

By this time, excitement for everyone was at its peak. The Team Jan Mein Leh was all set for the winter expedition.

Day 1 - 25th Jan, 2014.

The day started early. We had to be at the airport by 8.30 a.m. Though my excitement knew no bounds, I could sense nervousness creeping in. All sorts of thoughts were bombarding my mind. But there was no turning back now. While I had met Hitesh and Rajesh a couple of times during the last few months, I had not met the others, only interacted with them over chats. There were apprehensions galore, more so because I had never travelled with people I did not know. And this was a trip where we would be cut off from civilisation for a few days. All my apprehensions were put to rest as soon as I met them. They were very warm and welcoming people. This was going to be a fun trip.

The security check-in was a pain. I had to take off the jacket, the boots, empty the camera bag (that was a big one - camera, extra batteries, chargers, memory cards) and put them back in again, wear the jacket, wear the boots. Believe me, with so many layers on, wearing those boots was a task. While I was made to take off my boots, Rajesh went in like a breeze without having to take them off and Bhaskar had to take off only one boot. Why would they ask anyone to do that? Somethings will never make sense in the Indian context.

With the security check done, we were that much closer to the destination. An hour and fifteen minutes in the flight, I couldn't wait no more. The views from the aircraft on take-off were nothing to write home about because I was on the east side. The sunrise played spoilt-sport. As we approached Leh and prepared for landing, it was a different scenario. The mountain ranges were either brown or white or brown with splashes of white - just like a pencil sketch. It was as if one could roll down the windows and touch them. I could see a frozen lake from the aircraft, and just when we were landing, I saw the road going up to Khardungla. The sight of the zigzag line cutting across the snow-clad mountain was breath-taking.

Leh airport is a very small, quaint airport. One could feel the lack of oxygen and the dryness in the air as soon as one stepped out of the aircraft. For the first time in my life, I saw blankets being used as curtains. It was a cold wind of a very different kind. At the airport we were welcomed by our cab drivers Dorjey and Dorji. They were going to be with us through our stay. After reaching the hotel we had tea, sandwiches and some hot maggi. We placed the order for lunch and then settled into our rooms to freshen up. The rooms were comfortable. Heating was available from 5.30 a.m. - 10 a.m. and 6 p.m. – 11 p.m only. Wait!... What? No heating after 11 pm!! How would one survive the cold without heating?! And this was Leh, the warmest and the most comfortable we would be in days to come.

Harish, an officer posted in Leh, whom I had met at my school alumni meet in December came to meet us. He had helped us get all the Inner Line Permits and most importantly the permits for the drive through the Chushul Valley. That is an extremely restricted area due to its proximity along the Sino-Indian border. Post lunch, we left for a bit of sightseeing around Leh. First on the list was a lake which was frozen and had been converted into an ice hockey stadium for the winters. Then came the Kali Mandir which is co-located with the Spituk Gompa just on the outskirts of Leh. Kali Mandir is apparently open for a week at this time of the year. I took one look at the stairs I would have to climb, and it got me thinking whether I should do it on day one or take it easy. Good sense prevailed and I decided to stay back. Well, I don't know whether it was good sense or bad, but I sat at the base while the others went up to the mandir and further up to the Gompa. I believe the views from up there were fantastic. Well, I would never know.

After this we went to the Shanti Stupa. Shanti Stupa was built in 1991 by Japanese Buddhist Bhikshu Gyomyo Nakamura. The Shanti Stupa holds the relics of the Buddha at its base, enshrined by 14th Dalai Lama himself. The stupa has become a tourist attraction not only due to its religious significance but also due to its location which provides panoramic views of the surrounding landscape. The view of the Leh city from the stupa at night is absolutely mind-blowing, though I have seen it only in photographs. It is here that I realised how beautiful barren can be. The shades of white, brown and rust can paint such beautiful pictures. I could just sit there for hours if I had my way, taking in the calm, quiet, beautifully barren surroundings. Who knows, if I had the flair and a vocabulary to back it, maybe write some poetry too.

On the way back to the hotel, we stopped at Neha Sweets in the Leh market for some veg momos, samosas and idlis, dosas and chai/coffee. Neha Sweets is one of the handful places that are open through the year. Nothing fancy but decent food. Also, that is all that you can expect in Leh at this time of the year. While the others chatted till late, I retired to my room, had a handful of dry fruits, a cheese slice and a couple of chocolates for dinner and called it a night.

Day 2 - 26th Jan 2014

I woke up around 3.30 a.m shivering with cold. Sitting up, I realised the heating was off. I tried calling the reception but there was no response. That's when I realised that the heating was switched off at 11.00 pm and would come on only at 6.00 a.m. Two and a half hours to go and I was shivering badly. The hot water in the flask had also become cold. The only thing I could do was to add on layers on the body. After tossing and turning in bed for a bit, I dozed off to sleep to be rudely woken up at 6.45 am by my daily alarm.

I had my bed tea and requested for a bucket of hot water for a bath. As I hadn't had dinner the previous night, I was famished. I called room service and asked for an omelette and toast. What arrived was a very cold omelette. It was just about edible. Anyhow, I was hungry so I ate it. I got ready, packed a few things that I would need in a backpack, got the flasks filled with hot water and was all set for the day. Our first stop was at Neha Sweets, where the others had their breakfast. By 10.30 - 11.00 a.m. we were all set and ready for the day's tour.

Time for a flashback. Way back in 2013, I had done a road trip through Kashmir & Ladakh with the Husband and kids and a few friends. Something very strange happened with us as we were entering Leh. We had stopped at a small lonesome café in Nimoo, a small village just before Leh. This was around 5.30 in the evening. We all went in, and while the tea was getting ready the Husband was outside just organising the car a bit. While he was doing this, there came up to him a man and started chatting with him.

The man: "Kahan se aye hain?"

Husband: "Delhi se aye hain"

The man: "Leh ja rahe hain?"

Husband: "ji"

The man: "Yahan se jab aap jayenge to raaste mein pehle Magnetic Hill aayega, uske baad aayega Sangam. Sangam ke liye niche jane ki zarurat nahi hai, upar se hi haath jod lena. Last mein aayega Gurudwara Pathar Sahib, wahan zaroor jaana aur langar zaroor khana".

The Husband turned around for precisely a few seconds and when he turned back there was no one there. The man, it seemed, had just vanished into thin air. He did not pay much attention to it then. We had our tea and were on our way. By the time we finished with Magnetic Hill and the Sangam, it was almost 8 pm and we were all exhausted. The kids were almost asleep. We all decided that we would skip the Gurudwara for now, and since we were driving back on the same route, we would visit it on our way back. Three days later, we were on our way to Khardungla and Nubra Valley. When we left Leh that morning, it was bright and sunny. Leh to Khardungla is about 39 kms and within about 35 kms the weather changed suddenly and we landed ourselves in a snow storm situation. We somehow managed to reach Khardungla. Khardungla, at 18,380 ft is one of the highest motorable passes in the world. The air is extremely rarified and it is explicitly written there that one should not stop there for more than 30 mins. We were stuck there for 10 hours before we were evacuated at night!!

Once we were back at night at our army accommodation, we realised what that man had said. He had implored us to not enter Leh without visiting the Gurudwara, and we did not do as he said. It made us wonder if there was a connection there. Well, who can say. But that day I swore I would always pay heed to such things. Yes, it may be just superstition, but does it do any harm in taking blessings? I think not. In fact, the positive energies will always do you good.

So, when we were planning this trip to Ladakh, I was very sure that before I start out on the expedition, I would first go to the Gurudwara and then go anywhere ahead. Even if it meant going out of the way by quite a bit. Thus, on this day our first stop was Gurudwara Pathar Sahib. It is situated 25 kms from Leh on the Leh - Kargil highway. Gurudwara Pathar Sahib stands at the place where Guru Nanak is believed to have vanquished a demon. According to the legend, Guru Nanak was travelling to Srinagar. One night he halted at this place in Ladakh which according to the locals was haunted by a demon. When the locals asked Guru Nanak for help, the demon got very infuriated and threw a big boulder down at him while he was meditating. On touching the Guru's back, the stone turned to wax, which took the shape of his body in the sitting posture. Further infuriated, he tried kicking the boulder again with his foot, only to find his foot imprinted on the rock. He then realised that Guru Nanak had special powers and apologised. This shaped out boulder lies at this Gurudwara. The gurudwara is maintained by the Army. A very neat, clean and peaceful place. We ate the langar of chai and boondi. Anything served in a langar is always delicious, however simple the dish maybe. It is much later, in one of the conversations during my visit to Kashi, someone explained to me the effect of energy that becomes part and parcel of a place. "The spiritual energy of a place manifests itself in every part, every particle of that place. With passing time, it becomes stronger and stronger. The same can be said for negative energy too."

The Nimoo Bazgo Power Project, or the Alchi Dam is built on the Indus River, 70 kms away from Leh in the Alchi village. The village is famous for the existence of one of the oldest monasteries in Ladakh (a national heritage) Alchi Monastery. It is mainly known for its magnificent and well-preserved 11th & 12th century wall paintings, all in an Indo-Himalayan style. At this time of the year, it was a deserted village. There were just a handful of local people and a few cows. We walked around the village. It had the look of a village that had survived a holocaust. Not a soul to be seen or heard. The monastery was unfortunately locked, probably because of the winters. We went a little ahead where one could see the Indus River flowing by. The calmness of it all was very soothing. There is something about the sound of a river flowing in a calm, peaceful environment. In the days to follow, I would realise that at every stage of the trip I was experiencing the most amazing experiences I would ever have in life and I had no one to share it with at that moment. And these are times when one feels so homesick.

By the time we were done here, it was 3.30 pm. Hunger pangs were edging in. After a brief stop at the Zanskar-Indus confluence we were on our way back. On the way we stopped at one of the dhabas for some veg momos and maggi. The food wasn't great but yes, the tummy was full.

Back at the hotel, I remembered to ask for an extra quilt. I wanted a good night's sleep as the next day was going to be a drive of about 190 kms which in the mountains is a long one.

Day 3 - 27th Jan 2014

The next morning started at 5.30 am. I had a horrible excuse of a bed tea. I bathed for what was going to be the last time in the next few days, and I was all set for the day's journey to the mighty Changla and beyond. I called up home and told my family that I would be completely off the radar for the next four days. No phones, no connection with the rest of the world. It was just the eight of us and our two drivers.

We left Leh at about 9.00 am. A 10-15 kms from Leh, and our cab driver, Dorji got a call from Dorjey and we were told we had to turn back. When we reached the spot, we saw Dorjey burning some cardboard pieces under the Innova. Well, apparently the diesel had frozen in the pipe leading from the tank to the engine. That was new for me because I thought technology over the years had taken care of this. Then I saw two stoves on the carrier of the Innova and realised technology had to bow down in front of the cold temperatures that prevailed there. We checked the temperature, it was - 7.5° celsius and going down. Once the diesel was defrosted, we got back into our cabs. Our first stop was Karu, for breakfast. Breakfast was aloo paratha, curd, and rajma. It was, I realised later, the best, the tastiest meal I had in the whole trip. With breakfast done, we were on our way to the mighty Changla.

The drive upto Changla was pretty uneventful. The weather was bright and sunny. The humongous Karakoram Ranges made one feel like tiny specs in the huge universe. Zingrail is where the snow line starts. We were driving over snow. The Army vehicles had to necessarily put on snow chains at this point. A few curves and turns later there we saw the Border Road Organisation's (BRO) sign welcoming us to the Mighty Changla at the altitude of 17,888 ft above sea level. The 3rd highest (at that time) motorable pass in the world! Temperature was - 20° celsius.

There is something about Changla. Although it is a much bigger, broader pass than Khardungla, I felt it was more intimidating. I felt the thinness of the air more here than I did at Khardungla (which is a higher pass in terms of altitude) in June last year. Ten minutes outside the car and I started feeling the first signs of AMS. Dizziness hit me big time. Unable to stand outside, I quietly went and settled in the car and had some water. Water is the one stop shop for all ailments in Ladakh. I had a chocolate and waited for the others to come back. Dizziness was so bad that the 30 odd minutes that we spent there seemed like an eternity. I had to really try not to pass out there. Once we left Changla, it was a descent and slowly I started to feel better.

A drive of 58 kms brought us to Tangtse, which was going to be our place of stay for the night. We were to stay in a homestay. Tangtse is a biggish town, with a substantial army settlement too. It does have hotels and shops but it being winters, most of them were shut. My room for the night was a traditional Ladakhi kitchen. Beautifully decorated with carpets, small tables, mattresses to sit on, cushions, utensils, dry fruits, a bottle of whiskey too. I was impressed. I was told I would be provided with a heater that was run on LPG. It would be shut off at 10.30 pm and if I wanted, restarted at 6.00 am. Well, I really had no choice, so with the promise that I would get ample quilts for the night I agreed.

Then came the shocker. I wanted to go to the loo. I was shown a door. I opened it and the from the door I could see a thick green carpet on the floor, old yes, but nonetheless looked warm. I entered and didn't know how to react. The loo was all of 4 ft. by 3 ft. There was a hole with 2 blocks of wood on either side of it, and when you sat on it there was cold air coming from below. That was because there was a door below from where they came in and cleaned it. These were the kind of loos I remembered from my childhood trip to Ladakh 30 years back. Nothing had changed. Anyhow, where and in what part of me did my shit vanish off to, I don't know because I never felt it coming till I reached back home in Delhi.

Lunch was some kind of a yellow dal, aloo sabzi with paneer, rice and chapattis. I don't know about the others but I ate only because I had to. It was just about edible. Food in this trip, I realised, was basic and bland to the extent of being tasteless. Now when I look back, it was maybe because the supplies in winters are very limited.

The single point of focus of this trip from the very beginning was to drive on the frozen Pangong Tso. Naturally, we were all extremely excited. We all had seen the Pangong in its blue splendour in our previous trips. Now we would see it in its frozen state. The five-month wait was finally going to be over. We reached the lake. It was completely frozen. Dorjay inspected the lake and told us that this part was not frozen enough to take the weight of the car. To say that we were disappointed was an understatement. But there came a ray of hope. The next day, on our way to Hanle we were to drive the entire length of the lake. Probably some parts ahead could be strong enough. With that hope restored back, we had our fun on the frozen lake and drove back to Tangtse. On the drive back, I could feel dizziness creeping in again. Later, I was told that Shibu and Smitha were also not feeling well. In fact, Vineet was throwing up at Alchi. Not that I was happy, but yeah, it was a relief that I was not the only one feeling the symptoms.

Tired and exhausted, after an early dinner, similar to what we had in the morning I went into my den for the night. I got down to charging my phone and camera batteries. The phone was doubling up as a camera because my camera was not being able to withstand the cold. I slept with three humongous quilts. The only clothes I took off for the night was my quilted lower and my parka jacket. By this time, I had developed a bad headache and the medicine was just not taking effect. I had a very restless night, the pounding in my head just wouldn't stop. I got up sometime during the night to check the time and realised that my phone had also given up due to the extreme cold. There was no way to know what time it was and how long before one had to wake up. As I lay there, loneliness started hitting me. I did know Hitesh and Rajesh, but it was not like when you have someone you really know close to you. I didn't want to spoil their trip because of my health. So, I kept to myself, I had to pull through till Leh somehow. It surely made me wonder why I was doing this.

Day 4 - 28th Jan 2014

In the morning there was another challenge. How to brush my teeth? I had no energy to go down to the wash basin to brush. So, I brushed my teeth in the room, rinsed my mouth with warm water in the flask into the empty glass and washed my brush in the same water. Eewww! How could I, you'd ask. But I did. I also couldn't get myself to go to that "windy from below" loo. I wore my outerwear, shoes, caps, had a handful of dry fruits, chocolate and a cheese slice and was ready to face the next day's journey. The headache seemed better. At this point, I would like to point out that high on calories and high on carbohydrate foods along with a lot of water are absolute essentials at high altitudes. Always carry a stock of these with you.

Tangtse - Hanle is a 170 km ride through the Chushul Valley. The route we were taking was a restricted route. It was a drive through the valley plains. No roads. Just tyre marks and tracks to follow. After a breakfast of chai and salted poori, we were back on the road to Hanle, crossing the Pangong Tso, driving along it for its entire length in India. Pangong Tso is a saline water lake and it freezes completely in winters. It is a 134 kms long. About 70% of the lake lies in Tibet and China. The LAC of the Sino-Indian Border passes through the lake. We drove along the lake for quite a bit, before we stopped at a point where the lake seemed to be frozen pretty solid. Dorjay got off to inspect and he gave us a thumbs up. All of us got off the car. He drove the Innova onto the lake, skidding along, doing the doughnuts and then came to a halt. Most of us had captured it on tape and the consensus was that since the ice was a bit dicey, we would just click pictures sitting in the car and who is to know who was driving. Having decided that, Hitesh was the first one to get into the car. As soon as he got in we heard a big cracking noise! As if his tail was on fire, Hitesh pressed the accelerated and just drove off the lake on to the bank. We didn't know what the cracking noise was, but none of us had the courage to take it back again. We loaded ourselves back into the cars and were on the path merrily clicking away pictures of the barren landscapes. There were a number of snow crossings (in summers they would be river crossings). One had to be careful that the ice didn't give way. We also came across groups of wild asses called Kiangs, graceful in their own right. Enroute, we visited the Rezangla Memorial. This memorial was built in memory of the 114 Ahir soldiers led by Major Shaitan Singh, who died on Nov 18, 1962 during the Sino-Indian war. Maj Shaitan Singh was awarded the Param Vir Chakra for his supreme self-sacrifice. As per records, they killed 1700 Chinese soldiers. We also saw a number of bunkers belonging to both, the Indian and the Chinese sides. There was a strange exhilaration that one felt travelling on that route.

Somewhere on the way we stopped at the Chushul Village for a Maggi and chai lunch. As a kid, I had visited and travelled extensively through Ladakh as my father was posted here. I remember from that trip of mine to Chushul that there is a hill there called Garnet Hill. And I so vividly remember the Lamas brought us raw garnet stones from the hike up the hill. My brother still has those with him. In fact, not only garnets, he also has raw turquoise stone that we found in the Shyok River in the Nubra Valley. What wonderful memories of those visits.

Coming back to the Maggi, it was honestly, the most inedible maggi I had ever had. How can anyone mess up making Maggi. But there it was. For days to come, after the trip, the mere mention of maggi would nauseate me. This was the only place we could have got anything to eat. So yet again, out of compulsion and not choice we ate. The loo experience here was well, yet another nightmare. There were 2 loos by the roadside as big as what they were in Tangtse. One had half a door and the other had no door. The half door was a way to block the loo and make it non useable. That left me with the one with no door. I had no choice. I needed to pee desperately. It was again the hole in the floor with a room kind of thing below. Facing the opening of the loo, I realised it was facing the road with people gayly walking by looking at me trying to figure out things. Well, desperation took over, you gotta do what you gotta do.

We were back on the road taking in the barrenness and looking forward to the night sky that awaited us. A little before Hanle, is a village called Loma. At the check post here, you have to hand over your cameras etc. for security reasons. None of us were willing to part with our camera equipment. Dorjay suggested we hand over our mobile phones, since they were as it is useless because there was no connectivity. We were to collect them on our way back, enroute to Nyoma.

Hanle village has a population of only about 300 people. It also is home to the Indian Astronomical Observatory. One of the highest observatories in the world. The location of both the village and observatory is highly sensitive due to the proximity to the Tibetan/Chinese border. Special permission is required from the Indian Government to visit the observatory. We were at an altitude of 17,400 ft above sea level and temperatures bordering -25° celsius at this time.

In Hanle, we were again staying in one of the home stays. The loo here, thankfully, was clean and tiled with a wash basin. 7-star luxury as per the standards there. Here, I realised it had been 2 days since I had changed any part of my clothes, there were still 2 nights to go before we reached Leh and the comfort of the hotel. This realisation was put on the side. Taking off 6 layers and wearing them all over again, surely was a daunting task especially when AMS was threatening to take over. Come to think of it, eventually the "carry one set of change other that what you are wearing" was the most sensible advice.

The rooms here were 4 bedded rooms with a bukhari in the middle. The fuel for the bukhari was goat/sheep excreta. Little marble like stuff. Every 10 mins the guy would come in and pour two mugs full into the bukhari. Bhaskar, in his attempt to help our Ladakhi host decided to take on the responsibility of adding the fuel. In all his excitement he poured 3 mugs full at one time. And Oh boy, did it backfire! He burnt his hand and a bit of the carpet in the room too. The host was definitely unhappy at seeing the burnt carpet and well, made sure we paid for the damage. Hanle survives on solar electricity. They get the supply from about 6.00 pm to 10.30 pm. So, not only does the heating go off at night so does the light.

Hanle has one of the most amazing night skies. I have not seen so many stars in my life. And the best part is, they don't twinkle. That is how thin the air is. It was one of the most romantic night skies I had ever seen. Ten minutes out under the sky and I was back inside tucked into the warmth of my bed wanting to go to sleep before the heating went off. I did go off to sleep, but suddenly woke up, feeling amused and then suddenly feeling very sad. Part of me began laughing, part of me started to cry. At first, I thought I had lost it. I felt that the lack of oxygen had gotten to me and I had completely lost it. But then tears took over completely. I was so terribly homesick. I had just seen one of the most beautiful, amazing sights I had ever seen and I had no one with me to share it with. It had been 48 hours since I had spoken to my family. Disorientation began creeping in. I knew I was not alright and there was still 2 days before we reached Leh. I don't know for how long I cried, but I did doze off to sleep.

Day 5 & 6 - 29th and 30th Jan 2014.

I got up feeling very dizzy. Brushed my teeth, went to the kitchen and remember having a paratha and tea for breakfast and was ready with the others to leave for Nyoma. We collected our phones from the check post at Loma and proceeded towards Yaya Tso. By this time, the dizziness completely overtook me and I was in an absolutely zonked out state. Deep sleep took over. I have no clue how long we drove. All I recollect seeing is the team with the Indian flag on the Yaya Tso which we had been carrying since the Republic Day to hoist. I have no clue what happened after that. I only know what I have seen in the pictures clicked by them. I faintly remember the room in Nyoma. Ours was a triple - sharing room. I don't know whether I had any dinner or breakfast for that matter. Water was the only thing I remember drinking. The next day's drive to Leh is not even a blur. I was completely zoned out. I do remember throwing up a couple of times. But beyond that, nothing.

We reached Leh in the evening. I just went up to the room. I had a wash, asked the hotel staff to make some soup from one of the packets I was carrying. I had half a bowl of it and went to sleep. And yes, before all that, I called up home. I had to hold myself back from breaking down. Was I glad to speak to *the Husband*. Now I knew things would be okay. I just had to pull through another day. In any case, since now we were down to 11,500 ft, things were starting to get better where AMS was concerned. But dizziness was still there. I was very unsteady on my feet. Before I knew it, sleep just engulfed me. I vaguely remember a friend on call with me, telling me to use the oxygen cans I was carrying. I do remember Rajesh and Hitesh coming in asking me if I was okay. I remember wondering if I should lock the door of the room just in case I passed out. I think I did and crawled back into bed.

Day 7 - 31st Jan 2014.

The others had planned to go to Khardungla. Much as I had wanted to go originally, I really was in no shape to go. I just slept till late. When I finally woke up, I had a wash. I did not have the energy to bathe. I finally changed my clothes after almost 5 days. I had something to eat and went back to sleep. Come to think of it, I slept through most of the day. In the evening, Harish came to visit me. He offered to take me to the hospital but I said I was okay. Once he left, I had some dry fruits, cheese slices and went back to sleep again. The next day, I would be home, with my family. And everything would be fine. I just had to make sure I walked out of the airport on my feet.

Day 8 - 01st Feb 2014

The morning went by in a dizzy state. Getting ready, going to the airport, checking in, waiting for boarding, all of it happened in daze. When the flight took off, when it landed - I don't know. The others were somewhere at the back of the aircraft. I was in such a hurry to reach home that as soon as I got my luggage I said my byes and left.

As I walked out of the airport in my mind, I seemed to be filling in diesel in luggage trolleys at the airport. Hallucinations are much a part of AMS. I could feel some relief wash over me the moment I saw the black Scorpio. I left it to *the Husband* to put the luggage in. I just went to the co-driver side of the car and slid into the seat. I was home. Now I didn't have to worry about anything. And yes, I would finally have loads of hot water. And of course, my loo.

For the next two days, I was still reeling under the effects of AMS hallucinating at two halves of Mr. Manmohan Singh's face, one in a white turban and the other half in a blue turban coming from either side of my face and joining in between. Why Mr. Manmohan Singh, I have no clue. I was unsteady on my feet, dizzy, nauseated. I didn't want to speak with anyone. I didn't want to meet anyone. I just wanted to be by myself. But all that did not matter. What mattered was I was home.

These were seven days of my life. A gamut of emotions. I laughed, I cried, I was excited, I was nervous, I was very unwell, I was determined - all of this and more. It made me reflect on the mistakes I made in preparing for the trip. No amount of research really prepares you for what you get in Ladakh especially in the winters. I learnt never to take anything for granted. It made me realise what it meant to be alone in a crowd. That one night in Hanle, I realised how important it is to be comfortable in one's aloneness. Mind you, aloneness and loneliness are two very different aspects. It is not easy to be. It will not be untrue to say that perhaps it was this trip that taught me the wonders of sharing your thoughts with your own self vocally as you would probably do while writing a journal. It may sound crazy but believe me it is cathartic. It is the best way of getting your pent-up thoughts out of the system without the fear of either anyone getting to know about them or anyone judging you for your thoughts.

Will I do something like this again? I don't know. Despite not knowing what was happening for two days, those two days being a near blank, was the trip worth it? Absolutely yes. Was the trip what I was expecting it be? It was that and much more. Those were seven days of my life on my own - four days that were completely off the radar and two days that are still a near complete blank. A scary thought in today's times. But all of it really made it what it was - an unforgettable experience.

The Golden Quadrilateral – The beginning of the journey called 'India On My wheels' (March 2016)

Travel and driving have always been my most favourite things to do. In the two years that followed the winter trip to Ladakh, I did a few trips with my family. Some were chilled out, relaxing trips, some were exploratory, fun trips but there was something missing. I wanted to do something meaty, something with a little more substance. I had made a choice when the kids were younger to give up work and be a full-time mom. I had been very happy playing that role. Now that the kids were older and did not need me as much, I had a lot of time on my hands. How much can one travel with the family when there are multiple schedules to be matched at all the times. It would not be wrong to say that a certain level of frustration had begun to set in. Certain unresolved childhood issues had resulted in a very low self-esteem and that had started to make its presence felt in a big way. I had already been through two episodes of clinical depression earlier on and it seemed to me that this feeling was triggering a third episode. Believe me when I say it is not a good space to be in. I was desperate to do something.

One morning, while having our morning tea, a casual conversation with *the Husband* about the need to do something exciting brought up with the idea to do a solo drive. It was only natural, as travel and driving are the two loves of my life. He suggested a solo drive of 4-5 days. That would also give me some time to myself to sort my thoughts out. But, the state of mind I was in, it had to be bigger. It was going to be a first so it had to also be special.

A few days, and many hours of research later, I finally decided on driving the Golden Quadrilateral. The GQ is a 5900 km highway network connecting the 4 metros - Delhi - Kolkata - Chennai - Mumbai - Delhi. And in all my enthusiasm to do something big, I made out an itinerary that was about 18 days. But life is what life is. When has it ever gone as per what you plan. A certain unforeseen contingency happened and I had to cut it down to 11 days.

Finally, this is what I was going to do -

Day 1 - Gurgaon - Varanasi

Day 2 - Varanasi - Kolkata

Day 3 - Kolkata - Puri

Day 4 - Puri - Konark - Vizag

Day 5 - Vizag - Chennai

Day 6 - Chennai - Mahabalipuram - Bengaluru

Day 7 - Bengaluru

Day 8 - Bengaluru - Pune

Day 9 - Pune - Mumbai

Day 10 - Mumbai - Udaipur

Day 11 – Udaipur - Gurgaon

While there was a lot of enthusiasm around the planning, there was one thing that was worrying *the Husband* and that was my navigational abilities. I can get lost even on a straight road. Yeah!!

That part is my weakness. I cannot read maps and I am bad with directions. It made me think whether I should attempt a solo trip at all. Help came in the form of Ravneet, my friend for close to 30 years. She is also an avid traveller and a diehard foodie. She expressed her desire to join me and I was just waiting for her to ask. I jumped at the suggestion. Of course there was a clear understanding of what our roles would be - She would be the navigator who would make sure I do not get lost and I would be the driver who would lose my way nevertheless. As we were going to be driving 10 days out of 11, we would hardly have time for geographical exploration but local food was what we were going to surely explore.

Remember I had mentioned that I had joined a group of highway enthusiasts by the name of HV Kumar - Fan Forum & Message Board? This would indeed be the right time to tell you a little about it and the man behind it. HV Kumar is a Chartered Accountant by profession but he has spent what seems like a lifetime travelling across the length and breadth of the country. He is what they call the Human GPS. He has been, for many years, helping travellers by sharing his knowledge of the Indian highways in the form of route maps and virtual guidance through their travels. It is like when you travel, he travels with you, only virtually. So, for this trip, I connected with him. Chief, as we all call him fondly, helped plan the route and stays (when not staying with friends or family) along the way. One can safely say, with him guiding us and following us virtually, there was a lot of peace of mind.

We decided that we would have a Facebook page where we would give live updates of our entire trip as we progressed on it. There were several names that came up on our list but "India On My Wheels" seemed to top the list. It suited the ethos behind my travels which is to explore the enchanting landscape and the culinary palette India has to offer. It clearly encapsulated both the loves of my life -

travel and driving. This was also a name I could carry forward irrespective of who I travelled with.

As the days progressed, excitement became contagious. It was spreading amongst the friends too. One friend said he would help organise a flag off for us and will also manage our page while we were on our drive. The two weeks before the trip went by in a flurry. But there was also a huge apprehension. I had never been away from home all by myself for this long. There was an inherent false sense of being indispensable. I wondered how they would manage at home without me. *The Husband* kept me pepped up and every time I had these thoughts he stirred me away from them saying , "All will be well, sab ho jayega"

The day for our departure was 3rd of March 2016. The next day after my 45th birthday. I had a lot of my friends coming the evening before to wish me luck. There were cakes, flowers, phone calls. I have always been low on self-esteem and extremely low on self-confidence but that evening I was fully charged up. I felt like a celebrity. A flag off had been organised in our condominium and 5.30 a.m by the President of the Resident's Welfare Association. Honestly, I was expecting only my friends to be there. It was most heartening to find at least a hundred people waiting at that ungodly hour for us to be flagged off. Most of them, I had seen in the condominium but did not know. It was touching to have them come up to us and wish us luck. There was a tea and biscuit service also organised. A Panditji was also present to do a small pooja. I can say this for both Ravneet and myself, we were both so humbled by this gesture. We felt like we were truly on our way to achieve something big, although I doubt it was really such a big deal. Much as it made us feel special, I started to feel a certain pressure. What if I am not able to complete the drive? I had never driven such long distances alone. I had never had such long drive days before. What if I don't have the stamina to complete the circuit? All this would be such a waste. And more than that, I had made this out to be such a big achievement. I would just lose face in front of my family and friends. I went through the whole flag off ceremony with these thoughts but once we left, I decided I will go as far as I can, push myself as much as I can, no more apprehensions. I was not alone in this. It was going to be eleven days of a gypsy life. Every night in a different city. Experiencing a life I had never known, and I was going to make the most of it. Rest, as they say, Que Sera Sera! What will be, will be.

After a 5.30 a.m flag off from Gurgaon, we were off. Though we had a schedule for night pitstops but were travelling with no hotel bookings in hand except a few places where we were staying with family and friends. I had left all of that to my mentor, Mr. H V Kumar. All the route planning and on-the-go backend support was his effort.

The first stop for us was Varanasi. We reached pretty late in the evening. Although we barely spent one night there, we still managed to get a peep into the chaos where people come to find eternal peace. The ghats of Varanasi are crowded and chaotic and that may as well be an understatement. Walking through the crowded lanes I could sense a strange kind of pull. This pull continued to stay with me and years later I finally spent 10 days in Varanasi. And for me the city will always be Banaras or Kashi and never Varanasi. Believe me even 10 days were not enough to explore the vibe called Kashi.

More than the places, it was the food that was explored in this trip. We had stopped at one of the trucker's Dhabas in Dhanbad for lunch. Basic fare of dal, cauliflower and potato sabzi, rotis and raddish and onion salad. Very simple but very delicious food. The owner was a sikh gentleman from Sanewaal in Punjab. Curious, I asked him how he reached Jharkhand. He said he used to be a truck driver himself and at that time the erstwhile Bihar used to be very notorious because of which there never were any good eating places on the highways for the truckers. So, he decided he would open one. We chatted with him for a while. He asked us our story and was very amused by it. He treated us to some very delicious tea too. We had been warned about the notorierty of Bihar and Jharkhand. But believe me, sitting there eating our lunch, talking to the dhaba owner, we felt the safest. And why just there, I think throughout my travels across the country, I have never felt anything but safe. People, in general, are good at heart. Or maybe it is because I go looking for the goodness in people, I always find the goodness in them.

While having our lunch at this dhaba, I observed a few truck drivers and their cleaners going about with their work. In and out of the truck, cleaning, a bit of maintenance check et al. Something triggered inside me and I decided one day I will do a drive in a truck. Well, the drive has yet not happened but I did work on getting my HMV licence once I got back home. That is another story. For now, suffice to say it was a gruelling exercise. I am still waiting for this dream to take shape. Insha-Allah! It will happen.

We did take detours on the way, some for food and some for a bit of sight-seeing. Out of all the food that we sampled in the states we crossed, Oriya food was quite nice, the gur ki rasmalai in Kolkatta was mindblowing, and we had some Kerela food in Bangalore. That was super amazing, particularly a dessert that we had - Illaneer payasam. It is made by simmering milk with tender coconut water and pulp with condensed milk. Brilliant!! Topping the list was Andhra and Kathiawadi food.

Also, during this drive we met some exceptionally loving people in Belgaum. Rajneesh, an army officer based there, and his wife, Shilpi, welcomed us into their lives, made sure our stay in Belgaum was extremely comfortable, His CO (Commanding Officer) made sure we were treated like queens. Experiences like these make you really believe in the goodness that exists in the world. It is because of people like them, who have so much love to offer, the world is a better place to live in.

An unscheduled extra day spent in Belgaum landed us in a soup. I had to be back on the 13th of March under any circumstances. We were now a day short. Ideally, we would have taken 3 days from Belgaum to Gurgaon. Now we only had 2. Which meant day 1 was 1100 kms to Himmatnagar and then another 900 plus kms to Gurgaon. It was a crazy drive. With practically three nights of partying behind us it was a task. The saviour of course was Red Bull and coffee taken one after the other at least thrice that day and the 15-minute power naps every now and then. A very-very-very big disclaimer here – please do not do this under any circumstances. Sleep well before a long drive and stay hydrated. What we did was stupid and dangerous. There is a very fine line between adventure and stupidity and that day was nothing less than stupidity. I have never done something like this ever again.

And of course, there was this interesting little encounter with the cops too. So, when we got off the Mumbai-Ahmedabad Highway just short of Ahmedabad to go towards Himmatnagar, we were stopped by the cops. This was around 9.30 at night. One of the cops walked around to the driver's side while looking at all the stickers that said "India On My Wheels". He looked at me, then he peeped inside to look at Ravneet, then he looked behind us inside the car.

The conversation went like this:-

Cop : "Madam kahan jaa rahein hain ?"

Me: "Ji Gurgaon"

Cop : "Kahan se aa rahe hain ?"

Me : "Ji Gurgaon"

Cop (smiling) : "Madam kyun mazaak kar rahe ho?"

I explained to him that we had started from Gurgaon 10 days back, went literally around the country and were headed back to Gurgaon.

Cop : "Madam aisa kyun kar rahe ho?"

Me : "Bas, shauk hai gadi chalane ka."

Cop (extremely amused): "Madam aapko kabhi kisi police waale ne chai pilai hai? Aao aaj aapko hum chai pilate hain."

Well at that hour chai was such a pleasant thought, but well, chai with the cops? Avoidable, we thought. I am sure he meant well, but... We thanked him and excused ourselves and were on our way as fast as we could.

It was a marathon drive. We drove 6,810 kms over 13 States and a 100+ cities in 11 days. Actually, out of the 11 days, we drove 9 days. There are times in life when you think of doing something and in jest begin to make plans and slowly before you know it, the joke becomes a reality. This trip turned out to be a trip of many firsts. It was the first drive I did without my family. It was the first time I drove the entire distance by myself. It was a trip where for the first time I took a power nap by the road side and that was liberating in its own way. It was a trip where practically every night was in a different city. It was a trip in which I had the longest drive days I had ever experienced – 1,100 kms in a single day. It was a trip that got us featured in newspapers. In fact, in Belgaum we had a small little press conference for the local newspapers. The high we got out of the trip was something else. This drive turned out to be the one of the most important milestones for me. It would not be incorrect to say that it went on to become a turning point in my life. It helped me discover the gypsy in me.

Beyond the Untamed Horizon - Lahaul & Spiti (August 2016)

Post my GQ trip, there were a couple of road trips with my family in Himachal Pradesh. But there was this thirst for more. Something more adventurous, something that would push me a little beyond my limits. There was also this thought that I should take it a little slow and not ride on the high of the GQ experience. Ladakh came up in my mind, but I had done that twice in the recent years. There was a lot of talk about Lahaul & Spiti. The thought was worth evaluating. And as it would happen, it was only a matter of days before the group of three was in place. Manav, Ajay and me. Manav is a veterinarian by profession and is an amazing photographer. Ajay calls himself the Roadographer. Who is a roadoghrapher you might ask? Well this is a term coined by Ajay for himself (it is a registered trademark in his name) for his love for clicking pictures of the roads he travels on.

What was finalised then and there, was that the three of us were heading out up-north. For the "where", there were a lot of discussions. Two months of going back and forth and we zeroed down on Lahaul & Spiti, Sach Pass, the Cliffhanger route of Killar - Kishtawar in Himachal Pradesh and the Mughal Road in Kashmir. The Mughal Road is an 84 km road between Bufliaz, a town in Poonch District, to the Shopian District. It traces the historic route used in the Mughal period over the Peer Panjal Pass. Fun fact - Bufliaz was named after the horse of Alexander the Great (Bunifales) who died here. The Cliffhanger route of Killar-Kishtawar is one of the most dangerous roads to drive on not only in India but also the world. We wanted to do it all. The timeline was 8-9 days which was a bit less but then fortunately or unfortunately the circumstances in the valley were such that we had to shelve the Mughal Road plan. The final itinerary was Delhi - Chitkul - Kalpa - Puh - Kaza - Chandratal - Killar - Sach Pass - Kishtwar - Chamba - Delhi. It was still a very packed itinerary for 8 days but we were all excited and raring to go.

Day 1 & 2 - Delhi - Ambala - Shimla - Narkanda - Rampur Bushahr - Chitkul - Puh

On the D-Day, Ajay and I left Delhi at 6.30 in the morning. We were to meet Manav (who was based out of Meerut) at Ambala. Since we reached Karnal at the same time, we decided to have breakfast at one of the dhabas there, shift the luggage into Ajay's car and then head towards Ambala, where Manav was to leave his car. Our first stop was Rampur Bushahr, about 70 odd kms ahead of Narkanda. By the time we finally left from Ambala, it was 12.30 and we were running terribly late on our schedule. We had lunch at Giani's in Dharampur after which it was a pretty uneventful ride upto Rampur. We reached pretty late, and it also took us some time in searching for the Army Mess where we were to stay at. We had our dinner and crashed out soon after, as the next morning was an early start. It was going to be a long ride. We had planned to go upto Chitkul and Kalpa before heading out to Puh.

Chitkul, a small little hamlet on the banks of the Baspa River, is the first village of the Baspa Valley and the last village on the old

Hindustan-Tibet trade route. It is also the last point in India one can travel to without a permit. By the time we finished with Chitkul it was already 5.30 in the evening and we still had to go to Kalpa before heading out to Puh. We decided against Kalpa since we would get terribly late reaching Puh. There was a drive planned to a very remote area close to Puh the next morning and I for sure did not want to miss that for anything. That was an area one could go to only with the Army connections. I would probably not be able to go again. We had a quick cup of tea and headed out towards Puh. Kalpa would happen another time.

To say Karcham - Puh was a bad stretch of road is an understatement. I doubt most part of the stretch had even seen tar in its lifetime so far. Crazy stoney path is all I can say it was. We reached Puh at about 10.30 at night. Tired and exhausted, we checked into the Army Mess, had our dinner and called it a night. The next morning again was an early start to one of the most adventurous and challenging journeys I had done so far. Yes, it was steps above the two trips done in Ladakh in the recent times.

Day 3 - Puh - Sumdo - Gue - Kaza

It was 6.30 a.m. The three of us were ready and all set for the drive of the day. First was a drive into a remote and restricted part of Puh. Winding roads up and the amazing barren landscape just made the ride worth every mile that we covered. I wish I could say more about that area. Somethings are meant to be experienced and not shared. This would be one such drive. Calm, peaceful, stunning landscapes. All that and much more. We wandered around the mountains for a couple of hours before heading out towards Kaza. Thankfully the roads towards Kaza were mostly good.

Well, not all of it. There were parts which were prone to

landslides. One such place was where we noticed stones sliding down the mountain. Naturally we stopped. First it was small stones and then the big stones slowly started sliding down. The logical thing was to go back a bit and steer clear of an impending landslide, which is what Ajay did. We got off the car and began wondering what should be done. There were dozers standing there but no drivers to move them and get them into action, if necessary. And needless to say, we had no phone connectivity on that stretch. In my mind there were thoughts racing by as I am sure they were in Ajay's and Manav's too, when we noticed a tipper truck coming from the other side. We waited to see what the truck would do. The smaller stones were still sliding down. Nothing major though, but one never knows in such situations. With great ease it crossed the area and moved on to cross where we were parked. And then there came a Bolero pick-up and with great ease that too crossed over to our end. Maybe this was new to us and therefore we were a bit wary of what was happening, but then we too decided to cross over. We got into the car and just did what the other two vehicles had done and in between a couple of small sliding stones, crossed the area. I for sure, heaved a sigh of relief to get out of that one.

Sumdo is where Kinnaur Valley ends and Spiti Valley begins. We took a tea break here. And there I had one of the most soul satiating plates of chowmein I have ever had. Of course, I doubt there was anything healthy or hygienic about its preparation, but yeah soul satiating it sure was. The right amount of oiliness, the right amount of spice heat, the generous helping of soy sauce and topped with the local pumpkin-tomato ketchup and the green chilli sauce… Ooooh! It was soulful. A little ahead of Sumdo is a bifurcation on the road. One going to Kaza, the other going to Gue Village. We took the road to Gue. As the story goes, in 1975 an earthquake struck the region. And while digging on a rescue mission, the ITBP forces found a mummy of a monk. It is also said that apparently blood came out of the mummy and the hair was also visible on it. It is said to be about 500+ years old and has been identified as that of the monk Sangha Tenzin. The mummy is hunched in a meditating position, draped with shawl. The holy beads are in his hand, and the head bowed towards the holy book kept in front of him.

From that point of bifurcation, the village is about 12 kms. We had gone in about 10 kms when the car just stopped. Well, it was a case of engine overheating. I think it was because the car was over loaded. There were 3 of us and then our luggage, tents, camping stuff et al would easily be equivalent 2-3 people in terms of weight. Combine that with the altitude and rarified air, I think it is only fair that the car would also feel the brunt. While trying to figure out what to do, one of the options we thought of was to leave the car there and walk up the 2kms to the village. But then, on the flip side, it was already 5.30 p.m, and we had no clue if there were any timings for visiting the mummy. We did try walking a bit, but I guess acclimatisation was an issue, I couldn't walk, I felt breathless and my head began throbbing. So, with a very heavy heart and great disappointment, we turned back. There was still a long way to go before the day ended and chances were not what we could take.

On our way to Kaza, we came across this village called Chandigarh. And it had trees laden with apples. It was too tempting not to pluck a few. And that is what I did. I felt like a kid while stealing the apples from the tree but it was good fun. I told the care taker I was going to pluck only one but of course that is not what happened.

The next 75 odd kms were a mix of good and bad roads. It was well past 10 pm when we reached Kaza. But before that we had stopped somewhere for a loo break and I just happened to look up at the starry sky. And I fell in love with it. The Milky Way was so clearly visible to the naked eye and there were so many stars in the sky. Romantic, beautiful, amazing. I would probably run out of adjectives. So many stars on a dark, moonless night. Never have I ever seen something so beautiful. Hanle had stars, here it was the Milky Way. I had seen so many photographs of the Milky Way and had always wondered if they were photoshopped. No, they weren't and no, the photographs do not do the real thing justice. If I had my way I could have just laid down there and kept gazing at the starry sky all night for the rest of my life.

But we had to move on. We had a destination to reach. The next day, although would be a long day, seemed lighter as we were going to be in Kaza itself for another night and Kaza is where I went off the communication grid for the next 2-3 days as there was no mobile connectivity available. Ajay and Manav had their BSNL connections so that was a saving grace.

Day 4 - Kaza - Pin Valley - Kibber - Key Monastery - Hikkim - Komic

Fortified with a breakfast of aloo parathas and tea, we headed off to Pin Valley. But before that we went to get the car tanked up on fuel. The reason I mention this here is because Kaza apparently has one of the highest retail fuel stations in the world.

Pin valley is about 20 kms short of Kaza while coming from Puh. It is also home to the Pin Valley National Park which is known for its protection of the endangered snow leopards. We had a lot to cover that day so we set a time limit upto which we would drive into the valley and then come back. Scenic barren landscapes marked the drive. While we had stopped at a point to click some pictures, I heard my name being called out. I turned around and was pleasantly surprised to see fellow traveller friends Neha and Puniet. It is always nice to find familiar faces in the middle of nowhere. We chatted with them, exchanged travel notes and also got some pointers on the impending Sach Pass ride.

After Pin Valley, we headed towards Kibber and the Key Monastery. Kibber is a small village 16 kms from Kaza at an altitude of about 14,200 ft. According to the demographics available on the internet, Kibber had a population of about 366 people. Some 80 stone made houses with about 77 families. Through the Kibber village, we drove to Chicham Village. Actually, you go upto 3 kms short of Chicham and then there is a gorge that you cross on a ropeway trolley. Now there is a bridge that has been made over it. One look at the gorge and the size of the trolley was enough for me to just forget about giving it even a thought in my wildest dreams. Back at Kibber we had lunch and headed towards the Key Monastery.

The spectacular monastery is located at a height of 4,116 mtrs. and is 7 km from Kaza. It is the largest monastery in Spiti Valley and is a religious training centre for the Lamas. Ajay wanted to stay in the car, so Manav and I walked up to the monastery. While we were looking around the Gompa, one of the Lamas offered us some tea, which was quite an interesting one. I have never had tea that like this before. It was a sweet, cinnamon and clove flavoured black tea. After a brief chat, he opened two rooms of the Gompa, one of which had the sacred writings of Buddha. This was apparently the room where Dalai Lama stayed when he visited here. This room also had a statue of the person who, the lama said was the future Buddha.

It was already about 5.45 p.m by the time we got out of the Gompa. The photographer in Manav was itching to click the monastery in light of the setting sun. He just mentioned that to Ajay and Ajay took it like a man on a mission. It was a longish ride to the other side of the river, but he managed to reach the spot in time for Manav to capture the majestic monastery in the light of the setting sun. We then headed back to Kaza. Komic and Hikkim were still left to be covered.

Hikkim, is a village at an altitude of about 14,500 ft. The claim to fame for this village is that as per the Limca Book of Records, it has the world's highest Post Office. To reach the post office (which is open through the day) one has to walk down a steep slope to a house. We all wrote a post card for our respective families and posted it there. The post master told us that it would reach in 6-7 days. While Manav received the post card, I still await the arrival of the postcard. It seems it just got lost somewhere.

After Hikkim, we headed another 3 kms to Komic. Although the board in Komic says it is the highest village in the world with motorable roads, apparently it is the highest in Asia with an elevation of about 4,587 mtrs. It was quite dark by the time we reached both these villages, so that is about all that we could explore. Back at the hotel, we had our dinner and crashed into bed. The next day was an early start to a long ride to Chandra Taal and then onwards to Keylong.

Day 5 - Kaza - Kunzum La - Chandra Taal - Batal - Gramphoo - Keylong

Originally, we had planned the day until Chandra Taal and were to spend a night there, pitching our own tents and getting the camping experience. That meant that the next day we would be doing Chandra Taal - Batal - Gramphoo - Keylong - Udaipur - Tindi - Killar. A total of 250 odd kms which we had thought were a pretty manageable distance to cover in a day. Apparently not. When we had met Puniet and Neha at Pin valley, we had discussed our plan with them, and they asked us to rethink on it. The same was reiterated by the local cab driver they were with. Apparently, the Batal - Gramphoo stretch was an extremely bad stretch of roads and so was the Udaipur - Tindi stretch. To do all of that in one day was stretching it a bit too far. And then there was also the issue of car over heating which we needed to keep in mind. So, we reworked the route and decided to do Kaza - Kunzum La - Chandra Taal - Batal - Gramphoo - Keylong. Initially, our families knew that we were going to be off the grid for the next 48 hrs, but then with the change in plan we told everyone that we would be contactable by the end of day when we reach Keylong.

We had decided to have breakfast at Losar. We left Kaza at about 7.30 am. As we were crossing Key Monastery from across the river (from where we had taken the sunset shot the previous day), Manav realised the first sunlight had still not touched upon the Gompa, it was probably minutes away. We were just in time to see the magnificent sight. And what a sight was! The first rays of the Sun coming in from behind the mountain and and gently touching the tip of the monastery. It was surreal. Naturally, we stopped right there. Manav got his soul satisfying sunrise shots, I got my selfie of the day, and Ajay got his "roadographs". So far so good. We went a little ahead and as we were crossing a flat plateau, Manav got some dramatic photography ideas. He and I got off on the road and he asked Ajay to go off the road and drive upto the end of that plateau. So, half an hour and some fantastic photographic shots later, we were back on the road driving towards Losar.

By the time we reached Losar, we were all famished. I was, by now getting a little sick of aloo parathas, so I ordered a maggi for myself while the guys ordered aloo parathas. Of course I had an aloo paratha too. Next to where we were sitting, was a group of Austrian bikers having their breakfast of Black tea and omelettes. They were with us in the same hotel as ours, and were heading towards Leh. One of them was very fascinated by what we were eating so asked me to help order the same for them. I was having pickle, which he tried and quite liked it. The next I see him having it with his omelette. This just reiterated what I always believe and that is, how we are all so tied up with traditions and cannot imagine things beyond that. He was relishing the pickle with his omelette and I could not even imagine what it would be tasting like.

With our tummies full, we headed towards Kunzum La. As you exit Losar, there is a check-post where you have to make an entry. While Manav and Ajay had gone in to get the entry done, I saw an open tap with water gushing out. This was the 3rd such tap along the route that I had seen. It was only natural for the mind to think that there was so much of wastage of water that was happening. I went upto the tap to shut it and saw that there were specific instructions written to NOT turn it off. Curiosity got the better of me, as it always does. When we asked the guys there, they told us that if they shut the tap, there are chances that the pipe would burst because of pressure. And they would have to go quite a distance and height to go and repair it. Hence, they do not turn the tap off. Well, you cannot fight that logic.

The road upto Kunzum La is a steep one. There were times when Manav and I had to get off so that the car would lighten up, for whatever it was worth. We would walk some distance, till we reached the flatter part of the road and then get back into the car. Since the day before we had worked out a system to manage the issue. Pre-emption kept the car from heating up or losing speed at the wrong time. Slowly and steadily our lungs were beginning to support us on that. Kunzum La is one of the easier passes I have been across. Its where Spiti Valley gives in to Lahaul Valley. From the point where you turn off the highway for Chandra Taal, you can take your vehicle about 13 kms or so. 12 kms to the camp sight, then a steep drive of about a km to the parking area and then a walk of about a km to the lake. We reached the camp sight, with Manav and me getting off the car and walking 2-3 times. When we saw the last mile of the road, we all had the same thoughts - the car will not make it up. Not only was it steep, but extremely narrow and well, let's just say very very stoney and 'bouldery' if I can coin that term. And no way were we going back without going upto the lake. While we were thinking what to do Ajay came up with a brilliant idea, that we ask for a lift in another vehicle. We looked around and we saw a Bolero Pick-up standing next to a camp site. Ajay and I trudged down to find the owner. It happened to belong to one of the camp owners. We pleaded and bargained with him and he agreed to take us up there. The ride up for me was quite alright as I was sitting in the front, but I am not too sure how it was for both Ajay and Manav. They were standing at the back. Chivalry does have its disadvantages, I guess. The 1 km walk had been psyching me out for a long time. We were at 14,500 ft, and I have never been an exercise person, and I did not know how my lungs would react to the walk at that altitude. The driver said they take 10 minutes but a friend who had been there earlier told me she took 40 mins. We started the walk slow and steady, mentally prepared for it to take a long time, but we did it in 13 minutes. Was I impressed with myself or what!!

Chandra Taal is a very small lake, but it is so peaceful, serene and calm. The blue and the green of the water was simply breathtaking. The first thing I did was go to the edge of the lake and sit down by its side just to take in the peace. The sound of the water lapping on the sides was sheer music to my ears. It was simply magical. What I wouldn't do to spend a night under that gorgeous, romantic, starry night sky next to this peaceful lake with the added Milky Way that I so fell in love with. The only thing that shook me out of the dreamland that I was in, was the fact that we still had the Batal-Gramphoo ride.

By the time we came down to where our car was, it was 5.30 pm. We met Neha and Puniet again on our way out, and they suggested, as did the other drivers that we spoke to, that we should stay over at Chandra Taal and maybe leave very early the next day. As it was going to get dark soon and the Gramphoo stretch was a treacherous one. Our only worry was car breakdown. In case it got heated up or something like that happened there would be no help around. So, we decided to stay on for the night. While Manav and I went to find out a deal for the night, Ajay had a thought and a valid one at that. We had told everyone we would be reaching Keylong and there was no way we could pass on a message that we were staying over in Chandra Taal. The thing is, this entire stretch from Losar to Koksar (A little before Keylong) did not have any phone connectivity. It still does not have any even after so many years. If they did not hear from us, they could get worried. So, we decided to move it. We were going to Keylong. Somehow, we would manage. Against all sane advice we set off and reached Batal by about 6.15 pm.

Batal is home to Chacha Chachi Dhaba. From the outside, it looks like a small hut. But when you enter it, it is a world in its own right. It's a decent sized space where they have tables and benches for people to sit and eat. And there is another room, a dormitory of sorts where there are beds lined. One can sleep here for a minimal charge. It was warm and cozy. They served aloo parathas, maggi, omelettes, tea and cold drinks - what more can you ask for in the middle of nowhere. They also had a satellite phone which was out of order that day. Had that been working, we could have called home and stayed back the night.

What was to be just a quick cup of tea led to a bread omelette dinner and we set off towards Gramphoo by about 7.30 pm. This was utter madness by all standards. To call it a road would be absolute insanity. It is not even a track. It had water crossings, it had boulders, it had a big circle of stagnant water, it had a rivulet flowing through the road, it was sheer craziness and the dark of the night only added to the madness of it all. There were places where one had to get out of the car to figure out where the road was going. One wrong move and well, that would be it. It took us 3 and a half hours to cover the 60 kms stretch but yes, we did it. It was past midnight by the time we reached the hotel at Keylong. After calls to family were done, tired and exhausted, I slept off. I have no idea when I slept but the next thing I heard was my morning alarm go off. The next day, we were hoping would be a lighter day. A 130 kms travel was all we had to cover. That would be easy and for a change we would reach our destination, Chiari, in day light. Maybe we could do a sample of the Cliffhanger on the Killar - Kishtwar route. But that was another day and destiny had other plans for us.

Day 6 - Keylong - Udaipur - Tindi - Chiari

We were very happy that we had covered the worst of it all the day before. We were a bit chilled out. A 130 odd kms would surely not be a very long day. In the mountainous terrain 130 kms generally translates to about 5-6 hours of travel time. It so happened that I needed to be back in Delhi by Sunday morning and we needed to choose between doing Sach Pass or doing the Killar - Kishtwar route. We chose Sach Pass, with the agreement that since it was a shorter drive day, we could do a 30 - 40 km sample of the Ciffhanger in the evening. Refreshed and excited, and yet again, after a breakfast of aloo parathas (I will strangle anyone who even mentions aloo paratha!!!!) we set off towards Killar.

Keylong to Udaipur is a distance of about 55 kms. The roads were excellent, tarred roads. Narrow, but pretty good. As it is by now our concept of good roads had taken a whole new meaning. By noon we were in Udaipur. We had the whole day and just 70 kms more to travel. We did 60 kms of Batal - Gramphoo in 3 and a half hours the previous night. How bad could this 70 kms stretch be? Life was good. Indeed, a very relaxed day. Ajay was taking photography lessons from Manav and while that was happening, we just stopped by at a small tea shack and spent another hour or so chatting, took some more photography lessons. All we needed was some chilled beer and it would have been the perfect setting. We were totally operating on a relaxed mode.

It was, I think, past 1 o'clock when we left Udaipur. The road was narrow, untarred but still manageable. Nothing like what we had seen the day before. At one point, Manav wanted to take a photograph of the car by the waterfall. While he was guiding Ajay to get the perfect angle, one of the tyres got punctured. Since we were in water, and on a curve, Ajay drove a little ahead where there was space and parked it by the side. We tried opening the spare tyre and the nuts wouldn't budge. So, we decided to fill in air from the compressor we were carrying and go up till the next village which was about 5-6 kms and get it fixed there. With the air compressor in place, we took out the camping chairs we were carrying and sat down in the middle of the road. It was bliss, at least for the moment.

While we were sitting in the middle of the road, I realised that this was a road which was not frequently used. There may be a vehicle coming the next second or there may not be one coming till the next day. We were also cut off in terms of phone communication. If something were to happen, no one would know of it. There would be no help coming on time. Surrounded by all the huge mountains, we were just about a spec which would not be found. That moment of realisation was a truly humbling one for me. I have been carrying a lot of emotional baggage with me. And at that moment something happened and I felt some of that baggage offloading and I was feeling a little lighter. The importance I was giving myself due to the emotional hurt I was carrying all these years felt like it was withering away. That was also the moment I realised that travel was going to be the best therapy I could find for myself.

Air filled in, chairs back in the car, we piled in and off we went. A little ahead stopped to check on the tyre - all good. We were in action. Drove some more till we came to a bulldozer clearing the road and we had to stop. That is when we realised the tyre had gone flat again. The BRO guys helped us open the tyre. And that is when also we realised that our proverbial honeymoon was over. The stepney was also flat. Luckily, while they were taking the flat tyre off, I noticed the puncture spot. Ajay checked the tool kit, there was a puncture repair kit. There was still hope left. Manav and I got down to repairing the puncture. Both of us had never done it but only observed it being repaired. We managed to fix it. By this time, the BRO guys had left. It was just the 3 of us. All we now had to do was fill in the air and we were good to go. About half an hour of the compressor being on, we realised that it had stopped working. It was not filling any air. Now what? There were three of us, with 2 out of the 5 tyres punctured, in the middle of nowhere! All we could do was wait.

Fortunately, there was a guy who came by on a bike. He told us that at Shoar, the next village about 5 kms away, there was a BRO Detachment, we were sure to find help there since they would definitely have a workshop. If not that, we would have to go to Purthi, which was 10 kms away. He also told us that a Sumo from his department was following and that they would give us a lift to the next village, but no promises on how we would come back.

Ajay suggested that Manav and I take the 2 tyres in the Sumo and go along and see what we could manage while he waited by the car. Time was well past 5 pm. We reached Shoar, and right at the border of the village was the BRO office. Long story short, as luck would have it there was a fair happening close by and everyone had gone off to the same. The resident engineer was also about to leave, when we caught him just in time. He was an extremely sweet and helpful guy. He called the driver of a tipper truck who filled up air into the tyre from the air compressor of the truck. He couldn't help us with repairing the stepney though, but at least one tyre was fixed. Then he offered us his Bolero, along with the truck driver to drop us back and also fix the tyre for us. Not to forget, also offered us some soul satisfying tea and bhujia which of course, both Manav and I devoured.

By the time we finished with all this it was around 7.00 pm. We still had about 20 plus kms to go. Just before Shoar is where you enter Pangi Valley. There is a big, beautiful waterfall here called the Kallu Nullah. The water of this waterfall, the driver told us, was very heavy and viscous water. Curiosity was getting the better of me, but much as I would have loved to stop and check out what it actually felt like, I just kept quiet, since a lot of action had already happened.

We reached Chiari by about 9.30 pm. We had a booking in the circuit house there. In the dark of the night, it seemed like a lonely cottage on a slight slope. There was one lonesome light bulb on a pole near the gate and everything else was pitch dark. All you could hear was the River Chenab flowing close by. Definitely a scene out of an old Bollywood movie. The caretaker seemed clueless about our booking but by the looks of him, I just felt he was pretending about not knowing of it. Anyhow, it just meant that naturally he had prepared no dinner for us. The way the day was progressing, I was not surprised. We were famished, since all we had had were aloo parathas for breakfast. Good for us that we were carrying some stuff including a camping stove. Well, we could have simply cooked the maggi in the kitchen, but adding a little more chaos to the day was fun. So, we sat in the room, made maggi for dinner. We had chocolates for dessert. And we called it an early night for a change. But sleep did not come easy. While my room was in the main cottage, the room Manav and Ajay were sharing was in a block about 100 metres away. For some reason I had a very eerie, uneasy feeling. I am not really the kind of person who is scared of being alone, but I guess it was just one of those days when I was. Fear really has no logic. My phone had no signal and there was no way for me to ask the guys to give me one of the BSNL phones. It took a lot of courage on my part to run across to their block and get a phone from them. Once I had the phone with me, I felt a little at peace and finally slept off.

Day 7 - Chiari - Killar - Sach Pass - Chamba

We had heard that the drive to Sach Pass was a very challenging drive. We had heard it was a steep climb with stoney tracks. It is in fact called the "Baap of all Passes" because of the kind of drive it is when going from Killar side. All of this had definitely left us feeling very anxious. Also, because the car was not a 4 x 4 and even without the steep climbs we were having issues with it. The three of us had come a long way, through a lot of challenges and this was the final one. We had to get through this one too. There was no turning back.

Finally, the day arrived. The much-awaited drive upto the Baap of all Passes. I don't know about Ajay and Manav, I never spoke to them about this, but I was extremely anxious. Every local driver we met enroute reiterated only one thing and that was "saab, poora raasta khadi chadhai hai." (All through the way it is a steep climb up). Although we never really got stranded anywhere, it was still there in the back of my mind as to how we would take the "khadi chadhai". Deep inside I knew I would have to walk stretches. So far, all the walking at high altitudes had not led to any AMS issues except in the initial couple of days when I couldn't walk without the pounding headache kicking in. Would I be able to walk up steep slopes? I had no answers to it. I think it is more the fear of the unknown that creates all the issues in the mind. You hear stuff that is someone else's perception, and you start believing it to be your's and the others' fears become your own. Anyways, there was no turning back now. There were 3 routes out of Chiari to go back home. One was Sach Pass - Chamba , the other was Killar - Kishtwar and the third was via Manali. Let's just say in terms of road conditions for the car each was equally bad. So, with that thought in my mind I just prepared myself for whatever was to come.

The first thing on the priority list was to get the stepney fixed. A few kilometres from Chiari towards Killar is a village called Phindru. We found a guy to fix the tyre. And while he was doing that, Manav went and found a place for breakfast. Guess what I had for breakfast? Bingo!! Aloo parathas... again!! Though I must admit that it was one of the best I had had during this trip. With a satiated tummy and the car stepney in place, we set out for the final leg of our journey.

The road upto a few kilometres from the Alwar bridge were pretty decent. It did make us wonder if it was all over-hyped about it being a challenging climb. We had covered a much worse on the Batal - Gramphoo stretch. There was nothing of what we had heard there would be. Just when we had begun to settle in with the idea that it was indeed all an over hyped thing that we experienced the first bout of it. Sharp and steep hairpin bends, and the tarred road that vanished into being a track. It was probably all very well for the two sitting in the front. But for me it was an ordeal. Imagine a scenario where 2/3rds of the back seat was full of luggage and loose luggage mind you, which also included 3 high end cameras which both the gentlemen refused to put into their respective camera bags. I was hanging onto the door to one side, fixing my two feet under the front seats and with one arm trying to stop the stuff lying on the seat from falling over. All this while the car was running up steep slopes, through sharp frequent hairpin bends at 3,000 plus rpm (revolutions per minute). Up to a point, I was still clicking pictures, but then, I gave up. I couldn't multitask to that extent.

We were to go up 7,500-8,000 ft in altitude in about 35 kms. There were times when we would stop and give the car a breather. Wait for it to cool down. I did wonder quite a few times whether that was the car's way of telling me that I need to stop thinking of food all the time and begin to lose some weight. Slowly and steadily, we were covering the distance. We were in no hurry. There were places where we even had to clear the roads off the boulders that had come sliding down. It was becoming cooler and the wind was beginning to hit the head. We came across a couple of beautiful waterfalls where the car actually went from under the waterfall. We crossed a couple of big water crossings too. Sitting behind the driver, while the car is going on a steep uphill direction, can give you a feel of a vestibule effect. And because you cannot see the road ahead, the fear adds on. There were 2-3 places where I felt the car going too close to the edge of the road for my comfort, so much so that for someone like me, whose religious knowledge begins and ends with the Gayatri Mantra, the Hanuman Chalisa flashed in my mind at those times. Both Manav and Ajay looked cool probably because they could see the road and what it was outside. For me it was a nightmare doubled by the fact that I was being rolled around like a dice. It also did not help when I saw the steep gradient we had come up on and the steep gradient we had to go up to. In bits and pieces, slowly and steadily, we covered the distance. Finally, we reached the top. It took us a good about 2.5 - 3 hrs but yes, we did it. In-spite of all that had been going on in the mind, we did it. We had heard that quite a few cars had had side cuts on the tyres, but nothing of that sort happened to our car. Ajay managed it beautifully. Hats off to him and hats off to the car. The suspension, the alignment, the tyres stood the test of nature perfectly.

Once we crossed the pass towards Chamba, it was a different landscape. The roads had a gradual gradient. The condition was a lot better. They were much easier on the car and the mind. And after we crossed Satrundi Check Post, the topography changed completely. From absolutely stoney, barren mountains we came to absolute green mountains. Waterfalls lined the roads. In fact in one semi-circular stretch, we counted 7-8 waterfalls. We reached Bairavgarh by about 5.00 in the evening. That is where for the first time in 5 days I got a proper signal on my phone. I Facetimed the kids. Oh yes, I was suddenly very home sick. We had lunch and were on our way to Chamba which was where we were ending our day. It was time to celebrate.

Day 8 - Homeward Bound.

We were tired, exhausted, happy, sad , all of it and more. It was a very quiet, uneventful ride back home. A lot had happened in the previous 7 days. I had pushed myself beyond what I had thought I was capable of. I lived a dream. Did Sach Pass prove to be the proverbial Baap of all Passes? Yes, it did. Did it live up to the reputation it has? Yes, it did. Would I come again? Yes, I would. Would I want to do it any differently? I don't know. What went on in my mind when I reached up there? I was happy, I was proud of myself for achieving what I dreamt of doing, but in a strange way I was also blank in my mind. And I was sad too. Yet again I did not have my loved ones with me to share that moment with. I don't know how long we were there at the pass, but in my heart, I went through a gamut of emotions. However much a tough nut I maybe on the outside, inside I am a real softie. And yes, I missed that hug! In spite of everything, I am mighty proud of myself. I have come a very long way in life. Travel has taught me to be happy. It has taught me to live my life.

Mesmerising, Magical Rajasthan - A Solo Journey (August 2017)

With every trip that I did, my definition of a "meatier, more juicer trip" kept changing. Life is like that. You always want more. The "more" for me now was a solo trip. Well, the seed of a solo trip was already taking shape during my GQ trip planning. It did not happen then but then as they say, there is a time and place for everything. Now was the time to step into the world of solo travel. I had been travelling without the family, so in a sense I had stepped out of the security of the family cocoon. During the planning stages there was much contemplation on where to go. There was the temple trail in the south of India, there was the North-east and there was also the thought to do a solo back packer's trip in public transport and whatnot. It all sounded extremely exciting in thoughts. But the more I spent time on it, I realised it was better to take baby steps. I also needed to be sure that I was comfortable with my own company. Though after my Ladakh trip in the winter experience I was somewhat convinced that I would be able to do it but I wanted this to be the first of many and not first and the last. Rajasthan came out tops as the preferred destination to be explored in my own car. Eight days, closer to home, in the comfort of my own car was a great way to start. Rajasthan, of course, has a lot to offer and it is a great place to be in the monsoons. Awesome weather and no crowds thronging the places. So, there it was the itinerary set, Bikaner, Jaisalmer, Jodhpur was the circuit.

Day 1

The drive to Bikaner from Gurgaon is about 8-9 hours. And believe me it was an absolutely amazing drive. Roads were fantastic, the landscape was lush green and there was no traffic on the road. I reached Bikaner at about 2.30 pm. I had booked Laxmi Niwas Palace. A beautiful palace converted into a hotel, which has been the setting for many a Bollywood movies. One of the recent ones being Fawad Khan's Khoobsoorat. I could just visualise each and every scene out of the movie right there. I checked in to the hotel and the best thing that happened was that I was upgraded to a suite. The advantages of being a solo woman traveller. My room was on the 4th floor so we naturally needed to take the lift. The lift goes up until the 2nd floor and then you take the stairs. This palace was built in 1902. The manager told me that the lift was one of the first ones to be installed in India. It has a two-way opening lift, which had metal grill sliding doors. You get in and it is all wood panelled and has a red velvet bench on one side. It is big in size but can carry only 4 people at a time. And when it moves, it was one very rickety lift. Despite the rickety-ness, sitting in it felt so royal. The one and a half days that I stayed there, I was like a kid who had found a toy. I have lost count on how many times I went up and down in that lift - with or without reason.

After freshening up, I requested the manager to organise an auto for me, for him to take me into the city, show me around some Havelis and the markets. The first stop was at the havelis. I had never really been to any havelis earlier, and in my mind, I had this image of the havelis as time and weather-beaten buildings which would probably be very unkempt. I reached the site and what I saw was totally unexpected. The havelis were extremely well maintained on the outside and the surroundings were spic and span. At the cost of sounding clichéd, it felt like one of the old time European lanes. Unfortunately, most of the havelis are shut to the general public. The auto driver took me to one which is called Rampuria Haveli, part of this is now converted into a hotel called Bhanwar Niwas. The haveli, belonging to a wealthy merchant family, was built in the 15th century. It is made out of red sandstone. These havelis are built with both, the Rajput and Mughal architectural influences. Amazingly fine carvings and lattice work were done on these havelis. The opulent interiors just take you into another world, another time, another era.

After the haveli visit, he took me to a 500-year-old Jain temple called the Seth Bhandasar Jain Temple. This temple was built by a wealthy merchant Bhandasa Oswal in 1468 and was dedicated to the 5th Tirthankar Sumatinathji. This temple is an architectural masterpiece. It is said the 40,000 kgs of pure ghee (rarified butter) was used instead of mortar to build this temple. It is also believed that this ghee trickles out of the walls when it is extremely hot. The temple is beautifully carved and painted in bright colours. It does make one wonder how evolved technology was in the times gone by. The kind of workmanship that existed in those times cannot be replicated anywhere closely with all the progress we have made today.

Bikaner is also home to the famous Bikaneri Bhujia. Now it was time to go find some of the same. So off we went to this shop near the railway lines called Bishanlal Babulal. A friend of mine who had been here earlier had given the reference. A small little place but it had an amazing range of savouries. What caught my taste buds was the paneer bhujia. A very tangy bhujia with loads of raisins and cashews in it. I picked up 2-3 different varieties for myself, and some that my friend had asked for and was on way back to the hotel. It had been a long day. I had had only sandwiches on the go since the morning and was now totally famished. Lal Maas was awaiting!

Day 2

When you say Bikaner, the one thing that comes to mind instantly is The Karni Mata Temple, or the more famously known Temple of Rats. Ever since I had seen it on one of the travel programs years back, I had wanted go and see it for myself. Although I must say, if there is anything that I feared besides lizards, it is rats. So it was with absolute mixed feelings that I got up the next morning and set out driving to Deshnoke, a small town 30 kms from Bikaner on the Bikaner - Jodhpur highway.

The Karni Mata Temple is about 600 years old. According to the story the priest told me, Karni Mata was originally the wife of Depoji Charan of the village of Sathika. However, she later expressed unwillingness to her husband to engage in conjugal relations. He initially humoured her, thinking that she would relent in time. Instead, Karni arranged for him to marry her younger sister, Gulab, so that he might have a proper married life. She herself remained celibate all her life. She apparently lived upto the age of 151 years. Folklore has it that Karni Mata's sister's eldest son, who was also her favourite, drowned in a pond in Kapil Sarovar in Kolayat, while he was attempting to drink water from it. Karni Mata implored Yama, the God of Death, to revive him. First refusing, Yama eventually gave in, permitting him and all of Karni mata's male descendants to be reincarnated as rats. It is also said that these rats, once they die are reborn in the human form.

When I was taking off my sandals to get into the temple, I had no idea how I would react to the rats scampering all over. It was playing on my mind. I am not a religious person at all. And thus, I guess it is natural that in such situation repulsive thoughts come to mind. I walked in and there is no sight of any rats. I had this picture in my mind of them being there in hoards. Then suddenly out of nowhere these 3-4 rats came running after each other. I jumped out of their way and in the bargain lost my balance. And there I was flat on my backside on the floor. I was extremely embarrassed. I first checked on the camera and then took a deep breath. All was well. And strangely, just in that instance, my fear of the rats vanished. I got up and walked towards the place where the deity was placed. In the nooks and crannies, I saw these bunches of rats sleeping over each other. The priest took my pooja thali, did what he had to do and gave me Charn Amrit to drink. Which I did. After this I went around the temple. At various times even sat down next to a group of rats to photograph them. What I also noticed was that the rats looked very sick. A lot of them had these tumour-like growths. When the priest was telling me the history behind the temple, he told me that it is all the sweets that they eat that makes them like that. And he also told me that the Charn Amrit that I had was part of the same milk that the rats drink. I cannot even begin to describe the thoughts that bombarded my mind at that time. I went numb. And it is at times like these that you realise faith and belief override all sense of logic and science. Anyhow, it was too late now for me to sit there and entertain any of the crazy thoughts that came to mind. There were so many people who would have had it before me, nothing happened to them, nothing would happen to me. With that thought, I headed out of the temple. At least one thing is for sure now, I know I will never fear a rat anymore. But lizards? Well, that will stay with me.

My friend who had visited Bikaner earlier this year had mentioned a road side dhaba enroute for some nice Rajasthani food. I had skipped breakfast as I wanted to have brunch there. This dhaba is called Brahman Hotel and it is about 12-14 kms from Deshnoke while going towards Bikaner. It's a stand-alone dhaba, so you cannot miss it. I ordered a thali which had Dal Batti, Gatte ki sabzi, malai kofta, dal, Ker Sangri, pyaaz ki chutney (basically chopped onions sautéed with green chillies) and pyaaz ka raita and bajre ki roti, it was quite delicious but Pavana ka Dhaba near Beawar still gets the brownie points. I accidently discovered Pavana Ka Dhaba on one of my drives through Rajasthan. It is about 4 kms short of Beawar when going towards Delhi. The choorma is to die for and the daal baati is delicious to the next level.

With my stomach happy, it was time for the next stop. The Junagadh Fort. For the longest time, I knew of Junagadh being in Gujarat. My uncle used to work there and that is how I knew of the place. So, when I was researching Bikaner, Junagadh Fort being in Bikaner completely shook the foundations of my as it is weak geographical knowledge. I am not kidding, I opened the atlas and looked for Junagadh and was relieved to know that I was right about where it was. For the life of me I cannot understand why Junagadh Fort is not in Junagadh. I do admit Geography was never my strong subject.

Bikaner came into being only around the mid-15th century. Rao Bika, the second son of Maharaja Rao Jodha, the founder of Jodhpur city, knew he would never inherit the kingdom from his father, so he decided to build his own empire at Bikaner, which was till that time called Jungladesh. Bikaner, though a part of the Thar Desert, was considered an oasis on the trade route between Central Asia and the Gujarat coast since it had adequate spring water sources. The history of Bikaner and the fort within it started with Bika. It was only about 100 years later that Bikaner's fortunes flourished under Raja Rai Singhji, the sixth ruler of Bikaner, who ruled from 1571 to 1611. The Junagarh Fort was made during his reign, though it took about 5 generations to come to what it is today. His successors, Maharaja

Karan Singh, Maharaja Anoop Singhji, Maharaja Gaj Singh, Maharaja Surat Singh and Maharaja Dungar Singh subsequently kept adding to the Fort. Maharaja Ganga Singh was the best-known Rajasthan prince and was a favourite of the British viceroys. He built the Ganga Niwas Palace which was designed by Sir Samuel Swinton Jacob. The building was called Lalgarh Palace and he moved his residence from the Junagadh Fort to the palace in 1902. Ganga Singh's son Sadul Singh acceded his state to the Union of India in 1943. His son Karni Singh succeeded him in title in 1950. Karni Singh died in 1988 and he did not have a successor. The royal family continues to stay in a suite in the Lalgarh Palace, part of which is now converted into a heritage hotel which is called Laxmi Niwas Palace, the place I stayed in. Now I realise why I felt like royalty.

The one thing that catches your eye as you enter the fort is the cleanliness. The entrances have chain curtains hanging down and the open spaces have been covered by a net roof so that the birds don't come in. The floor, made of Italian tiles is absolutely spic and span. Really, it was a pleasure to go around the fort. The Diwan-e-khas, made in red sandstone, is so beautifully and intricately carved. I had some interesting conversations with the guide who accompanied me. According to what he told me, Maharaja Ganga Singh was responsible in getting the first railway line and the water canal system to Bikaner.

Another conversation with the guide about the natural colours used in the fort for painting the murals took me to the studio of Raju Swami, a miniature painting artist based in Bikaner. A soft spoken, unassuming guy, Raju Swami is an extremely talented artist. Apparently, and that is what he told me, each room in Udai Vilas, Udaipur has his paintings hanging. He has also exhibited in The Galleries Lafayette, Paris a number of times. He explained what miniature paintings actually meant. He told me about the natural colours, their sources - from the earth and vegetable colours. He took me through his paintings. I was awestruck by his work. Each of them looked like prints rather than paintings. A look through the magnifying glass and you see how fine the work is. It was truly amazing. Apparently, they have a lot of dietary restrictions to help maintain a good eyesight. His two sons are also exceptional artists. And this is a family tradition going back generations.

It was indeed a very educative day that I spent. And I would like to believe that had I not been solo, I probably would not have done all this. Somehow one is more receptive, more aware, when one is alone. Whatever it was, I had an amazing day. Bikaner was quite a surprise package. I felt it is a very underrated city. I completely fell in love with the it.

Day 3

It was time to move on to the next destination - Jaisalmer. Jaisalmer is named after Maharawal Jaisal Singh, a Rajput king who founded the city in 1156 AD. "Jaisalmer" means "the Hill Fort of Jaisal". It is also called the "Golden City of India" because the yellow sand and the yellow sandstone used in every architecture of the city. It gives a yellowish-golden tinge to the city and its surrounding area. Believe me when I say it is so yellow, that I began to feel jaundiced. I am not exaggerating there. It shares almost 470 kms of the border with Pakistan on its west and southwest side.

Since it was only about 320 kms drive, I knew I could drive at leisure. I had the time to explore places enroute. My first stop was at a place called Gajner. Gajner is about 30 kms from Bikaner on the Bikaner-Jaisalmer highway. Gajner Palace, now a hotel, was originally a hunting lodge for the Maharaja and his family which was built by Maharaja Ganga Singh on the banks of Gajner Lake. The entry to the lake is necessarily through the palace premises. And if you are not staying at the hotel, they charge you INR. 250/- for entry (which also includes a cup of tea or coffee and cookies at the lake side coffee shop). I reached at 8 am. The boats were still not ready. I requested the person at the reception and he agreed to contact the concerned person. I was told that the boatman would be there by 8.30 and that I could in the meantime look around the property and then have some tea at the coffee shop. I did just that. It is a very peaceful place with nice walkways along the lake. It is the perfect place if you want some peace and quiet. There is this thing about being at such places when you are alone. It was so quiet that I could actually hear myself think. I was so aware of all the sounds around me. There were these two crows who gave me company while I was having my tea. Well, it is another matter that they stole my cookies. By the time I finished my tea, the boat was ready. Never had I ever done boating alone, but it was fun. The boat man had his own stories to share. The whole setting was so beautiful. From where I was in the boat, the palace looked like a place right out of fairy tale set in an English County. I was amazed when I realised I had been boating for an hour.

18 kms from Gajner towards Jaisalmer is a small town called Kolayat. This was my next stop. I heard about Kolayat for the first time when I had gone to the Seth Bhandadas Jain Temple in Bikaner. The priest there had told me about it. The temple at Kolayat is a mythological temple, which is believed to have been closely linked with the life of the Indian saint Kapil Muni, the propagator of the 'Sankhya' philosophy. Sankhya is a philosophy that regards the universe as consisting of two realities, *purusha* i.e., consciousness and *prakriti* i.e., matter. *Jiva* i.e., a living being, is that state in which consciousness is bonded to matter in some form. According to the Sankhya scholars, this fusion led to the emergence of *buddhi* i.e., intellect and *ahaṅkāra* i.e., ego. Kapil Muni is said to have been the

incarnation of Lord Vishnu. According to mythology, the saint had achieved salvation and shed his body under a 'Peepal' tree situated here. Thousands of sadhus and pilgrims take a dip in the sacred waters of the lake nearby to purify their sins and to attain salvation. Kolayat has a series of marble temples, sandstone pavilions and 52 ghats, which are basically bathing places, built around a large artificial lake which never goes dry. The colour of the water also is a very different blue - a powder blue. I guess it is because of the colour of the sand. I have to admit, it was a very clean lake. This is also the same lake that I mentioned earlier where Karni Mata's sister's eldest son, drowned. A walk around the ghats and the lake was an extremely interesting experience. There were so many people, all from different walks of life, in different kinds of moods. In the half an hour that I spent there I witnessed happiness, sadness, loneliness, celebrations and mourning. It just reiterated to me the power of religious faith and belief in human life. Observing such sights was indeed very humbling.

After Kolayat, it was a straight drive to Jaisalmer. Absolutely excellent roads to drive on till Pokhran, after which there was road widening happening. But since there was no traffic, I faced no delays.

Just 10 kms short of Jaisalmer, on the highway itself, is the Jaisalmer War Museum. This museum showcases the glorious history of the Indian Army. It displays vehicles and equipment captured during the 1965 and 1971 Operations. It also has two Honour Walls with names of Param Vir Chakra and Mahavir Chakra winners engraved on it. It took me about 40 mins to go around the place and watch the 15-minute documentary and I was on my way to the hotel.

I had enough time before dinner and I also need to refuel since I had an early morning start to what was going to be an epic drive, so I quickly checked in and went out for a drive around the city. After refuelling I asked around and got to know there was a small lake close by - The Gadsisar lake.

Gadsisar Lake was excavated by Maharawal Gadsi Singh in 1367. It is a rain water lake surrounded by small temples and shrines. It was made more like a water conservation tank. This reservoir controlled entire water supply to the arid city. Apparently, it attracts a lot of migratory birds in the winters.

Bikaner was a lot cleaner, so in that sense I was a little disappointed. But the next day was going to be a great drive, so the excitement of it overshadowed the disappointment.

Day 4

Any itinerary to Jaisalmer is incomplete if you do not visit Tanot and Longewala. Tanot is a village 120 kms from Jaisalmer. It is more famously known for the Tanot Mata Temple. Tanot Mata Temple is about 1,200 years old and is 16 kms from the Pakistani Border. It is said that during the Indo-Pakistan War of 1965, Pakistani Army dropped over 3000 bombs targeting the area around the temple but none caused any considerable damage, about 450 of these bombs were dropped within the premises of the temple and none exploded. In 1971 when Pakistan and India went to war this area was again targeted by the Pakistani Tanks for four days. Again, all the tanks got stuck in the sand and the Indian Air Force picked them out easily by bombing them where they stood as they were unable to move even one inch. Over 200 Pakistani tank troops were killed here and the majority actually left their stuck tanks and ran for their lives. The legend exists since 1965 and was re-affirmed in 1971 and it is a recorded fact that each and every enemy soldier who dared to attack this area was killed. The dud bombs are kept as exhibits within the temple.

As a practice, Tanot Mata Temple is the last point upto which civilians are allowed. One needs to take permission from the district or military authorities and only after proper documentation, the permission is granted. A dear friend of mine who is in the Army organised the permits for me. Naturally I was extremely excited. I left Jaisalmer at 7 a.m after a tasty breakfast of aloo ki sabzi and parathas. It was an awesome drive. The entire landscape was scattered with windmills. As you cross Ramgarh (60 kms from Jaisalmer) there is one windmill that is pretty close to the road. I stopped there to take a picture of my car with the windmill in the back drop. And for the first time I actually observed a windmill. It was quite fascinating. The sound that it makes as the blades cut through the wind, the sheer size of it all, it was really mesmerising. I must have stood there for quite some time before I realised I had to reach somewhere.

Just after Ramgarh my phone network vanished. I later got to know that only BSNL works in that whole area. And beyond Ramgarh, the traffic also seemed to vanish. There was not another soul on the road other than me, just beautiful roads and an amazing green landscape. Yes, I was driving in Rajasthan, which is supposed to be a desert, but it was all green. The first sight of the desert and sand dunes came at Ranau, a small little village 30 kms from Ramgarh. Much as I was itching to get off the road and drive in the sand, I had to keep myself on the road. For one, I was alone with no back up and two, there was neither any phone network nor anyone on the road for me to call for help.

I reached Tanot at about 9.30 a.m. There were 2 BSF men standing there. I asked them where I could park the car. And one of them came up to me and asked me my name and where I was coming from. Once my identity was confirmed, he told me that they had been waiting for me. He had instructions to escort me through the entire bit and make sure I was comfortable and then direct me on the way to Longewala. I suddenly felt all important. Tanot Mata Temple is maintained by the BSF and within the premises is the BSF guest house. I was first taken to the guest house. They offered some really tasty tea and refreshments. While I was having tea, I was chatting with them and they told me the history of the temple. After having tea, they took me to the temple. The panditji made me sit down and did a pooja for me. As I mentioned earlier, I am not a religious person, but I totally respect the beliefs and rituals such places have. Blessings in any form never hurt anyone. While coming into the temple I had noticed that there was a Pir Baba ki Mazaar outside. According to the panditji there was this Pakistani soldier who was a devotee of Tanot Mata. During the war, he kept discouraging the Pakistani army from attacking the temple and its surrounding area. The Pakistanis in anger, cut off his limbs. He kept fighting them and somehow reached the temple and died there. It is his mazaar that was built at the temple.

I was then taken to another section of the temple where there were hundreds of thousands of handkerchiefs tied. It is a belief that when you tie a handkerchief and make a wish, the Tanot Mata fulfils it. Once the wish is fulfilled, you need to come back and untie any one handkerchief. There is something about these temples which have such strong beliefs that give me goosebumps, and I say that in a good way.

After the temple visit, one BSF jawan was assigned to me for escorting me to the border post. We set out after the register entry and identification check. It was a 16 km drive to the border post. What an amazing drive it was - just miles and miles of flat land. It felt like a scene right out of a western movie. I was just waiting for Clint Eastwood to come out riding from somewhere.

All these days I had been alone on the road, so I could not get any pictures of me with my car. Now that I had the BSF jawan with me, I made sure I got my fill of pictures on the road. He also patiently obliged as many times as I asked him to. He was very amused when he got to know that I had been driving all alone from Delhi. Once we reached the border post, the first thing he told the 2 guards there was that I was here driving by myself. I spent a good half an hour with them. I talked to them about life at the post and I had my questions and they answered them all. My love and respect for the men in uniform just went up by notches. It is not an easy life. The loneliness, the monotony, the extreme weather conditions - it is not a comfortable job but they do it with so much passion.

After that, we went to the base camp. Where I was shown around. And I guess, its only right that for security reasons what I saw there should stay there. I had a great time. And once again, thank you my friend (you know who you are) from the bottom of my heart for making it possible for me to experience this.

By the time we came back to the guest house it was 12 noon and I was famished. Yes, I had lunch waiting for me too. A simple yet delicious lunch, I must add. After Lunch I was given directions to Longewala and I set out on another beautiful drive.

Longewala is about 45 kms from Tanot. A beautiful desert drive. Here I could not resist it and the heart won over the mind and I went off the road. I did not try too many antics, but yes, I had my fun. My family and friends were going to be joining me in a few days and we would be going to Sam Dunes, that kept me going. I knew I would get the fill of action then.

Longewala is a small little village. The war memorial is bang on the road. So far, I had been driving through a landscape that was green, because of that I did not feel the heat. Longewala is sandy and when I got off the car, the heat hit hard. The sun was reflecting off the sand and hurting my eyes. I have no clue what the temperature was but it was extremely hot. The war memorial is a small little place. There is one room that has all the exhibits from the Battle of Longewala, and then there is the AV room where you see the war documentary. Outside, there is a captured Pakistani tank.

Visits to war memorials always leave me in a sombre mood. Though I must admit that I was most affected by the Kargil Memorial, but that was probably because we lived through it and could relate to it. Nonetheless, the mood had suddenly become very pensive. I sat in the car for a while, gathered my thoughts and started driving towards Ramgarh and then on to Jaisalmer. Needless to say, the drive to Ramgarh was as lonely as what I had done so far.

As soon as I reached Ramgarh, my phone started pinging as if it had gone nuts. I saw a lot of missed calls from the family. I parked on the side and called them up. I assured them I was fine and I was on my way.

About 6-7 kms short of Jaisalmer is a place called Bada Bagh. Maharaja Jai Singh II had commissioned a dam to create a tank during his reign in the 16th century. After his death, his son Lunkaran, made a beautiful garden next to it and constructed a cenotaph in his memory. Later cenotaphs were made in memory of other maharajas too. Though I had all the intentions of going in and exploring the cenotaphs, something held me back. There were these 4-5 guys who made me feel uncomfortable and unsafe. So, I listened to my gut feeling, and left. Though, I did manage to take a few pictures. My research on the internet showed me some beautiful cenotaphs that I missed by not going in, but it is alright. There is always another time.

It was about 4.30 pm and I was not tired as yet. So, I looked up how far Kuldhara was and then decided to go there as well. It is about 20 kms from Jaisalmer. Frankly, I was in two minds whether to go there alone or not. I have said this before too, in case of the unknown, the perceptions of other people sometimes become your own and as a result their fears become yours. Your own sense of logic goes out of the window. At one point, I almost turned back. But then I decided to go ahead.

As the folklore of Kuldhara goes, about 200 years ago, it was home to the Paliwal Brahmins. It was during this time that Salim Singh, the Diwan of Jaisalmer, known for his debauchery and unscrupulous tax-collecting methods, set his eyes on the beautiful daughter of the village chief. The Diwan was absolutely hell bent on marrying the girl and he told the villagers if they came in his way he would levy huge taxes on them. Fearing the wrath of the Diwan, the residents of the entire village fled one dark night, leaving behind their homes and everything within them. Kuldhara was abandoned by its very own people. No one saw the thousand-odd members of the village leave. For generations now, no one knows where the Paliwals have resettled. All that is known is they cursed the town when they left – that no one would ever be able to settle down in Kuldhara again. It is probably one of the most mysterious migrations known in Indian history.

I reach Kuldhara and I see this big gate. I call out to this guy sitting near it, he happens to be the ticket seller. He guides me in. Inside, I am met by this 12-13-year-old boy who is eager to tell me the story. He said I could pay him whatever I felt like. He seemed like a cute kid so I went along with him. I knew the story, but still went along. To be really honest, I was extremely disappointed. It was nothing like what I was probably expecting. To top it all, there was construction happening to recreate the village. And let me be honest, there was nothing ghostly about the place. And to think that I was in two minds, was absurd.

It was one of the best days of my trip so far. The solitude, the drive, the landscape, the historical importance of the places I visited, everything just made it a complete package. The total distance between Ramgarh-Tanot-Longewala-Ramgarh is about 200 kms. This was truly the solo part of the journey. Complete solitude and no connection with civilisation when I was driving made it the most confidence boosting, empowering 200 kms that I have ever driven! For someone who has had confidence issues all through her life, it was truely a day that has left a mark for life. It was surely a day that needed to be celebrated. Back at the hotel, I asked the manager to book a dinner table for me at Trio, a roof top restaurant with a beautiful backdrop of the Mandir Palace. A befitting setting to drink to an absolutely awesome day.

Day 5

It had been a long day, the previous day. Ever since I started on this trip, I had been getting up early every day. This morning I slept in. I woke up at about 9, had a very leisurely breakfast and planned my day. It was the day to be a typical tourist.

My first stop was Ludrava. It is 15 km to the north-west of Jaisalmer. Ludrava was the ancient capital of the Bhatti Dynasty till 1156 AD when Rawal Jaisal founded the Jaisalmer State and shifted the capital to Jaisalmer. It is famous for the Jain temple dedicated to 23rd Tirthankara, Parsavnath which was destroyed by Mohammad Gori in 1152 AD but was reconstructed in 1615 by Seth Tharu Shah.

Ludrava has a very different architectural design, it was more on the pagoda style with very fine carvings and lattice work. In Jainism, there are 24 Tirthankars. The idols of all the Tirthankars are identical, but what differentiates one from the other is the symbol. The symbol of Parsavnath, the 23rd Tirthankar is the snake. The idol at this temple is made of black touchstone. There are about 100 snakes that are carved like a hood behind the idol. There is also a place where there is a hole from which it is said a snake comes out every Nag Panchami and drinks milk. There is also a kalpavriksha in this temple enclosed in a stone structure. It is supposed to be a wish fulfilling tree. I wonder if it still works.

After this, I headed to the Patwon ki Haveli. It is a cluster of 5 havelis. The first one was constructed in 1805 by Guman Chand Patwa and his 5 sons. These were completed in a span of 50 years in the 1st half of the 19th century. In those days, it was estimated that in total Rs. 10 Lakhs was spent in constructing these havelis. Hindu and Muslim craftsman hailing from Gujrat, Malwa and Sindh worked in constructing these havelis. These were known as "mansions of the brocade merchants". There are also theories that these merchants made a lot of their fortunes through opium smuggling and money lending.

What really had me in awe was the carvings. Such fine work. I have not yet got my fill of it. How I would love to live in times of such grandeur and opulence. The things on display in the haveli gave an interesting insight into the life and times of the "patwas". There is a whole gallery that displays the different kinds of Rajasthani turbans. It is the way a turban is tied by which you can identify the caste, culture, profession of the person wearing it. Another section has a range of weighing stones used in those times. Also, there is a copy of the 'Tajeraat-e-hind" or the IPC in Hindi.

I was by now done seeing most of the touristy places that were there to see in Jaisalmer. The one thing that was left, was the fort. During my research, I got to know that the Jaisalmer fort was a living fort. For some strange reason, I did not know where to start and how to go about seeing it, what to expect. I don't know if it is just me or others have also had this conflict in the mind. Anyhow, I finally did manage to reach the fort.

Jaisalmer Fort was built in 1156 AD by Rawal Jaisal atop the Trikuta Hill. It is apparently one of the largest in the world, and is called the Sonar Qila. Almost 1/4th of the city's population resides in the fort. It is most unlike any fort I have visited. I guess because of the people living in it. I visited a Jain temple which was inside the fort. If I remember correctly, this one was dedicated to the 8th Tirthankar whose symbol was the half-moon. The thing about these temples in Rajasthan is that in none of them has any cement or mortar been used. These are all interlocked. That is the reason that there are so many pillars in each of these temples. One can see the metal interlockers that look like oversized staple pins. The guide took me to the palace too, but by now I had had enough of palaces and temples. I was not inclined to go see another one. Actually, I will be honest, after the previous day's action, this was just not exciting enough.

It was time for lunch and found this cozy little restaurant serving Italian food right at the gate of the fort. Had my lunch and headed back to the hotel. The rest of the evening I lazed around the poolside with a book, something I had not done in a long time. That evening, the chef made some amazing laal maas for me in addition to the delicious buffet – like I said earlier, some advantages of a lady travelling alone - room upgrades and the extra bit of pampering; I am not complaining!!

If you really ask me, I was pretty disappointed with Jaisalmer city. I had a very different image made up in my mind of Jaisalmer, which it wasn't. Secondly, it is a city which survives on tourism, and one would think that it would be an extremely warm (and i don't mean that in the climatic way) and welcoming city. It wasn't so. I have been to a number of cities in Rajasthan and warmth and hospitality is one thing I have associated with each one of them - but not Jaisalmer. It just felt that all they wanted to do was fleece the tourist. This is one city, probably I would not want to come back to. Except of course if it is a focused visit to Sam Dunes for some self-driven dune bashing.

Day 6

The next destination was Jodhpur. Jaisalmer to Jodhpur is about a 5-hour drive. So, I had planned on going via Osian. Osian is an ancient town famous for the cluster of ruined Brahmanical and Jain temples dating from the 8th to 11th centuries. The city was a major religious centre of the kingdom of Marwar during the Gujara Pratihara dynasty. Of the 18 shrines in the group, the Surya or Sun Temple and the later Kali temple, Sachiya Mata Temple and the main Jain temple dedicated to Mahavira stands out in their grace and architecture. It is also known as the 'Khajuraho of Rajasthan'. The town was a major trading centre, at least as early as the Gupta period. It maintained this status, while also being a major centre of Brahmanism and Jainism for hundreds of years. This ended abruptly when the town was attacked by the armies of Muhammed of Ghori in 1195.

On my earlier visit to the area two years back, I had wished to visit Osian, but it never happened. So, this time I was quite certain I would take the detour enroute Jodhpur and visit the temples. On the way to Pokhran, I came across hoards of people on bikes and cars. They were like men on a mission. Unruly was an understatement. I stopped at one of the roadside camps that were erected for them to ask what was happening and I was told that they were all headed towards Ramdevra for a fair. Ramdevra is a village 12 kms from Pokhran on the Bikaner Highway. The village is named after Baba Ramdevji, a Tanwar Rajput and a saint who took Samadhi (conscious exit from the mortal body) in 1384 AD at the age of 33 years. Maharaja Ganga Singh of Bikaner constructed a temple around the samadhi in 1931 AD.

Ramdev is considered to be an incarnation of Vishnu. Muslims venerate Ramdev as *Ramshah Pir*. He was said to have had miraculous powers and his fame reached far and wide. Legend has it that five pirs from Mecca came to test Ramdev's powers. Ramdev, after the initial welcome, requested them to have lunch with him. But the Pirs said they only ate in their personal utensils, which were lying in Mecca so they could not have their meals. On this, Ramdev smiled and said look your utensils are coming and they saw that their eating bowls were coming flying in air from Mecca. After being convinced of his abilities and powers, they paid their homage to him and named him Rama Shah Pir. The five pirs who came to test his powers, were so overwhelmed by his powers that they decided to stay with him and the samadhi of these five are also near samadhi of Ramdev. Ramdev, a ruler of fourteenth century, believed in the equality of all human beings, high or low, rich or poor. He devoted his life for the upliftment of the downtrodden and poor people of the society. His worship crosses the Hindu-Muslim divide as well as the distinctions of caste. His followers are spread across caste-barriers in Rajasthan, Haryana, Punjab, Gujarat, Madhya Pradesh, Mumbai, Delhi and also Sindh in Pakistan.

August - September are months when a huge fair is organised in Ramdevra, and the entire crowd was going there - in cars, on bikes, even on foot walking hundreds of kms. At Pokhran there is a bifurcation, one road going towards Bikaner which would have taken me to Osian (via Ramdevra, of course) and the other straight to Jodhpur. I stopped at one of the dhabas at the crossroads for tea and thought over what to do. The hundreds of people on the road were kind of deterring my thoughts. I had no inclination of crawling any more than I had to. So, while having tea at the dhaba I just put in query to my friends on what I should do. They suggested I head straight to Jodhpur. And I did just that. I guess visiting Osian was not meant to be.

Anyway, the road to Jodhpur from Pokhran is a two lane toll road, a new toll road so the toll booths were still not operational. All through the way I came across these people travelling to Ramdevra. I reached Jodhpur at about 2.00 pm. ITC WelcomHotel is on the outskirts on the Jaipur highway beyond the Cantonment. I had read in someone's travel blog that the hotel had a sumptuous 6 course royal Rajasthani meal on its menu. So, the first thing I asked the lady at the front desk was about this. She asked me when I would like to have it and we fixed the date for dinner. I had just about settled in the room, when I got a call from the Chef. We had a little chat about my preferences, if I had any allergies, what I liked what I did not and all of that.

I called up Arjun, a friend in Jodhpur, who I had got to know in the Scorpio Owner's group that I am a part of. As there was a lot of news doing the rounds about floods in Rajasthan, I had connected with him in that regard before I left. And on one of the numerous chats we had, he had offered to show me the Jodhpur that is usually not on the tourist map. I took him up on his offer and we fixed up a time for early next morning. Since I had nothing else to do, I just chilled through the evening, dreaming of the dinner, wondering if it all was a hype, more so because I was paying a bomb for it.

I was having a drink in the bar when I was called in for my meal sharp at 9.00 p.m. A nice table was set for me in a separate corner. There walks in the chef, introduces himself and sits down at the table. His name is Chef Akshraj Jodha (love the name). Chef Akshraj is from the lineage of none other than Rao Jodha, the founder of Jodhpur. Chef Jodha is known for his ancestral Akheraj Deolia cuisine. He is the custodian of Rajasthani cuisine across ITC Hotels. An awarded chef, he has also featured on David Rocco's show, been part of a Hollywood movie and feaured in various publications. Oh man! The feeling to have a celebrity chef cook a meal for you is out of the world. Well, I did not know all of this then. Since then, I have kept in touch and had the privilege to experience his dishes and his hospitality even in the later years too. We chatted for almost 45 minutes, talked about what I do, and what brought me to Jodhpur and then went on to tell me a little about the meal he had prepared for me. It was a Rajput meal that he had prepared that evening.

The first course was what is called Raab. Raab is a warm drink made with chaach (buttermilk) and Bajra (millet flour). Delicious is what it was. I loved and savoured every sip of it.

The next course was a vegetarian kalmi kebab and mutton ki bootein (mutton boti). This recipe is basically of game meat, but since game meat is not used anymore, mutton is the next best choice for it. The mutton was served in a cute little toy pressure cooker. It was cooked to absolute tender perfection, with the right level of spice for me. I wanted to have more of it but, well there was more on the menu so I stopped myself. The veg kebab was quite nice too.

Next came in fish. Fish, per se, is not part of Rajasthani cuisine, but it was served prepared in a Rajasthani way. It was dipped in a batter of sabudana and garlic and then fried. Frankly, I am not a fish eater and the dish itself did not sound very appealing to me but it was DELICIOUS. The garlic and the sabudana simply added to the taste of the fish. And the fish was served atop an empty Jägermeister bottle.

In between the courses the Chef would come and ask me how I liked what I was eating and would tell me about the next thing on the plate. The next was the thali. The thali had a Dal Batti, Ker Sangri, Chakki ki shaak, Murg Jodhpuri and Laal Maas served with Bajre ki roti. Murg jodhpuri (I think it was prepared with yoghurt and kasoori methi) was the star on the plate followed by Laal Maas.

Chakki ki Shaak is basically a dish made out of wheat flour. It is an interesting dish for sure.

By now, I was kind of full upto the brim. But there was more yet to come. The next thing that came was a digestive and an interesting one at that. It was a small roll of slightly sautéed onion layer, stuffed with gram paste (hummus like) and rolled over charcoal. Yes, I also cringed at the thought of eating it. But with the Chef standing right there I could not even dispose it off. I had to eat it. Surprisingly, it was not as bad as it sounded. But ... yeah .... Let us just keep it as purely medicinal!!

The next thing that came was gulkand ice-cream. The presentation was so visually captivating. A dollop of pale pink ice-cream with red rose petals in it on a nest of golden caramel. I just did not feel like cutting into it. It was heavenly. I could just feel the cold ice-cream trickling down my system. It was so soothing after all the spicy food I had consumed. I just did not want it to finish. It must be showing on my face because the Chef and the steward, both were smiling, almost laughing, looking at me. It was really the "mmmmmmmm!" moment.

The last thing that came was a liqueur – a chocolate-mint-vodka liqueur. There was no way, I could consume another morsel or another drop after this. I was done. It was death by food. The whole experience lasted 3 hours. But what an experience! This was totally worth every penny I paid.

Day 7

I met Arjun at 8 a.m at Ghantaghar (Clock Tower) in old Jodhpur City. I parked the car and we both went on his Activa. There is no other way to go into that area, the lanes are so narrow and crowded. Our first stop was the Gulab Sagar Lake. Gulab Sagar Lake was actually constructed as a source of water storage in 1788 by Maharaja Vijay Singh. There is a Kunjebehari temple of Lord Krishna and the Raj Mahal Garden palace on the bank of lake, but unfortunately it is unkempt and in a state of neglect.

Next, we rode to the Toorji Ka Jhalara. A baoli in Rajasthan is called a jhalara. Toorji ka Jhalara was built in 1740 by Maharaja Abhay Singh's Queen consort. It was primarily used by women. Its recent drainage, clean-up and restoration has uncovered over 200 feet of hand carved treasures in Jodhpur's famous rose red sandstone including intricate carvings of dancing elephants, lion and cow shaped water spouts and beautifully designed deities. It is one of the very few step wells that have fish thriving in it.

The day I went there the weather was breezy and cloudy. And at the stepwell, we found a whole lot of people jumping off the height into the stepwell and thoroughly enjoying themselves. We sat there for some time. It made me wonder - we, in the metros are only stressing through life. And these people, are so stress free. It was a week day, 9.00 in the morning, and these men had not a care in the world. I am sure they have their families, they too need to pay their bills, but they also believe in having a life, a fact, which we in the metros don't even give a thought to.

After this we went to Ranisar and Padamsar. Ranisar Lake and Padamsar Lakes are two adjacent lakes built five hundred years ago for natural water conservation and rarely run out of water in this parched landscape. Ranisar lake was built in 1459 by Queen Jasmade Hadi, Rao Jodha's wife and Padmasar was made by Queen Padmini, daughter of Rana Sanga of Mewar. Out of the two lakes, Ranisar, I found, was a much more serene place. Though the water could have been cleaner, but it still seemed like a place I would like to go to when in the mood for some peace and quiet. Because it is not on the "tourist" grid, it has that bit of tranquillity to it.

After this was a crazy Activa ride to a place called Pachetia Hill. Part ride, part walk up absolutely narrow lanes, in the back lanes of houses. At the end of it is a small temple and beyond the temple was sheer heaven. There was a ledge from where one could get a nearly 270 degrees view of the city. It was windy and it was BEAUTIFUL! What a sight it would be at night, especially a no moon night, with twinkling lights from the houses down below and the millions of stars up there.

By now I was famished. I had lassi at Mishrilal on my mind. Arjun, first took me to the shop called Chaturbhuj. Chaturbhuj is famous for gulab-jamun. This is an absolute must have. It is very light brown in colour, extremely delicious and are not syrupy, which is the best part. Don't ask me how to reach Chaturbhuj. Just take an auto from Ghantaghar, he will get you there. The next stop was Mishrilal. Mishrilal is easy to find. His shop is right at the entrance of Ghantaghar. We took lassi and a mirchi bada and kachori. The lassi is what he is famous for and it was addictively delicious. I can still feel the taste lingering in my mouth. I am salivating as I write about it.

Since it was only about 11 a.m, I decided to make a trip to Om Banna Temple. My family and 3 friends with their families were coming to Jodhpur the next day at and then we were going back to Jaisalmer for some action in the Sam dunes. Why going back, you would ask. Well, let it suffice that madness knows no bounds. I had been to Jodhpur for a day about 2 years back, and had explored the Mehrangarh Fort at that time. Had no inclination of doing that again. Jaswant Thada was one thing I wanted to do, which I would the next day. The drowsy effect of the sweet lassi had begun to take over, but I was sure I would not miss out on a visit to the Om Banna Temple.

Om Banna (also called Shri Om Bana and Bullet Banna) is a

shrine located on the Pali-Jodhpur highway in Pali District, about 50 kms from Jodhpur in Rajasthan, devoted to a deity in the form of a motorcycle. The motorcycle is a 350cc Royal Enfield Bullet. As the story goes, on 2 December 1991, Om Banna (formerly known as Om Singh Rathore) was travelling from the town known as Bangdi near Sanderao of Pali to Chotila, when he lost control of his motorcycle and struck a tree. Om Banna was killed instantly, his motorcycle falling into a nearby ditch. The morning after the accident, local police took the motorcycle to a nearby police station. The next day it was reported to have disappeared from the station and was found back at the site of the accident. The police, once again, took the motorcycle, this time emptying its fuel tank and putting it under lock and chain to prevent its removal. Despite their efforts, the next morning it again disappeared and was found at the accident site. Legend states that the motorcycle kept returning to the same ditch. It thwarted every attempt by police to keep it at the local police station; the motorcycle always returned to the same spot before dawn.

This came to be seen as a miracle by local population, and they began to worship the "Bullet Bike." News of the miracle motorcycle spread to nearby villages, and later they built a temple to worship it. This temple is known as "Bullet Baba's Temple." It is believed that Om Banna's spirit helps distressed travellers. Every day, nearby villagers and travellers stop and pray to the bike and its late owner Om Singh Rathore. Those who pass by stop to bow their heads, leave offerings in honour of the helpful spirit, and some drivers also offer small bottles of alcohol at the site. It is said that a person who does not stop to pray at the shrine is in for a dangerous journey. Devotees also apply the 'tilak' mark and tie a red thread on the motorbike. The tree that caused Om Banna's death remains ornamented with offerings of bangles, scarves etc. A 24-hour diya is kept lit at the temple.

On the way to Om Banna, I encountered the Ramdevra bound traffic by the hoards. The fact that I was reeling under the lassi effect was not helping at all. It seemed like hours before I reached the shrine. To say it was crowded was an absolute understatement. I paid my respects and was on the way. All I had in mind was sleep. And that is what I did.

The lassi induced sleep was heavenly. I slept through the afternoon and the evening. I woke up, actually forcefully pulled myself out of the bed at about 8 pm. I freshened up a bit and went the restaurant to get something to eat. Hunger was beginning to creep in. I was just about thinking of what to eat when I got a message from Arjun asking me if I was interested in some street food. Of course I was, but I had neither the inclination nor the energy to drive. He said he would pick me up, so the plan was set. The first thing we had was a Bombay Sandwich. I had seen this a few days earlier on one of the travel programs and was wanting to have it and there it was. It is basically a slice of bread with butter and grated cheese and cucumber and then a slice of bread. This is grilled over fire and then topped with some more grated cheese and bhujia. It tasted heavenly. We sat in the car and ate it, devoured it is what I did. One of this is enough to fill you up for hours. The next was a stop at Gypsy. Gypsy is a vegetarian restaurant. The fun part is you don't need to go in and eat. You are served in the car too. Arjun ordered a pav bhaji. I have to say this, I have not eaten a pav bhaji like this in ages. The pavs were soaked in butter and the bhaji was just right. While we were waiting for the pav bhaji to come, I saw this bakery store called 15 AD. My friend who frequents Jodhpur had mentioned the molten chocolate cookies from this place. Naturally I went there and picked up a couple of boxes. Whenever any of you go to Jodhpur, please remember, these cookies from 15 AD are as important as lassi from Mishrilal

It was the last day of my 'solo-ness'. And was really the time to sit back and go over the last 7 days. But nothing of that sort happened. Before I knew it, I was in slumberland again.

Day 8

The last bit of my 'solo-ness'. In the evening, I would have my family with me and friends too. The last 7 days were fun, solo travel really is the way to travel. I have never been so aware of what was around me as I was in these 7 days. Not once did I feel lonely. Not once did I question myself on why I was doing this all by myself. In fact, I think I would do this all over again. Before I embarked on this trip, I was worried whether I would be able to bear my own company for so many days. Surprisingly I did, and I loved it. There has been something very empowering about the experience. But I will also not deny that I was happy to be meeting my family. There was nothing much that was slated to be done that day before the family arrived. Jaswant Thada was one place I wanted to visit.

The Jaswant Thada is a beautiful Cenotaph built by Maharaja Sardar Singh in 1899 in memory of his father, Maharaja Jaswant Singh II and serves as the cremation ground for the royal family of Marwar. The mausoleum is built out of intricately carved sheets of marble. These sheets are extremely thin and polished so that they emit a warm glow when illuminated by the sun. The cenotaph's grounds feature carved gazebos, a tiered garden, and a small lake. There are three other cenotaphs in the grounds. The cenotaph of Maharaja Jaswant Singh displays portraits of the rulers and Maharajas of Jodhpur.

The cleanliness and the way the monuments are maintained is remarkable. The lawns are beautifully manicured and green. Its not just Jodhpur, every city that I have visited in this trip, the cleanliness is very noticeable. Even the public washrooms at these monuments are clean. Something that is missing in Delhi, unfortunately.

The evening was spent, relaxing with family and friends. The next two days were a whirlwind. The morning was spent back at Ghantaghar. Actually, Pushkar and Karan went to Ummed Bhawan, and I took Vinod and my family to Mishrilal, after which we went to Chaturbhuj, bought gulab jamuns for everyone. On the way back, the auto driver insisted we stop at this particular shop and have their onion kachoris. The thought of having one made in pure ghee was just not appealing but, on his insistence, we took one. And boy, was it delicious! Finger-licking good! We bought some more and then headed towards 15 AD, of course for the cookies and then met the others at Ummed Bhawan. No, I did not go in. I had had enough of palaces and forts. Only dune-bashing was on my mind now. After that we headed to Jaisalmer via Osian - yes, finally Osian happened but never got around to seeing the temples. We went looking for dunes, never found them because Rajasthan is all green at this time.

Early next morning, we were on our way to the dunes at 5 a.m. My first experience with driving in the soft sand. I almost gave up in the first 2 minutes when i got stuck. But I am glad I did not. It was so much fun once I got the hang of it. Finally understood the power of 4L. For the uninitiated, 4Low and 4High are modes for different driving conditions in a 4-wheel drive vehicle. While 4H is used when you need better traction and stability like for driving on snowy, icy, muddy or rocky surfaces, 4L is designed for very slow, controlled driving on rough terrain or in situations where the vehicle may get stuck.

Since the trip was a "solo" trip, it was natural that the drive started from Gurgaon and it ended in Gurgaon. So, the 950 km straight shot drive from Jaisalmer to Gurgaon (via Sonipat since I had to drop my daughter at college) was driven by me. I did not let *the Husband* drive. The roads were very good. I did not feel an iota of tiredness even after being behind the wheels for 17 hours.

It was a crazy, fun-filled 2 days that were really a perfect end to superb holiday for me.

Kutch Nahin Dekha To Kuchh Nahi Dekha (January - 2018)

Part 1

The Kutch district in Gujarat is the largest district in India, spread over about 45,500 sq kms. In literal terms, Kutch means something that becomes wet and dry intermittently. The Rann of Kutch forms a large part of this district. It is a shallow wetland that submerges in water during the monsoons. And when the water dries up, the marshy salt flats become snow white. And that is what the Greater Rann of Kutch is famous for - The White Desert or the Great White Rann.

The thing with visiting Rann of Kutch is that your timing needs to be right. Water in the Rann can spoil the fun. It is a major dampener for people like me who wish to drive on the Rann. Statistically speaking, it is at its driest by end January, beginning February. But my trip was to be a family trip, and school plays spoilt sport during that time. Exams are around the corner and of course no holidays. And *the Husband's* year-end leaves also needed to be taken into consideration. Between the school and the office, the timeline finalised was 1st Jan - 7th Jan. Not the best time for a break from office but that was the best I could work out. 7 days, 7 stays, 7 places. The gypsy life I so love on my road trips.

The team started with 11 people from 3 families and by the end of it, consisted of 4 people (2 mother-daughter duos) – Khyati & Ria, Gitanjali & me. Family and work commitments took the balance of people out of the team. We were all at Ranthambore for New Year's Eve. The trip started from Ranthambore on the 1st of January. The first stop in Kutch was to be Zainabad. The distance from Ranthambore to Zainabad is about 750 kms. We could have easily accomplished that in a day, but the late-night party to bring in the New Year made us spilt the distance over 2 days. The first stop was Udaipur.

Before getting on with story of Kutch, I would like to tell you about this place we visited on the way to Ranthambore from Gurgaon. Chand Baori, in a town called Abhaneri, near Alwar. Chand Baori was built during the 9th century by King Chanda of the of the Gujara Pratihara Clan, who claim to be the descendants of Laxman. At its deepest point it is 20 metres. It has 3,500 narrow steps arranged in perfect symmetry split into 13 levels. The stairs encircle the structure on 3 sides. The fourth side boasts what was the summer palace of the King, with 3 storeys of beautifully carved jharokas and galleries and 2 projecting balconies. As the folklore goes, during celebrations, each step would be lit with a diya. One can only imagine how beautiful 3500 diyas would look. The "abha" or the light from these diyas is what apparently gave the place its name "abha nagri".

Adjacent to the Baori or the stepwell is a small temple - Harshat Mata Temple. The temple was built between the 7th - 8th centuries but was destroyed by Mahmud Ghazni. The temple is dedicated to Harshat Mata, believed to be the goddess of happiness and joy, who spread her glow and brightness around the town. The other folklore says the town got its name from the "abha" or brightness that the goddess spread.

There is one thing you must remember while going to visit the stepwell. When you use the Google Maps to search, search for Abhaneri and it will take you straight to Chand Baori. If on the other hand you search for Chand Baori, it will ultimately take you the destination but via a route which is at least 60 kms longer - so be careful. In fact, a friend made that mistake and when at some point in time they asked the locals, the locals laughed and said "aap bhi map dekh ke aaye ho?"

Now coming back to the Ranthambore - Udaipur stretch. When one does this stretch, one necessarily crosses Kota. I had only got to know recently that Kota is the hub for engineering entrance exam coaching. That was quite a surprise for me. But no, that is not why I mentioned Kota. The reason why I mentioned Kota is because there is a hidden gem about 40 kms from Kota - a place called Garadia Mahadev. Garadia Mahadev is a small temple dedicated to Lord Shiva. Locationally, it is situated at a gorge of the River Chambal, a point where the river takes a u-turn. It was very peaceful, beautiful and mesmerising. I had seen photographs of the place and wondered if they were edited pictures. No, the place is actually beautiful. It is an absolute must visit. I only wish it was better maintained, considering the kind of money that they charge. (Rs. 75 per person; Rs. 20 if you have a valid student's ID and Rs. 250 for 4-wheeler)

We reached Udaipur by about 8 p.m. We called it an early night after a lovely dinner at the roof top restaurant of the haveli we were staying in by the Lake Pichola. The next day was when we parted ways with the original team. 7 people became 4 and 2 cars became 1. The first road trip experience for 2 out of the 4 of us. I wonder if they had any idea of what they were getting into. As for me, this was going to be a first where I would have no break from driving, it was 7 days of driving every day, from one place to another, seeing sights enroute and moving on.

Part 2

Conversation with a cop on the Rajasthan-Gujrat Border;-

Cop : Madam, kahan se aa rahe ho?

Me : Gurgaon

Cop :Aur ja kahan rahe ho?

Me : Kutch

Cop : Aao madam phir gadi check karva lo.

Me : Ji bilkul. Lady constable hain yahan ?

Cop : Lady constable to nahi hai madam.

Me : Phir, kaise hoga ?

Cop : Phir kuchh nahi. Aap chalo.

Me : Thank you, sir!!

And on we went on our way. The thing with Zainabad and where we were staying was that we had to reach by 2.30 pm. The last safari into the wild sanctuary was at 3.30 pm. We had planned on leaving Udaipur by 6 am but that never happened. We left at 8.00 a.m and there went our chances of visiting Rani ki Vav at Patan and the Sun Temple at Modhera.

Rani ki Vav is a UNESCO World Heritage site, a step well built on the banks of River Saraswati. Constructed during the times of the Chalukya Dynasty, it is believed that it was made as a memorial for King Bhima I by his queen Udaymati. The Sun Temple is a Hindu temple dedicated to the Sun God, Surya, located at Modhera village of Mehsana District. Situated on the banks of the river Pushpavati, it was built in 1026-27 AD during the reign of Bhima I of the Chalukya Dynasty. The temple is built on 23.6° latitude (approximately near Tropic of Cancer).

Both these places are a must visit, and we missed it. Honestly speaking, at that point in time, we thought we would take a detour on our way to Ahmedabad and then visit these places, since we missed it now, but I guess these go into the list of things to do next time. I am not really worried, because there is a lot of Gujarat that I am dying to see. So, there will be a next time most definitely.

Zainabad is a small town on the fringes of the Little Rann of Kutch (LROK). We reached the Resort, Desert Coursers. It is the best the place has to offer. Cute little eco-friendly cottages. We were asked to take the car upto the cottages, unload the luggage and park the car outside. The best part is it is a pick your own luggage place. Never heard of that? Well, it is more or less a self check-in place. And when you leave, you get your car, load it yourself and leave. Payments are all done in advance. Lunch was vegetarian Gujarati fare. It was quite tasty I must say.

I must mention one thing here. When I booked Desert Coursers, I had started with 11 people. (They have a per person charge, not a per room charge). I spoke to the owner, Dhanraj Malik at that time, insisted on paying an advance to confirm booking, but in spite of all of that he never sent me the bank details assuring me that my booking was confirmed. Later I reduced the number of people to 7 and as late as 4 days before we were to be there, he confirmed my booking for 7 people. Finally, only 4 of landed there. What I was amazed at was, that they charged me for only 4 people. They did have 3 rooms ready for us and would have been completely within their rights to charge me accordingly, but did not. Thank you, Mr. Malik.

My stop at Zainabad was not so much to see the wild asses as to drive cross country into the Little Rann of Kutch. For this, one needs a permit. It costs Rs. 400 per vehicle, one person's ID and INR. 200 per camera. While asking him to help me get the permit, I had a long conversation with Mr Malik on the do's and don'ts of driving in the Rann. One of the things he told us was that it is a territory that can be very disorienting. It is just miles and miles of nothingness. What you drive on is a path of tyre marks. He warned us that while on the drive, not to try any antics, stick to the path, and not go driving off the path because

1) if you get disoriented you will never be able to get on to the right path and

2) if there is water, the ground becomes like quick sand and you get pulled into it.

He may have painted an extreme picture, but in such places, you can never be too careful. We would know the next day.

When we were getting ready to go for the safari, he suggested I drive in my own vehicle behind his safari jeep, so that I could get a feel of what driving in the Rann would be like. For a moment, and I would not lie about it, I felt as if he was trying to underestimate me and my driving capabilities. But then I realised he had a point. I was not here to prove a point to anyone, and it wouldn't hurt if I did what he suggested. So, there we were all set to follow in our own vehicle. The drive in the Rann was amazing. It left me wanting more. I was now looking forward to the next day's drive.

The Indian Wild Ass, also called the Gudkhur, Khur or the Indian Onager is a subspecies of the Onager that is native to Southern Asia. It is listed as "near threatened" by the International Union for Conservation of Nature. It was once found in areas extending from Western India, Southern Pakistan (provinces of Sindh and Baluchistan), Afghanistan and Southern Iran. Today, its last refuge lies in the Indian Wild Ass Sanctuary, Little Rann of Kutch and some areas of the Great Rann of Kutch. Its preferred environments being saline deserts, arid grasslands and scrublands. A surprising fact that came up while I was researching the animal was that it is one of the fastest Indian animals clocking a speed of 70-80 kms per hour, easily out running a jeep.

Also dotting the Little Rann are a number of salt farms. In the monsoon months the Rann is submerged in water and once the water begins to recede in October, the Agariyas (a local tribe) move in to make square shaped salt fields and begin the herculean process. Wells are dug to pump out briny ground water and then rely on the natural evaporation process to leave the white crystals. The Agariyas live in shacks beside their salt flats for about 8 months in those unrelenting conditions, braving blistering heat during the day and extreme cold during the night. Children begin working in the salt flats from the age of about 10.

About 12-15 tons of salt is produced every 15 days from each salt pan and is sent to salt companies and chemical factories across the country. What was extremely shocking was that these people sell the salt at a price as low as 20 paisa per kilo. And we buy salt at INR 18 per kilo. In a good year, a family at a maximum saves about INR 25,000. Most of the times it is much less. Skin lesions, tuberculosis and severe eye problems caused due to reflection off the white surfaces are some major health hazards faced by them. I drove back to the resort in a very pensive mood. Life indeed is not easy and we take so much for granted. Back to the resort, we had another Gujarati meal. We slept early as next day was really a big day, a big drive. We were headed to Dholavira driving almost a 100 kms cross country through the Little Rann.

Part 3

We were on our way at 6.30 am with packed breakfast of sandwiches and a loaf of bread that would probably make our lunch.

The first stop was to get the permit to drive inside the Little Rann. The office is about a kilometre from Desert Coursers enroute Zinzuwada from where you get into the Rann. Actually, it was hardly an office. The person who gives the permit lived in that house. We just rang the bell and woke him up. Even at that hour he made the permit with a smile. You could go in without the permit too, but in case there was a checking, it was a hefty fine you would need to pay. The permit is needed for any part of the Rann and is valid for a period of 4 hours. The only thing that Dhanraj Malik at Desert Coursers told us was that we needn't unnecessarily give explanations as to where in the Rann we wanted to go.

By 7 a.m we were well on our way to Zinzuwada. You enter the Little Rann from the Madapol Gate and you are welcomed with mounds of salt crystals looking amazing as the rays of the rising sun reflected on it. Interestingly, the first light comes only after 7.30-7.45, till then its dark. The Rann is an expanse, miles and miles of nothingness. What you follow while driving, is a path made of tyre marks and marked with white stones. What I followed was all that and the RoutO. What is a RoutO you may ask, well that is a trump card of an app (customised route co-ordinates) a privileged few get when you have the human GPS by your side. 8 kms into the Rann is a temple dedicated to Vachhara Dada. The story the panditji told us was that he was killed while fighting dacoits who were taking away all the cows from the village. My search into reading up more came up with something more bizarre. According to the Wikipedia site, while taking the pheras at his own wedding, Vatsrajsinh Solanki or Vachhara got to know that the dacoits were looting the village and taking away all the cows. He left the ceremony in the middle and went to fight them. While fighting the dacoits his head got severed and inspite of that his body kept fighting the enemy. It is said that his wife wanted to commit sati but was stopped by a saint who advised her to go to her in-laws' house. Vachhara was blessed by God and was asked consummate his marriage in the vayu form. Twenty-two sons were born to them. This just makes me wonder about a lot of things, but I am not one to question folklore and religious beliefs. Folklore also has it that Vachhara was born 7 times, and every time he was interrupted by acts of dacoits taking away cows. In the 7th life he successfully killed the dacoits. Thus became a shurveer and a demigod after that. Another interesting thing, the panditji told us we could have all the prasad we wanted, but we had to eat it there not take it with us. It only struck me later that I should have asked why so. Khyati and I tried to analyse the logic behind it concluded that it is maybe to avoid any wastage of the prasad that one takes and do not end up consuming.

And we were on our way again. The RoutO showed that we were to keep the temple on our right and then move, which we did. Till a point there were the white stones marking the path. Then we came to a fork. There was a board that read Plasava. We took the left path. As we moved ahead on this path, I could see we were moving away from the path RoutO was showing. Not wanting to mess around, we turned back and came to the place where the board was. We realised there was an arrow pointing towards the right path. So, we started on the right path. But a little ahead we realised we were still moving away from the RoutO. We stopped and well, it was serious discussion time. This route had the stones marking the path, the board pointed this path as going towards Plasava where we were headed to and yet it was going away from the path that RoutO showed. What do we do now - follow this or do what RoutO was asking us to do? After a lot of contemplation, we decided to stick with RoutO, so we turned back and got onto the path that coincided with RoutO. This path had no stone markings. We drove on. Keeping our eyes on the RoutO and on the path ahead.

I will be lying if I said we were not stressed and psyched by the expanse of nothingness. It did not help that there was no phone connectivity either. But after driving some 10 kms, I began to ease. I did not speak about it with the others, but I assume they too felt a little at ease. We stopped and spent some time walking around, clicked some pictures. As for me, here I was literally in the middle of nowhere, completely off the grid, in a part of the world most of us do not know existed. And if we were to get lost and something were to happen, there was a good chance of no one finding us till it was too late. The fact that there were three other people depending on me was also playing on my mind. No, I won't call the thoughts negative, just plain philosophical. How much we gloat about the self in our everyday lives. That thought, at that moment, in that place had the power to simply shake me up once again. It was a reiteration of how miniscule we are compared to this vast universe – and we make the mistake of believing we are the universe. There was a moment of realisation during my Spiti trip last year, when I shed a huge part of the baggage I had been carrying in my heart. Right there, at that moment, in the middle of nowhere I parted with some more. I have carried far too much baggage for far too long. And I am happy that with each of my travels I seem to be able to shed it little by little. It felt nice to be slowly getting rid of the sadness and hurt.

We drove on for about another 10-15 kms when we encountered a wet patch. There was no way I was going to risk crossing it, not when I had been warned about the quicksand effect the water added to the Rann. It was time to take a U-turn. It meant going back the 30-35 kms we had come in and then taking the much longer route via the highway to Dholavira. As I was turning around there was a slightly wet patch which the right rear tyre went over. As it went over, I felt this sudden pull. It wasn't just me being paranoid. The others felt it too. And it was not just the "tyre in the slush" spin.

I kept the accelerator pedal pushed down and after a few spins (it helped that the other 3 tyres were on firmer ground) the car lurched forward and was out of it. I looked back and saw that a big pit made by the tyre. In all this split-second madness, the RoutO went off. I restarted the app, it took a while and the RoutO started. I heaved a sigh of relief and started to head back. Till we reached the temple, the RoutO was behaving itself and we followed it in reverse. Just as we reached the point where we had seen the board showing the way to Plasava the RoutO went off again and in spite of trying a number of times, it did not bring on the route map we were following. At this point, we once again contemplated taking the path pointing towards Plasava. Then Gitanjali remembered part of the conversation we had with the guys working at Desert Courser's who had mentioned that there was a lot of water and we would not be able to cross the Rann. So off we went towards Zinzuwada and thankfully from here on there were the white stones to follow till Zinzuwada. And also, deep tyre marks left by a tractor which we had noticed were running besides us all the way. We followed the tyre marks and the stones back to civilisation. I was reminded of the story of Hansel and Gretel. Once we were out, the first call of course went to *the Husband*. The second one to Chief (remember the human GPS I mentioned) I usually don't give a point-to-point update when I am on my drives. I do so if there is a change in plan. Once that was done, we were on the way. The sandwiches really hadn't filled us up and by now we were famished. Post Radhanpur, we hit NH 27 (my favourite highway from this drive) and the first thing we did was find a place to eat an early lunch. I don't remember the name of the place, but we had the most delicious missal-sev there.

Dholavira is an island (during the monsoons when the Rann is covered in water). It's claim-to-fame is that it is home to the ruins of the Indus Valley Civilisation. It is one of the top 5 Harappan sites.

But more on that later. The drive upto Dholavira is a long straight road with the Rann on both sides. White salt as far as you could see reflecting the sun rays falling on it in an almost blinding manner. While driving to Dholavira, a thought came to mind. I had heard that it is the most beautiful sight to see the moonlight being reflected on the salt Rann on a full moon night. This day was a day after the full moon night - as good, so to speak. We decided we would come back later that night to see it for ourselves. This would probably be the only chance since I had also heard that in the Greater Rann they allow you on the Rann only on the full moon night. From the point where this bridge starts (bridge in the monsoons, road now) the resort was about 30 kms away.

We reached the resort at around 4 pm. The plan was to drop the luggage, and then go on to visit the Harappan site, the Wood Fossil Park and then the Sunset point. We were informed that a trip to all these in the safari jeep was part of our package. We parked our car and were all set to go exploring the island.

Part 4

Indus Valley Civilisation as a lesson in History was taught to us in grade 6. I hated it. I was never really been a history buff and I admit that I have somewhere down the line passed that disinterest to my kids too. I now realise the wrong in it. But I am hoping that as in my case, my travels are igniting my curiosity towards stories behind the what and the how of things that have happened, it will be the case with them too. While planning this trip, I almost gave the Harappan ruins a miss. I am so glad good sense prevailed and I did not.

Dholavira is the larger of the 2 Harappan sites found in India, the other being Lothal. The Harappan city of Dholavira on the island called Khadir, or Khadir Bet, dates back to the 3rd Millennium BCE. It is said to be in occupation for about 1,500 years and the excavations document 7 different stages of its rise and fall. The city was surrounded by a protective wall which was about 11 meters at the base narrowing in thickness as it increased in height. An amazing aspect of Dholavira is the water management system. Dholavira is surrounded by brackish water. The main source of water was 2 seasonal water streams - Manhar and Manhas. The city was made on a gradient most suitable for reservoirs. The town planners dammed the 2 streams and diverted all the water into the city through reservoirs and channels. This site at Dholavira also has the unique distinction of an inscription being excavated with 10 signs of the Indus script. The city plan also had a citadel, middle town and lower town, a cemetery, a stadium and an annexe. There is also a museum which has the artefacts found during the excavations.

The one hour or so that we spent there left me thinking of how the inhabitants lived as compared to how we live today. Their houses, their meeting areas, their stadia, what kind sports they played, the hierarchy of their society, I wonder what life would have been like in those times. From the ruins, one could see that in terms of town planning they were quite advanced in their thinking, but by the same measure, I am sure their lives were a lot more simpler compared to what we lead.

From the Harappan site we went to the Wood Fossil Park. The wood fossils at Dholavira were apparently accidentally discovered during a plantation drive by the forest officials in December 2006 and are said to date back to the Jurassic age. They are what is called petrified wood fossils. More than the wood fossils, what I really liked was the landscape. With the Kala Dungar or the Black mountain across the river, it made a pretty sight. During the monsoons and much after that too, I believe this area is flocked by migratory birds including the pink flamingos. Flamingos were one of the main reasons I wanted to come to Kutch, but on reaching here I got to know that the timing was wrong. Oct-Nov is when they are here in abundance. And if Dhanraj Malik was to be believed, that year the flamingo count was at an all-time low. Nonetheless, we did see flamingos at a distance, flying in their signature straight line. No that did not satiate me. I will not even mark it as "seen".

The next stop was the sunset point or the Karni Mata Temple, or the BOP Karni. This is a point not far from the Wood Fossil park. It has a small temple and a BSF post. It is a beautiful sunset across the river. I have a weakness for sunsets and this one was particularly a pretty one. Sitting there in the quite surroundings with only a few other people dotting the landscape, it was indeed a peaceful hour spent.

Back at the resort, the first thing that needed to be organised was hot water. We had a 4.30 a.m start the next morning. There was no way anyone would give us warm water that early in the morning. We did manage to get an excuse for hot water. Let's just say we managed somehow. It was dinner time by then. There was very delicious Gujarati fare. I stuffed myself crazy and now I was ready to go to the salt pans I had mentioned earlier.

All through the visit to the Harappan site, and the Wood Fossil Park, we had a dedicated guide, Nagraj. I did ask him if it was safe to go alone at night as we were planning. While he assured us that it was completely safe, there was something about it that was nagging me at the back of my mind. So, while coming back from the sunset point, I fixed up with him to accompany us to the salt pans. Post dinner when we met him, he suggested we go to this area about 4 kms away instead of driving 30 kms to what we had seen in the afternoon. Sounded like a plan. We headed out in our car. About 200 mtrs. from the resort he asked me to get off the road and follow a very narrow off-road path. Pitch dark and ghostly was the only way to describe it. We must have driven about half a kilometre when he himself suggested we could go ahead or go to the originally decided place. I asked him why and he said that this was in the middle of the BSF area and if caught we could get into trouble. None of us had spoken aloud about it, but all of us were probably waiting for a suggestion like this. Without another word, we just took a U-turn and were relieved to be back on the road.

On the way, we had a long chat with the guide. He was basically from Haryana but his ancestors had settled in Dholavira. Their prime occupation was farming. Cumin and castor are what they cultivated. At regular intervals we would see a lone bike standing by the road side. Honestly speaking the whole scenario - dark of the night, full moon, one odd bike parked by the road side and the silence - all made for a very spooky scene. Upon asking we were told that it was the farm owners who spent the night at the farms to ensure no damage was done to the crops by the wild boars. I for one was not envying those guys who spent their nights in the farms, with snakes and wild boars as companions. Vipers are pretty common they say.

We reached the Rann. And for a while after getting off the car I just took in the sight. It was peaceful, quiet, beautiful, romantic. All that was missing was probably a pan flute playing a soulful piece. The salt was wet and I refused to venture onto it. I set up the camera on the tripod and clicked. Nothing happened. I tried a few times and nothing happened. Then Gitanjali suggested that probably the camera is not finding anything to focus on. That sounded like a probable reason. Here I must tell you that I had recently upgraded on my camera and was still exploring the machine and the technicalities of the art. I am technically extremely challenged and it takes me a lot time to get the hang of it all. It is only later I was told that for such times one just needs to put the camera setting on manual focus.

So, Nagraj was made to stand in the wet salt till such time the camera focussed and then the moment the camera clicked he was to run out of the frame. He took his own sweet time to walk out of the frame and what we got was a shot with ghostly shadow. Then Gitanjali was put to the job of being the model. Nagraj was much a part of it all, coaxing us to go on further into the Rann. He also told us that in the month of March a marathon is organised by the name of Run the Rann. We had a great time trying to figure out the settings and trying photography at night. And Gitanjali, of course, 'Ran the Rann', trying to get the camera to focus. I was so glad we got him along. At least we could enjoy our time there without worrying about being alone.

It had been quite a day for us, starting with the drive through the Rann and ending with the time spent on the salt pans under the full moon light. I was a tired but, a very content soul when I lay down to sleep. The smiles I saw on my co-travellers' faces were so satisfying for me to see. It was a first of a kind road trip for Khyati and Ria, and I felt so nice to see them having a blast. For me, I always have a plan, a things-to-do list, where to end the day itinerary, to begin with. But as I go along, the days' destinations stop mattering. It is the memories and stories you make on the way that mean so much more. And that is what most people I know never do. There is always a rush for them to reach somewhere.

Part 5

4.30 am was departure time, 4.30 am we were out of our tents. Another do-it-yourself place - load back your own luggage, open the gate, quietly drive out so as not to disturb the other people staying there, latch the gate behind you and drive off. No need to wake up anyone. I found this system quite cute. We needed to leave at 4.30 because we were to meet this officer from the BSF at Bhuj around 9 for the permit for Vighakot. Remember the lone bikes from the night before? Well as we went by, one of them was now parked about 2-3 feet onto the road. And there started the whole ghost thing again. We, of course all in jest, started figuring out the possibilities of ghosts and their existence there and what we would do if we would encounter one. By the time we were an hour into the drive, the villagers had woken up and some of the tea shops had begun to open too. We stopped at one of the tea stalls for some tea. That's when I noticed the tea tasted salty. I guess it is the brackish water, even though made potable, still has the residual salt in it.

We were in Bhuj by 10 a.m and went straight to the BSF headquarters, met the officer, got the permits, eagerly jumped at the offer of tea and we were on our way. Well, it wasn't all that quick, the officer was nice enough to tell us all about Vighakot and what we can expect there. We were in Bhirandiara by 1 p.m. First things first, we got the permit for the Greater Rann and then went and checked in to our resort. Again, a small set up, nothing fancy but quite comfortable, run by one of the locals who also had their house within the resort. Dumped our luggage and we were off on our way to Vighakot. The plan was to do Vighakot, then kala Dungar on the way back and then end the day with the sunset at the Great White Rann. I of course, was looking forward to some shopping at the Rann Festival.

Around 35 kms from Bhirandiara is a bridge called India Bridge. Once you cross the bridge, you come to the BSF check post where you have to get the first entry done. Handover the permit, show your ID, handover your cameras and phones, the car is checked for any hidden phones etc and then you proceed. There was a thought of keeping one phone hidden for taking pictures later, but the thought got trashed as soon as it came. People do it and that is their way doing things. I for one, could not get myself to do it. I somehow felt, there was a reason for the rule and we must respect it. And the bhaiyas at the check post were so polite and humble that I just not feel like doing anything I was not supposed to.

Before one gets on to the road to Vighakot, there are 2 more checkpoints that one needs to cross, same procedure, entry and sign on the show of the permit and ID. There is a Memorial and a Hanuman Temple that is about 25 kms from the check post. Beyond the last check post is this narrow road with the Rann on both the sides. During the monsoons it would probably be more beautiful sight with water on both the sides. The road in patches is lined with Keekar trees and dried golden coloured tall grass which give the effect of velvet from a distance. Enroute we saw some lovely sambhars, deer, neel gais, and wild boars. We would stop and admire them, they would look at us with curiosity. There were no cameras to distract us. The 66 odd kilometer distance were one of the most enjoyable drives we have had in this trip. No humans other than us. In hind sight, had we snuck in a camera or phone, we would have not really had such a great time. While I am one for capturing memories through a camera, I also feel sometimes the best way to store a memory is to live it without a distraction so that it just embeds itself in the mind for posterity. We reached the BSF base, had a look across the border from the vantage point had a chat with the people there. And were getting ready to leave when I told the girls to take out the loaf of bread and the cheese and all we were carrying from the boot and keep it in the car so that Khyati could make us sandwiches on the go. The BSF jawan there heard me and asked me if we would like him to put out a table and chairs for us so that we could have our lunch comfortably. We said we'd love that. So out came the table and chairs for us. We made our sandwiches - bhujia and cheese sandwiches with my fav Maggi Hot & Sweet sauce (it goes with me everywhere) with cokes and sprite and some tea cakes for dessert. It was a lot of fun.

On the way back, I was suddenly hit by sleep. So, I just parked in the shade and switched off the music and went off to sleep for 15 minutes. It was a great feeling to be able to just park in the middle of the road and do that. In middle of the road? Yeah, the road is just wide enough for one car to fit in, so anywhere on that road is the middle of the road.

By now, it was already 4.30 in the afternoon. We decided to skip Kalo Dungar. This is because if we went there, we would get late for the white Rann the sunset there is something I did not want to miss. Kalo Dungar or the Black Mountain is at the altitude of 462 mtrs. and probably the only place in Kutch which gives the panoramic view of the White Rann. Also, there is a temple dedicated to Dattatreya. According to Wikipedia, the legend says that when Dattatreya lived on Earth, he stopped at the Black mountains and found a band of starving jackals. Being a god, he offered them his body to eat and as they ate, his body continually regenerated itself. Because of this, for the last four centuries, the priests at the temple prepare a batch of cooked rice as prasad and feed it to the jackals after the evening aarti. When I see the pictures, I feel we should not have given it a miss. It would have been interesting to have a chat with the priests there, but I guess, there was only one thing we could have done.

The White Rann is about 30 kms from Bhirandiara. On the way to Dhordo comes a place called Hodka. For all of you who are shopping buffs and have the time, do spend some time exploring the lanes of this village for some amazing Kutchee stuff at throwaway prices. I, sadly did not have the time. But I did manage some beautiful stuff. More on that later.

The White Rann was a very crowded place. To our dismay, it was littered. We found ourselves a side that was without any humans and spent our time there. It was wettish salt, it felt more like snow. It is such a beautiful natural phenomenon, just wish the authorities were a little more stringent on the cleanliness bit, and just wish that the people were a little more sensitive to the idea of keeping it clean. Sunsets are my weakness. And this one too, was dreamy. In spite of the number of people there, it was beautiful. I find sunsets very peaceful to watch. They have such a calming effect. And sunsets always bring the promise of a new dawn.

Now was the time to explore the shopping part of the Rann Utsav. Contrary to what I was expecting, the fare being sold there was not obscenely priced. The stuff was good and well if I had my way I would have bought a truckload of stuff. I bought some beautiful bedcovers, bags, wind chimes, cushion covers and torans. When I had bought enough for me, I bought for gifts. There was so much more I wanted to buy. Sadly, space was a constraint. We ate some very delicious Pav Bhaji and Kutchee Dabelis and were quite done for the day.

Back at the resort, started the struggle for the warm water. The owner handed us one small little aluminium bucket and an immersion rod and that was it. While the water was getting heated, the owner's son asked us if were interested in some sari borders, to which Khyati and I said we could have a look though we were done with shopping. We went to their house, the lady brought out the packet and took out the stuff. I quite liked one and comparing them to the Delhi rates just out of curiosity asked the price. The lady said she was not sure if the roll was the required 9 mtrs but it was for Rs. 150. We thought she as saying Rs.150 per meter, but no, that was the per roll rate. These were clearly machine made, but even for that Rs.150 was a steal! Khyati did not want any, so I picked up the best three I could find.

I usually do not like to shop on my trips because where shopping is concerned, I come with no breaks. Whoever said shopping was the best therapy was absolutely bang on. Well, driving and travel still tops the list for me, but yes shopping comes close. I was one very happy woman who went to sleep that night. Did I tell you guys that the place to shop for silver is Bhuj? No, I did not explore silver shopping. Probably the next time I shall come more focused.

Part 6

The last leg our journey through Kutch was White Rann to Mandvi. After that, it was a home run, Mandvi-Ahmedabad-Gurgaon. The White Rann to Mandvi stretch via Lakhpat is a stretch which is sans any places to eat. It is quite surprising because there is a lot of traffic on the road. We did find one truckers' Dhaba, but the guy said we would get anything eat only after 12 noon. All he had to offer us was tea and biscuits. We took the tea, and our breakfast that morning was buttered rusks (we were carrying those) and tea. It was a decent tea though.

Our first stop was a place called Mata No Madh. Mata No Madh is a village about 95 kms from Bhuj going towards Lakhpat. It is known for a temple dedicated to the deity Goddess Ashapura. We asked a guy selling prasad the story behind the temple. According to his version, a baniya (businessman) was touring the area to sell his wares and stopped at the place where the present-day temple exists to spend some time. He was a big devotee of Goddess Amba and it was Navratri time. He also had no children and always prayed to her for a child. While sleeping one night, the goddess appeared in his dream. She asked him to build a temple for her on that very spot. He was not sure if it was a dream or was the Goddess really speaking to him, so as a token to prove that it was indeed no dream, the Goddess left a coconut and a dupatta by his pillow. The Goddess also gave specific instructions that once the temple was completed, its doors were to remain shut for a period of 6 months by which time she would appear therein. A few months before the 6-month period was over the baniya began to hear celestial music after sunset everyday. Thinking that probably the goddess had appeared, he opened the temple gates. He saw the deity outside the surface knee above as if she was attempting to stand up. That is how she appears to be in the stone that is in the sanctum sanctorum of the temple. The baniya's wish for a child was fulfilled and since then the deity has been called Ashapura, one who fulfils dreams.

The next stop was Lakhpat. Lakhpat is the last town on the western end of India on the India-Pakistan Border. It is an entire town within the Lakhpat Fort. Known as the "Basta Bandar", it was a very important trading post connecting Gujarat and Sindh. At one time the waters of the River Indus used to flow into Lakhhpat. It prospered from the maritime trade that flourished at that time. It used to be a town of millionaires. Lakhpati literally means millionaire. The town lost its maritime significance when, after the earthquake of 1819, the Indus changed its course to an area which in now in Pakistan's Sindh Province, and the port dried up.

The first time I ever heard of Lakhpat was from a very dear friend. We were chatting about our respective trips and plans to visit Kutch and he mentioned Lakhpat, the reason being that there was a Gurudwara here. I do have an affinity to Gurudwaras, even though I cannot really be called one with a religious bent. I find them extremely peaceful places to be in. Guru Nanak Dev ji, during the early 1500s, visited Lakhpat on his way to Mecca during the 2nd and 4th missionary journey's. As the legend goes, this was a house that belonged to a brahman with whom the Guru stayed on his visits. The house was converted into the Gurudwara as it stands today, some 200 years ago. The Gurdwara has the unique distinction of being awarded the Asia Pacific Heritage Conservation award for the year 2004 by UNESCO. It houses relics associated with Guru Nanak ji. These relics are said to be bestowed by the Guru to the Brahmin in whose house he stayed. These include Charan paduka or the wooden footwear and a Palki of the great Guru. They say these are perhaps the holiest relics of Guru Nanak ji on the Indian soil. This is one of the daintiest, prettiest Gurudwaras I have ever been to. It has such an old-world charm to it. And one that is so remarkably clean. They also have 3-4 dormitories and rooms where one can stay.

We visited another small Dargah. The Dargah of Pir Kamalshah. According to the legend, Kamalshah, a holy man revered by both Hindus and Muslims came from Kokilya, a village near Mandvi, and wanted to be buried here in Lakhpat. On his funeral party's arrival, the gatekeeper refused entry. The saint came back from the dead and anounced his intentions to enter town. Now alive, he was not stopped and he lived in Lakhpat for a month thereafter. Today, a family from the Pathan community cares for and maintains the structure.

There is also, I believe, a tomb of Pir Ghous Mohammad. Pir Ghaus Muhammad was a Sufi saint, half-Muslim and half-Hindu in his customs, who was believed to have supernatural power. He died in 1855, and his brother Bava Mia or Sa Saheb, from contributions made by Ghous Muhammad's followers, began to build a tomb locally known as *Kubo*. This tomb, of black stone, on a platform fifty-four feet square and seven high, rising in a conical dome 63 feet 3 inches high, is octagonal in shape, with four side doors arched and richly carved, and the walls decorated with patterns of flowers and leaves. Inside, the floor is paved with white and black marble, and the grave is covered with a white marble canopy. On the walls are passages from the Quran. It is still unfinished. There is a water tank opposite the tomb is believed to have healing properties for skin diseases. We did go in a little into the village, but could not find it. The deserted look kind of got to us. There seemed no sight of habitation. The ghostly quiet felt eerie. Though I am sure there are people living there because we did see goats roaming around. We decided to head back.

By the time we were done from here it was around noon. It would be time for lunch soon but from what we had found out this whole stretch was sans any place to eat. So, we decided to have the langar at the Gurudwara. It indeed turned out to be a brilliant idea. It was a simple langar of daal, roti, and rice but one of the most delicious preparations of daal that I have ever had so far. We had an extremely satiating meal, washed our utensils, thanked the lady who served us and we were on our way. Once a thriving town, it is now more like a ghost town. It had a deserted, lonely vibe. They call Kuldhara a ghost town, well that was a disappointment in that sense. For some strange reason, this ghostly town, one that is completely lost in time, has left a mark on me.

Our next stop was Narayan Sarovar. Narayan Sarovar Lake is one of the 5 holy lakes of Hinduism, alone with Mansarovar in Tibet, Pampa in Karnataka, Bindu Sagar lake in Orissa and Pushkar in Rajasthan. According to the legend, in the Puranic times, Lord Vishnu or Narayan appeared in response to prayers of sages and touched the land with his toe, creating the lake. Though it is a lake revered as holy to bathe in, it is not recommended because let's just say, it is really not clean enough to go bathing in.

There is a temple on the banks of the lake. The story of Koteshwar begins with Ravana, who won, as a boon from Lord Shiva for an outstanding display of piety, this shivalinga of great spiritual power. Ravana, in his arrogant haste, accidentally dropped and it fell to earth at Koteshwar. To punish Ravana for his carelessness, the linga turned into a thousand identical ones, some versions of the story say ten thousand, some a million. Unable to distinguish the original, Ravana grabbed one and departed, leaving the original one here, around which Koteshwar Temple was built. The temple is also known as Kotilingeshwar Temple.

While I was researching the itinerary for Kutch, a friend's itinerary had Guhar Moti as a point of interest. According to Google, Guhar Moti is the westernmost point of India. Naturally it found a place on my itinerary. Google Maps shows it coming after Narayan Sarovar when going towards Mandvi. Now the thing is there is no connectivity (atleast Airtel did not work) from about 30 odd kms before Narayan Sarovar when coming from Lakhpat. Though I had downloaded the route, it only showed 'limited information' which meant only showed the point not the route. We asked around at Koteshwar Temple and we only got vague glances from the people. So, we decided to keep the point on Google maps and driving towards it. Since it was in the direction of Mandvi, we were good with the idea.

As it is the road to Mandvi is quite a narrow, lonely road upto a point. And to top that we turned into a narrower road perpendicular to the road we had been driving on. A good distance in we see a milestone with "Guhar 0" written on it. I was pretty happy, we found what we were looking for and turned into the village. Well, that was not really the place because half a kilometre in and the village finished and so did the road end. We turned back and decided to go further down the road. Must have gone in about 7-8 kms when good sense suddenly prevailed. I saw the time, it was 3.30 pm, we had no phone signal and there was not a soul in sight. Suddenly it hit me that we were alone in a place that we do not know anything about. One look at Khyati and I knew she was also thinking the same. We turned back. And was I happy getting back onto the road leading to Mandvi. For us the resort at Mandvi meant the luxury we so desperately yearned for at this point. After 4 days of roughing, all we were looking forward to was unlimited hot water. The little things that we take for granted are the things that we end up valuing the most.

The next 2 days were the home run. The first stop being Ahmedabad. Since we had not been to Rani Ka Vav, Khyati, who is from Ahmedabad, suggested we visit Adalaj ki Vav. Adalaj is a quiet village on the outskirts of Ahmedabad. This has served as the place to rest for pilgrims and caravans for hundreds of years. It was built in 1499 by Queen Rudabai, the wife of the Vaghela Chief, Veersinh. This 5-storey step well, was not just a cultural and utilitarian space, but also a spiritual refuge. It is believed that villagers would come every day in the morning to fill water, offer prayers to the deities carved into the walls and interact with each other. May not be an alternative to Rani ki Vav, but it was quite a beautiful baori.

I spent a wonderful evening at the IIM campus visiting a very dear friend. The next day was a long drive back home - 970 kms, 17 hours. Tired, exhausted, aching but an absolute happy soul, is how I would describe myself at that juncture. That is how I came back from this trip. There is something about Gujarat that is pulling me to it. Not just the places to be explored but also the food. Their ability to balance the flavours is amazing. The sweetness just so subtly compliments the spiciness. Kathiawadi cuisine is another level of deliciousness. I feel Gujarati food is most underrated. It is just so sad that people don't understand the unique nuances of the cuisine. The next time, I will plan with some extra days in hand. This was too short a trip, but I had no choice. It was this much or not at all.

Enchanting Shekhawati
(March 2019)

My first rendezvous with the Shekhawati region was Churu. I came across Churu during a drive into the dunes that I did with some friends of mine. Up until then it was a town that one had studied in Geography as one of the hottest places outside the Equator. I made nearly four trips to Churu in less than a year ever since the first trip. It also became the venue of a very special family celebration. There was something about Churu that made me feel very connected to it.

Churu is known as the Gateway to the Thar Desert situated near the shifting sand dunes of the Thar. It used to be essentially a trading town on the Silk route. It is home to some amazing sandalwood artists and a whole load of lac bangle makers. It is home to some humongous havelis. I am sure in their time they must be really beautiful. Even in the present state of neglect, with all their faded fresco paintings, they are beautiful. The Surana Haveli is known as the haveli with no less than 1,100 windows. The haveli owned by Malji Kothari had Belgian glass on its front façade. When you walk through the lanes it feels like time has stood still in this town. There is so much that can be done to make it into a lovely tourist place. It is a town with people who have so much warmth with which they welcome you.

I wanted to explore more of this region. So, when I was planning a short trip with my mom, there were 2-3 things I had to bear in mind, one was the driving distance and two, there should be things to do yet it should not be very strenuous for her. Naturally Rajasthan was the choice. Well, let's just say I love Rajasthan and it is really my one stop shop for any trip ideas. And since I had done Churu a lot the year before, Mandawa was the next favoured pick. I had heard about it's havelis and the frescos and by what I had seen in Churu, I was excited. Of course, this trip was supposed to be about mom, but.... well....

Shekhawati mainly comprises of the towns of Mandawa, Nawalgarh, Jhunjhunu, Fatehpur, Ramgarh, Mahansar, Dundlod and Churu. These lie on the Old Silk Route and were basically meeting points for traders from the Middle East, China and India, mainly trading in opium, cotton and spices. Up until the early 19th century, a vast amount of the trade was diverted through this region. This merchant community that grew then is still a prominent class in the Indian Society - the Marwaris.

As the British set up grew stronger, more emphasis was laid on developing the port towns of Bombay and Calcutta to establish the monopoly for the East India Company. And by the end of the first quarter of the 19th century, it was clear that the traders would have to move base from Rajasthan. Soon the Marwaris carved a big niche in the economic scenario and flourished in their businesses based out of Calcutta, Bombay, Surat and Hyderabad. Between 1830 and 1930, these Marwari businessmen built palatial homes back in their homeland and commissioned painters to paint these havelis as symbols of their success and opulence. Even today, majority of the industrial houses are managed by Marwaris.

The Marwaris gathered a lot of wealth when the trade was flourishing, and they travelled the world spreading their trade. A natural progression to travelling is collecting articles from places travelled to. And in the havelis of Shekhawati, one finds such antiques on display. And honestly, for the first time I was actually fascinated by the antiques on display. Some of the things I could relate to from the stories I heard from my grandmoms. In fact, Vivaana, where we stayed, has quite a collection of these antiques.

Shekhawati is also known as the Land of Hidden Treasures. It is said that the Marwari traders of Shekhawati invested their wealth in expanding their business, as hard cash, as gold, silver coins and other valuables and in property. It is because of this that there have been incidences of these treasures being found buried in the floors and walls of these havelis. If folklore is to be believed 99kgs of gold, 28 kgs of diamond jewellery and 1850 kgs of silver was recovered from excavations of one of the Goenka havelis. Wonder if I should convince *the Husband* to buy a haveli? But first I need to find one which has such treasures buried in it.

Part 1

My natural choice of stay in Mandawa was Vivaana, a place my family and friends had visited twice earlier and spoken very highly of. Both the times I missed going with them. And whatever I had heard of the place, it was better than that. Actually, it is not really in Mandawa, but in a small village about 9 kms from Mandawa called Churi Ajitgarh. In fact, the museum gallery at Vivaana has a very interesting story about how the name got prefixed with the word Churi (bangle).

The village was named Churi Jodha after Jat Jodha who came with his family from the Pawa village and settled here. The village was founded by four traders named Malujee Brahman, Bhalojee Jat, Jhalayla Khati and Kadalaya in 1201. According to the local folklore, the ladies of Jodha's family used to get water from the nearby village of Ghodiwara. One day the women of both the villages had a fight and the women of Godhiwara taunted Jodha Jat's wife to ask her husband to dig a well of their own. When Jodha Jat failed to dig the well, the ladies of his family made him wear bangles and hence the village came to be known as Churi Jodha. It is now called Churi Ajitgarh after the then ruler Maharaja Ajit Singh who also constructed a fort in the village.

From the outside, Vivaana is quite an unassuming place. When we reached the place, I, for a moment did wonder why people went gaga over it. But it is a different story once you enter the place. The warmth of the Rajasthani hospitality I swear by is so apparent. Needless to say, the haveli set up did bring out the romantic dreamer that I am deep inside. Well, I am more and more convinced, I was a part of this life at some point in my past life.

Oh, did I mention, enroute from Gurgaon, one crosses a town called Chiraawa? It is home to some very delicious pedas - both the white ones and the brown ones. The white ones were the better ones according to me. They are not to be missed when crossing that town. Before Chiraawa on this route comes a place called Narnaul. One finds a lot of rasgullas here. I am told they are not so nice, but since I never stopped for those (surprisingly) I cannot say for sure, though the opinion of my source is pretty reliable.

Part 2

The next day started with a drive around the village. Ideally an early morning walk is wonderful, but we drove around with Peer as our guide. Peer was the Front Office Manager who very graciously volunteered to help me explore the town. Though it is a very small village, it has it's own school and health centre (a cute little 12 bedded hospital, a surprisingly very clean one at that - yes, I went in there too) in place. The 2 main havelis belong to the Nemani family. One is a humongous one, which is still in use by the owners and the other is a small one which I am told is sometimes let out to tourists. Since we did not have the permission to go in, we just saw these from outside, and Peer promised to organise the visit inside the next morning.

After dropping Peer back at Vivaana, Mom and I left for Mandawa. Mandawa, as I said earlier, is about 9 kms from Vivaana. I had just stopped at a place to figure out where to go when there came this guy on a bike and knocked at my side of the window. As it turned out he was a guide. A two-minute conversation and he was hired. INR. 500/- for the entire tour. We of course, only wanted to visit 3-4 havelis, but that was okay. He went and parked his bike and got in the back seat. Now before anyone says anything on how I could let a stranger into the car, well, that is how I have been exploring Rajasthan. And my experience in Rajasthan has always been a very nice one. I have never felt any reason to doubt their intentions. I even did the same thing while on my solo drive.

So off we went to the first haveli, Sneh Ram Ladia Haveli. It is said to be 140 years old. A bit restored and a bit as is. Right outside within the haveli complex is a shop selling antiques. I am sure if one went in one would find interesting stuff, but I did not venture in. Honestly because I was not very impressed by the haveli itself. I had heard so much about the havelis of Mandawa and I was definitely disappointed at the very start.

The next stop was at the Chokhani Double Haveli. It was built in the first decade of the 20th century. It got its name as Double Haveli because 2 identical havelis were made adjacent to each other for the 2 brothers and their families. We took precisely 10 minutes to walk through the haveli and we were out of it. Fun fact - close to this haveli was another deserted haveli which apparently was the Pakistani police station in the movie Bajrangi Bhaijaan.

By now, I was completely disappointed and dejected by the havelis. It was a sad state of affairs. I was kind of ready to go back, when the guide took us to Kedarmal Ladia Haveli. One of the rooms is painted in gold. I am told that 3 kgs of gold had been used in paintings in the room. This was better than what I had seen so far, but I had had enough. I just wanted to call it a day. Though the guide kept telling me there were more and prettier ones, I was just not up to it. It was time for lunch, and one of the staff at Vivaana had suggested Kothi Mandawa as a nice place for lunch, so that is where we headed.

Kothi Mandawa was desserted to say the least. A nicely done up place, but not a soul in sight. The staff was more than happy to cook us lunch so mom and I settled down. Gatta curry and Ker Sangri was what we ordered. It took some time for the food to arrive, and I was beginning to fear that the food would be as disappointing as the town was. But I was extremely pleasantly surprised. The Ker Sangri was one of the best I have ever had. And the amount I have travelled in Rajasthan, I have had a lot of it. Delicious is an understatement.

We drove back home and I kept wondering what was so special about Mandawa. Churu did not have havelis with a lot of frescos, but at least it was cleaner than what I found Mandawa to be. And I was told that this place was beautiful. Maybe I never went to the right places. I don't know but I was very dejected.

Part 3

Next morning, I went for a walk around the village. There are a lot of peacocks in the area. I had till now in life never seen a peacock with its feathers completely open. As I stepped out of Vivaana and walked a few steps I saw this peacock perched on a tree. I focused my camera on it and as if that was a cue, the peacock opened up its feathers and started moving as if posing for the camera. I was elated. The previous day's disappointment just fizzled away. My day was made. Needless to say, the walk never happened. I was too excited having seen a peacock with feathers open that too perched on a tree. It just gave me the feeling that the day may just turn out to be an awesome one. Our first stop was the big Nemani haveli.

Shivnarain Surajmal Nemani, the biggest seth in the village and can probably be given the credit for the school and hospital (which initially was built as a maternity hospital but now is a small 12 bedded general hospital) in the village. Also, the well that he built in his haveli is said to have provided water to the entire village. This haveli is built on a sprawling piece of land and still in use by the descendants. As you enter the gate, on the left you see a building which is a Shiva Temple, built for the women in the family so that they did not have to go out. On the right is the building that houses the living quarters. As you enter the drawing room you are transported back in time with furniture that reminds you of the furniture one had seen in one's grandparents' house. Humungous sofas which have springs inside, antique corner pieces, dainty dining chairs & high ceilings with ventilator windows. It gives a feeling as if your grandma will just be walking in from one of the doors. Actually, it was nostalgic for me because these were the kind of sprawling bungalows I have stayed in places like Lucknow, Bhopal and even Delhi, all thanks to my father being in the Army. I did not go to the upper floor as that is the area the owners presently use as their living quarters when they are in town. Behind the house there is a swimming pool, which was apparently used by the women of the house. And next to the well there is a room that houses a generator set which is more than 100 years old. It was imported from England.

After this we went to the smaller of the Nemani Havelis. According to what Peer told me the day before, this was gifted to the daughter in marriage. What this haveli is actually known for is one room on the 1st floor which is completely painted. There is not an inch of space that is left. That room was supposed to be the rangshala. Notable amongst the paintings are 3 paintings that are supposedly of Queen Victoria - one of her as a young girl, one with her 4 children and one of her as the old Queen Victoria. Also, there are 3 erotic paintings.

We dropped Peer back at Vivaana and left for Nawalgarh. Before leaving us, he called his guide friend in Nawalgarh, Shahrukh Bhai, and told him to expect us. A quick google search told me that the first destination should be the Poddar Haveli Museum. But Shahrukh Bhai asked us to meet him near Morarka Haveli - a five-minute walk from Poddar haveli.

Morarka haveli was built by Jairam Dasji Morarka more than a 100 years ago. I had been noticing in all these havelis that the doors have pointed knobs all over them. Shahrukh Bhai told us that it was a kind of a security system. Anyone trying to break open the door would hurt himself with pointed knobs. He also told us that the outside courtyard was the business area and the inside was for the family. The baithak in the outside courtyard was used to conduct matters of business. Another interesting thing that he told us was that in those times the fans used to be the fabric fans which had to be pulled by a rope. No, that is not the interesting part. The interesting part is that the persons pulling the rope in the business area were necessarily deaf and mute so that they could neither hear not pass on the business secrets to anyone. And the ones who pulled the ropes in the sleeping quarters were deaf, mute and blind. Hmmm ... I had always wondered about this!!!

Our next stop was the Poddar Haveli Museum. The haveli was

built in 1902 by Dr Ramnath Anandilal Poddar. It has exquisite frescos and murals and absolutely intricate artwork. It was beautiful. As you enter, on the wall is a painting of Dr. Ramnath Poddar and just above it is a very interesting paining. It is one of an elephant and a bull with only one head. If you see it from the perspective of the elephant and it becomes an elephant's head and see it from the bull's perspective and it becomes the bull's head. This haveli has been converted into a museum, hence it has antiques on display. One room houses dolls dressed in the various bridal costumes found all over Rajasthan. One room has a collection of miniature paintings, one has jewellery from back then, there is one room that houses documents from back then, bills, income tax challans and so on. Fascinating!

The target was to visit 3 havelis. There is only that much we could fit in. At the end of the day, it was supposed to be a relaxing holiday for mom, which it was not turning out to be. I had to constantly remind myself of it. Shahrukh Bhai insisted we go to the Bhagaton ki Haveli. Bhagaton ki Chhoti Haveli as it is called was made by Shivnarayan Bansidhar Bhagat. It has paintings of a tram, steam ship and a horse tram. Another thing that I came to know was that each of the rooms has a little stairway going up to an area like a balcony around the room. This was called the "duchhatti" used for storage or as a kids' play area. If you really ask me, though the Poddar haveli was beautiful in its grandeur, I found the Bhagaton ki haveli to be more interesting. It gave the feel of actually walking into the times gone by. In a way, it left me wanting more. I am sure there are more havelis worth exploring in Nawalgarh, but the heat had begun to get to us. All we wanted to do was get back to the comfort of the air-conditioned room and go into slumber mode.

Part 4

Later that evening, while we were having dinner, Simmons, one of the people working there, came up and told me that where they have the staff quarters, there is one peacock that comes, and for the last 3-4 days it had been dancing to his heart's content. He said he would have someone escort me in the morning and maybe I would get lucky a second time. So early next morning, I reached the staff quarters. There was this peacock who had already done his dance routine and was busy eating. It doesn't even begin to describe it when I say I was disheartened. In a bit, he flew away. I sat there a while looking at the doves and peahens flying in, eating and flying off. Observing them closely, I realised that the doves are such dainty birds with the ring around their neck and the peahens are so beautiful and we have only ever looked at a peacock.

After a while as I was about to get up, this peacock came in. He was there precisely for 2-3 minutes. And in that time, it was like he came, he performed and he left. I have never in my life seen something so gorgeous. The way he turned his back towards me and then opened up his feathers and slowly took a turn to show his magnificent feathers. It took a complete round and then closed its feathers. What a performer that guy was and what a performance he gave. It was as if he only came in for the performance. This totally made my day.

We were now headed back home. But before that, we went to a place called Dundlod. Our first stop was The Fort. Although the fort was founded in 1750, much of the present structure dates from 1840 onwards. Originally known as 'Shivgarh", it was built by Kesri Singhji, the 5th son of Rao Shekhaji, by whose name "Shekhawati" is known. It has since remained with the descendants of Rao Shekhaji. As you enter the big gateway called Suraj Pole, you get the feeling of having gone back in time. Two cannons adorn the walkway. You enter the Diwan Khana which is furnished with the

Louis the XIV furniture. It has a library that boasts a collection of some rare books. There are some family portraits and believe me when I say the men in the family were handsome to a fault. Totally drool worthy. The first floor was the "Duchhatti", the place from where the women saw the court proceedings in purdah. The fort is also a heritage hotel operational during the winter season. The owners have the largest Marwari horse breeding stud farm in the country and also run a programme for improving the Marwari breed under the name of Marwari Bloodlines.

The caretaker at the fort told me to visit the museum too. Although we were to head back, I decided to spend a little time and visit the museum. The interesting thing in the museum was one sealed urn containing water from the river Ganges which the family brought in 1902. One of the antiques that I loved was a 2-in-one turntable.

If Churu impressed me with its havelis and frescos, what was in store in these two days completely bowled me over, well the 2nd day more than the first. I wish I had planned on even a day more. But I guess, there is always a next time. Believe me when I say, Shekhawati may not have as much history as the rest of Rajasthan, but it has so much colour, so much beauty and so much character of its own. There is a place just outside Churu called Mahansar. This place is famous for its local liquor sold by the name of Maharani Mahansar. What is so special about it? Well, it is the flavours. Saunf (Aniseed), mint, rose, betel nut, somras, narangi, cardamom, kesar kasturi. Though I haven't been there but these are available all over Rajasthan. I have all of these in my collection. To me they are more like liqueurs. Interesting stuff.

Having visited these places, I honestly wonder how it is only a one-or-two-day destination for people. How can one explore this region and take in all it has to offer in one or two days. Three - four months back I mentioned to a friend that I was pretty much done with Rajasthan. But I was wrong. There is still more about Rajasthan that beckons me. I am far from being done with this state even though I have explored a huge part of it.

The City Of Nawabs – Lucknow (April 2019)

Day 1

I have lived in Lucknow for a year as a kid when my father was posted there. I have family in Lucknow who I have visited numerous times, but in all these visits I never ever went around exploring the city. And we all know Lucknow is famous for its food. As they say - closer to the temple further away from God. It was high time I did. What better way to do it than with a friend who is as much in love with food as me and loves the idea of going into the deepest crevices of the city to explore food. So, it was a 2-day trip - shopping, food and a little bit of sight seeing all bunged into the 27 hours that Neetu and I spent in the city.

We left home at about 5 a.m. It is a great drive on the YEW (Yamuna Expressway) and the ALE (Agra Lucknow Expressway). We entered Lucknow at 11.45 a.m and the first thing we did was park the car at the multilevel parking in Hazratganj. Driving in Lucknow is a pain and the areas we were planning to go, I personally had no idea what kind of parking spaces one would get there. So, our decided mode of transportation were cycle rickshaws and autos.

Right across the road from the multi-level parking is Janpath. The place to go shopping when you don't have much time. We were focused on what exactly we wanted and thought it would be a cake walk and we should be out in an hour at the maximum. But no, that is not what happened. We hopped shops and sadly never got the stuff we came dreaming about. Those guys are just not willing to understand what you want. They will hear you, give you the look as if they are on the same page and then go and get stuff they think you should buy. I almost lost it at one of the shops. Exasperated was how I came out. Anyhow, we picked up a couple of things because we had to pick up something and now that we had bought it, started loving what we bought. In all seriousness, the quality of stuff overall, is not what it used be earlier, workmanship has gone down to pathetic levels and what is good is obscenely expensive.

By the time we finished it was past 3 O'clock. Our food destination for the day was Chowk. Tunday Kababi, Rahim Ki Nihari and Idrees ki Biryani were the three places we wanted to go to. All of them supremely iconic places. All this while that we were going up and down the shops there were these cycle rickshaw guys hounding us to take us to Chowk - the wholesale market. Chowk was our food destination and we got the impression from the rickshaw walas that it was close by so we went to this guy and the deal was set at 40 bucks for the ride. He was to drop us at Tunday Kababi and off we went. The ride just went on endlessly and Tunday Kebabi was nowhere in sight. There were places where the road was a slight upward slope, so for a stretch I got off and walked a distance, then Neetu got off and walked a distance. We were feeling so bad for the rickshaw guy that we decided to pay him a Rs. 100 because we thought Rs. 40 was too less. All this while he kept saying "bas 2 minute". The heat of course was unrelenting. In all our goodness we gave him all the little bottles of water that we were carrying with us. He stopped enroute and we thought maybe he was lost, but no, he went chatting with a friend who owed him money (later realised he had taken the longer route to meet this guy). Finally at one place he took a turn, and we got this amazing whiff of food. We looked around and we saw Idrees Biryani. We asked the rickshaw guy to stop and he wouldn't saying it was not Tunday. After a lot of insistence, he did stop but also insisted he would wait. We went closer to the place and were told the biryani had finished. A fresh lot was being cooked and that would take time. We could come back at 6 in the evening. Dejected (and hungry) we sat on the rickshaw and told him to take us to Tunday. It was not much of a distance, and then there was a walk to the place. When we gave the guy the 100 bucks, he lost it at us. He said he wanted more. When I said he had only quoted Rs. 40 he refused to accept saying anything like that. He wanted Rs. 250. We gave him Rs. 50 more and walked away. Now the thing is, had he said that much in the beginning or even agreed that he had said Rs. 40 but was mistaken, I would have given him what he asked. The fact that he just refused to accept he said it inspite of me reconfirming at the beginning, he just lost it with me.

It was a Sunday, and there was the Sunday Bazar on the streets. The crowd was maddening. We asked directions and walked a good 300 odd metres and finally reached the iconic place called Tunday Kababi.

Tunday Kababi came into existence some 110 years ago by Haji Murad Ali. As the story goes, when he was a kid, he fell down and lost his arm. In the local dialect, such a person is called "Tunda". When he started selling kebabs, it in a natural progression started being called Tunday Kebab and the place was called Tunday Kebabi. The first one came in to being In the Chowk area. There is another one that came up later in Ameenabad. The Chowk shop serves only kebab and paratha and that too only buffalo meat kebabs. The Ameenabad shop serves both buffalo meat and mutton kebabs and also has kormas and all on the menu. Interestingly if you see the board hanging at the entrance of the shop says "Grandson's Tunday Kababi". This is the third generation who is running the place. The shop has table seating inside. If you are the kind who would only a go to a hygienic place or even a remotely clean place , this is most definitely not for you. If you see the way they serve the kebabs, you will simply walk away. The guy comes with a stack of plates. You would think he is setting the table for you, but no ... those stacked plates have kebabs in them. He lays them down depending upon how many you want. The kebab by itself is a very small one (priced at INR. 2.50 each). Each serving has 8 of these in a plate. The paratha is INR 10 /-. So, our meal costed us INR. 50. I have had the mutton galoutis from Tunday earlier, but when compared to the galoutis from Alkauser, I never liked the ones from Tunday. There was this flavour which I did not much care for. But the ones that I had in Chowk, were another level. Delicious is an understatement. The difference probably can be attributed to the meat then. If we were not on a food walk, we would have surely gorged on more of these kebabs.

About 100 metres from Tunday Kababi is a nondescript place called Rahim's. It has no board on the outside. And unless you are actually looking for the place, you will probably miss it. There is place to sit in the basement as well as on the first floor, more like a mezzanine floor. We were guided to the upper floor since that was where "families" ate. Again, hygiene and cleanliness were a big question mark. But that is never a deal breaker for me if I know the food is fresh and delicious. It seems we were the special ones, since the owner, a young boy, came to check if we had placed the order, and if there was anything else we wanted. Rahim is known for its Nihari and kulcha. Here you have a choice of meat - mutton or buffalo. We chose the mutton Nihari and Kulcha. The Kulcha was very different than any kulcha I have had before. It was like filo pastry. It was flaky. Paired with the nihari, it was a killer combo. The mutton however was a little chewy, but the gravy was delicious. It was extremely soul stirring. One plate of Nihari and one kulcha costed us Rs. 112.

Interestingly, in precisely 25 minutes, we had finished eating in 2 places. That is how fast the service is. We had thought that by the time we would finish Tunday and Rahim, it would be almost 6 PM, we would wait a while and finish off Idrees too. But since there was so much time, we thought of going to Dastarkhwan at the Tulsi Cinema Complex and come back for Idrees the next day. On the way back we took the electric rickshaw. The thing about an electric rickshaw is that it does not go at a very high speed, hence it is fun to sit in it and absorb the sights as the pass you by. It was a longish ride to Dastarkhwan since there was a lot of traffic. We really enjoyed the ride, slow and nice. On the way to Dastarkhwan, in Hazratganj comes this place called Laddoo Chanakya. He serves a thing called Kulfa. It is a something like a mixture of kulfi and rabri. The texture is like that of a sorbet, it is one of the yummiest desserts I have ever had. No visit to Lucknow goes without eating this. It is an absolute must have when in Lucknow. There is kulfa that is famous in Amritsar too, but I think the people who call that the best one have not had this.

We reached Dastarkhwan. They were just opening up for the evening. Took about 15 minutes to finish cleaning up and serving us. Now, on my earlier trips I had always gone to the Dastarkhwan outlet at Gomti Nagar. I've always loved and enjoyed the food there. My friends insisted that the one at Tulsi, which is the first outlet of the chain, is the best. My family in Lucknow always insisted that was not the case. This time I thought of giving the one at Tulsi a try and seeing for myself. Well, that is a different thing that I got to know later that the one in Gomti Nagar had shut down for renovation. We ordered Mutton Roganjosh and Mutton Botti and a Roomali roti.

My family was right. What I had was nowhere close to what was served at the Gomti Nagar outlet. That was way better than what we had that day. Rs. 300, the maximum we paid that day for food during the trip and the meal that we least enjoyed.

The time was 5.30 in the evening. We still had time before I had told my sister-in-law I would be home. So, we decided to head to the Residency. One part of the sight-seeing that was planned for the trip. The Residency was built by Nawab Asaf-Ud-Daulah and completed by Nawab Saadat Ali Khan in the late 1700s for the British. It was a large complex of buildings including residential quarters, armoury, stables, dispensaries, places of worships and so on. By the time we reached, the museum had closed for the day. Though the premises were open for another hour, there was no guide available for us. So, we went around the place much tired and exhausted all by ourselves.

The entrance is called the Bailley Guard Gate after Capt. John Bailley who became the resident of Lucknow in the beginning of the 19th century. There is one building which is named after Dr. Frayer, who was the resident surgeon during the siege of 1857. Within this building is a basement room or the tehkhana which was used by the women during the hot weather. There is a book written by Valerie Fitzgerald called Zamindar. The story is based around the time of the 1857 mutiny. She writes about this tehkhana as being used by the British to take refuge during the mutiny. I remember her describing a scene when the people are hiding in the tehkhana taking refuge, as bloody and gory as can be. The Residency is a place where one must take a guide, and if you can read up the history a bit before visiting, believe me you would enjoy it more. This is the only bit of sightseeing I had done in the one year I spent in Lucknow. I don't remember much now. But when I read Zamindar after the visit, I enjoyed it doubly more. For sure I will go back on my next visit and explore it with the guide. We were extremely tired and heat exhaustion was setting in too so just took a round of the premises and left.

A quiet ride back to the parking, a quieter ride back home where more food awaited us. We were tired and sleepy we called it an early night. The next day was an early day starting with some more food. With dreams of Sharma ji ke Bun Makkhan, I dozed off to sleep.

Day 2

Early next morning, we left home at 6.30 a.m., still in our jammies for some amazing bun makhan and chai at Sharma Tea Stall near Hazratganj. Even though the shop was not open yet for the day, there were people waiting. For people in Lucknow, Sharma Tea Stall is a meeting place, where they come every morning after their morning walk or exercise, or just like that to chit chat and catch up with friends before the routine of the day sets in. By 7 in the morning the place was buzzing with people who have come for the proverbial chai pe charcha.

The present Sharma ji who was sitting at the shop is the 2nd generation Sharmaji and he told us that his son has also joined in. The place has been running since 1955. The bun that he serves is as soft as soft can be. You have a choice of butter or double butter. Ofcourse the preferred choice is always double butter. Soft, fluffy, freshly beaten white butter generously spread between the bun – It is heavenly. And the tea, though the tea is served in glasses or Kullars as you want, I prefer to have it in a glass. Those glasses have probably never seen the face of a washing soap in their life but that is what makes the tea so tasty. Does it sound gross?! ... Believe me it is delicious. Also, if any of you visit Sharmaji, the butter is the freshest, fluffiest, tastiest early morning. Go by about 8.30 and it is not the same.

With our stomachs full and palette satisfied, we headed to the

Bada Imambara. The Bada Imambada was designed by Kifayatulla (the guide told us his original name was Qazam Ali, but people started calling him Kifayatullah because he was a miser) and built by Nawab Asaf-ud-Daula in 1784. It houses the graves of Nawab Asaf-Ud-Daula and his wife Shamsunnisa Begum. You enter through a triple archway gate. On the right is the Asafi Mosque, on the left is the shahi Baoli and straight ahead is the Naubat khana which has the graves and the Labyrinth or the Bhool Bhulaiya on the 3 floors above. Naubat Khana in its length is 320 ft., is divided into 3 halls. The Bhool Bhulaiya is made up of intricate passages and 489 identical doorways. It is quite a fun thing. And we had a guide, Maqbool Hussain, who made it all the more interesting. And the fact that he was taking amazing photographs was the icing on the cake. He knew just the places and the angles and frames where he clicked some very nice pictures of both of us.

After we finished with the Imambara, we realised we did not have much time. We had to head to Chowk for some shopping and Idrees Biryani before we started our drive back home. We took a quick round to the Chhota Imambara from outside and headed back home. When you go towards the Chhota Imambara, you cross what is called the Rumi Darwaza. When you look at it from one side it has 3 gates and 5 floors, while from the other side it has 1 gate and 3 floors. It is also referred to as the Turkish Gate as it is believed to be identical to a gate in ancient Istanbul. Both the Bada Imambara and the Rumi Darwaza were built for a good cause. During the time of Nawab Asaf-Ud-Daula, there was a massive famine that struck the city. The people being self-respecting people, refused to take food from the nawab for free. These 2 monuments were the brainchild of the Nawab as a sort of Food for work programme. The Architectural style for both these monuments is very different from what I have seen so far. The walls are lined alternatingly with structures that look like cloves and garlic pods. It is quite a refreshing change from the Mughal and Shekhawati styles I have been seeing in my previous trips to other places. The Chhota Imambara was built by Muhammad Ali Shah, the 3rd Nawab of Awadh in 1838. While I was googling what it was all about, I saw the picture on the internet, and now I am kicking myself for not having gone inside. It seems like a beautiful monument. Well, I guess I will just have to wait till my next visit to Lucknow to go and visit the place.

Moving on, after some more shopping in Chowk, we headed to Tunday again. Neetu wanted to get some packed to carry back home. That done we headed to Idrees Biryani. Oh, I forgot, as we stepped into the shopping side of Chowk, we saw this guy selling the famous makhan-malai. It is actually a Persian dish called Nimish, originally made from horse milk and cream. But the Indian version is made of cow/buffalo milk. Milk and cream is beaten to a soft fluffiness and sugar and saffron is added to it. This was the first time I was having it and honestly, I was very apprehensive. I can have makhan and malai separately, but cannot comprehend it together. It was mind-blowing. An absolute must-have. In Delhi it is called Daulat Ki Chat and in Banaras it is called Malaiyyo. The recipe is I feel a little different in Delhi and Banaras. I have had all three, but nothing comes close to makhan-malai.

Mohammed Idrees started in 1968 and now his sons run the place. It is a small shop that has one table that can seat 6-8 people. Neetu and I were probably one of the rare female customers who came and sat inside to eat. It takes about 3 hours to cook one degh of biryani and 16-18 deghs are cooked and served in a day. The biryani is lightly spiced, slow cooked with milk, cream and a whole load of saffron. I am not a fan of mutton biryani. In fact, I don't like it. But believe me this was amazing. I loved the flavour. This truly lived up to its reputation. I savoured every morsel of it.

And it was time to head back home. But we were happy with what we had accomplished. Yes, there is a lot that still needs to be had in Lucknow, but we at least covered the iconic places for non-vegetarian food in the city. The next trip I will for sure cover all that I missed out on this time, with the promise to tell you all about it.

The Sufi Trail
Ajmer - Sarwar - Sambhar – Nagaur
(Nov 2019)

Ajmer Sharif is a place that is special to me. One of the rear places that gives the agnostic in me a sense of peace even though it is one of the most crowded places to be. It was during my trip to Ajmer Sharif in April 2017 that I really got to know Riyasat Bhai. Riyasat Bhai is a Khadim at the Dargah Sharif and he is known to a very dear friend of mine. Khadims are families who for generations have looked after the upkeep and the affairs of the dargah. The time I spent in conversation with him after the ziyarat at the Dargah Sharif during that trip left me wanting more. Before that trip I had always gone in a bigger group so never really had the chance of having a conversation with him. This time it was just me and a friend of mine. We spoke about my travels and we discovered our shared love for food. And this is when he mentioned the Sufi circuit of Ajmer Sharif, Sarwar Sharif, Sambhar Sharif and Nagaur Sharif. Curiosity to visit them got me going and he promised he would take me there on my next visit. I made plans on multiple occasions but none materialised. Well as the they say, unless the Sufi saint of Nagaur, Hazrat Sufi Hamiduddin Khui wants you to visit him, you will not be able to go.

Sometime in August 2019, I was going through my son's school almanac and saw a long weekend opportunity in the month of November. The ideal time for me to travel out alone is when he has holidays. I connected with Riyasat Bhai to check whether he was free during that time, he confirmed and the plan was set. It seemed like finally I would do this. The way things had been going the last few months I was not so sure. But I guess going by the legend, it was my time to visit and nothing would stop me.

Ajmer Sharif

I reached Ajmer Sharif around 1.30 pm. As usual headed to Digghi Bazar, where I parked the car. There are a couple of car parks where you can park your car on a 24hr basis for a charge of Rs. 300. The usual auto guy, Zakir Bhai, was waiting to take me through the narrow lanes of Digghi Bazar to Riyasat Bhai's house where I usually stay on my visits. Now the thing is, when I am in Riyasat Bhai's care, it is not only about the ziyarat experience, it is also about the wonderful conversations with him and the most amazing food that his wife cooks up. This time I even got to feast on his sister's culinary skills. They as a family, have so much love to give and it shows in their hospitality.

The first thing Riyasat Bhai told me as we exchanged pleasantries was that I had come on an extremely auspicious day. It was Prophet Mohammed's birth anniversary. I was happy, as extra blessings never hurt anyone. I settled down in my usual room that is in a building 10 metres from his house. I had my lunch - delicious shammi kebabs and palak dal and rested for a while. I was to be ready by 6.00 pm.

Sharp at 6 o'clock, we headed to the Dargah Sharif. It is less than a 5-minute walk. It was already dark. We usually enter from the rear end and as one entered one could see the throng of people. But the crowd got completely overshadowed because all I could do was gape at how beautifully the Dargah Sharif had been decorated. Lights, flowers, fireworks in the background, all of it was so surreal. I had never seen it so decorated ever. I have visited the Dargah on Eid too, but this was something else. First things first, we went inside the sanctum sanctorum for the ziyarat. There I met Nawazish who is Riyasat Bhai's son, and both together offered the prayers on my behalf. I always say this there is something about a Gurudwara and a Dargah that bring me a lot of peace. After that finished, I stepped out and while I was standing there waiting for both to finish offering prayers on their own behalf, I just felt tears rolling down and they were unstoppable. Was I crying? No, I was not, but they just kept flowing. It just felt as if all the sadness and negativity was flowing out with the tears. I must have been standing there for 15-20 minutes with tears flowing out, and those 15-20 minutes were one of the most refreshing moments I have experienced in a long time. I felt somewhat cleansed, cleansed of the sadness I had been feeling for the last 4 months when I lost someone very close to me. I still feel a very important part of me is missing but I also know that that precious part of me is in safe hands up there and is being taken care of with all the love that he deserves.

After that Nawazish took me around the Dargah Sharif. I saw the mazars of Khwaja Moinuddin Chishti's youngest son, daughter, and wife. We went to the Akbari Masjid. Also, there is small room that goes down 32 ft. This is where Baba Farid used to do his chilla. Chilla is intense prayers done for a period of 40 days. The door to this room is opened only once every year in the month of Muharram. We spent a good amount of time walking around and talking. We went to the place where the daily langar is cooked. There are 2 huge karahis (woks) in which one sweet and one savoury semi solid khichdi like dish is cooked as langar. This is different from the badi and chhoti deghs which are cooked when someone sponsors them on fulfilment of their mannat (wish). The langar that is cooked, and the same goes for the Deghs is pure vegetarian without onions and garlic even. This is because people from all religions and beliefs visit here and these can be eaten by anyone. Non-veg langars made by people can be served in the Dargah, but the in-house langar is pure vegetarian. The Badi Degh can cook upto 4800 kgs of food and the Chhoti Degh can cook upto 2400 kgs. These deghs are usually cooked at night and distributed in the morning after the morning namaz. What is cooked is a kind of sweetened rice with a lot of dry fruits.

Whether you walk around or sit in a place at the Dargah Sharif, one gets to see people in different emotional states. There are people who come in happiness, then there are people who come looking for fulfilment, you can see some people sitting all by themselves and crying. Makes you wonder what all goes on in peoples' lives. It makes you wonder if at all your own problems are as big as you make them out to be. This is a place where your ego plays no part and each one is brought down to the same level irrespective of who you are in your life. Truly humbling.

After spending about an hour and a half at the Dargah, I came back to my room where my dinner of delicious methi keema and the most amazing aloo ki sabzi awaited. It had been a long day and I was tired. The next day was a 300 km drive Ajmer-Sarwar Sharif - Sambhar Sharif - Ajmer.

Sarwar Sharif and Sambhar Sharif

Garib Nawaz Khwaja Moinuddin Chishti had 3 sons and a daughter. While the mazars of the youngest son Hazrat Khwaja Ziauddin Abu Saeed, R.A and his daughter Bibi Hafiza Jamal are in the Dargah Sharif itself in Ajmer, the Mazar of his eldest son Hazrat Khwaja Fakhruddin Chishti is in place called Sarwar, about 60 kms from Ajmer. That is where we were headed. The drive took about an hour and a half, conversations with Riyasat Bhai are always fun, more so because we share the love for food. In fact, major part of our conversations was about food. And the best part is, we not only talk about food, he treats me to the most delicious food I have ever had.

As the legend goes, Hazrat Khwaja Fakhruddin Chishti was extremely short tempered unlike Garib Nawaz, who was extremely patient. For this reason, Garib Nawaz asked his son to go and practice religion elsewhere. It is also said that it is because of his short temper, when people visit Sarwar, they do not stay there, because the longer you stay, the more are the chances of any inadvertent 'Be-adabi" (disrespect) to happen that may anger the Khwaja ji.

The insides of the mazaar are beautifully made from exquisitely carved solid silver. The gate itself weighs 14 kilos. Inside the mazaar it is quiet and it is peaceful. Again, one gets to see people coming in with different expressions on their faces and expectations in their hearts. Life is a great leveller. And it is so apparent when one comes to places like these. When problems hit you, you just come down on your knees and pray for peace. You may be who you are to the outside world, you may follow whatever religion you are a part of in the outside world, but in that moment, it is just you and your belief and your faith.

We stopped for tea at one of the small chai tapris on the highway and headed towards Sambhar. Sarwar to Sambhar is about a 140 km drive. One needs to head towards Jaipur and then turn left at Dudu. Sambhar is better known for its salt pans. Sambhar Salt Lake or Shakambari Jheel as it is also called, is India's largest inland Salt Lake.

The Dargah at Sambhar houses the mazaar of Khwaja Moinuddin Chishti's grandson from his eldest son, Hazrat Khwaja Hisamuddin Sokhta Dil R.A. The suffix of "sokhta dil" got attached because they say that his ibaadat was so intense that his chest would get scorched with the heat of that intensity.

Inside the dargah sharif, the mazaar has a beautiful marble canopy, decorated with embroidered brocade and fresh flowers. Quiet and serene, one could hear a pin drop. Even though there were people sitting outside, it was quiet inside. Riyasat Bhai offered prayers on my behalf and after that I just stood in one corner for a while. The mind was blank and silent. There were no thoughts, just the heart and mind taking in the peace and quiet. I have often tried to silence my thoughts but have never succeeded in it. In fact, the more I try to silence it the more the noise in the head grows. And here without any effort it was as if I was thoughtless. It was all very new to me.

We left the Dargah Sharif and were back on our return journey. On the way back we stopped at a gurudwara, Gurudwara Charan Kamal Sahib. As the legend goes, in 1707, Guru Gobind Singh ji was travelling from Takht Shri Damdama Sahib in Talwandi Sabo to Huzoor Sahib in Nanded and on the request of the Mahant of the Dadoo Panth, Sant Jaitram ji, he along with his followers stopped here. Sant Jaitram ji requested them to have the langar that had been prepared. Guru Gobind Singh ji hesitated. On being asked if anything was wrong, he replied that all was well, but he would only have the langar when his baaj (the falcon) will be served food too. To this Sant Jaitram ji asked how it would be possible, they were strict vegetarians and the baaj was a meat-eating predator, they could not make anything that was fit for the baaj to eat. To this Guru Gobind Singhji requested his baaj, who then ate the bajra ka langar that had been prepared.

And this is when I realised in all the pictures of Guru Gobind Singhji, there is a baaj (falcon) perched on his hand. Some surfing on the internet, and I got to know that he is also called Dhan Dhan Sri Guru Gobind Singhji Chittiyan Baajan Waale. The falcon (I will refer to it as the baaj only) truly represents a Khalsa.

1. Cannot be enslaved - A baaj will either breakaway from the cage or die in captivity. A khalsa cannot be bound.
2. A baaj is independent. It will only eat what it kills and will never prey on leftovers of the other predators. The Khalsa is also expected to be self-reliant and never beg anyone for anything.
3. A baaj soars very high in the sky but has its eyes always on the ground looking for its prey. This represents humility that a Khalsa should have. He would soar high in life but he must always have his eyes on his weaknesses and be grounded in life.
4. Chakravarty - always moving, unattached. A baaj will never call one place as its permanent nest. It will never get attached. The lesson to the Khalsa is that he should not get attached to the material things in life because ultimately, we will have to leave everything when we die.
5. It is never lazy. Always alert, always on the go.
6. A baaj will always fly against the wind. Its unique. A khalsa is also unique, nirala. He does not wither under pressure.
7. A baaj is fearless. So is a khalsa.
8. A baaj is the king of the skies, it is royal. A khalsa is royal in his own right.

An interesting comparison there.

The Gurudwara is beautifully made in pristine marble, extremely peaceful and beautifully done up from inside. After paying our respects and taking the prasad we left for Ajmer. Unfortunately, did not have the time to eat the langar. But there is always a next time.

It was quite a day. But there was still the dinner that I was looking forward to. Delicious Paalak meat and Mutton Korma awaited me. But before that Riyasat Bhai treated me to his patent lemon tea. Believe me, one cup of it and all my tiredness and exhaustion just drained away. The next day was the final stop, Nagaur Sharif, the Dargah of Khwaja Moinuddin Chishti's successor, Hazrat Sufi Hamiduddin Nagori.

Nagaur Sharif

Nagaur Sharif houses the mazaar of Hazrat Sufi Hamiduddin Nagori, who was the successor of Garib Nawaz. They say one gets to visit Nagaur Sharif only if he wants you to visit him. Many a times people have tried to visit the dargah Sharif, but for one reason or the other gone back without completing the visit. Also, when you visit the dargah sharif, it is imperative that one has not consumed anything non-vegetarian, not even eggs. There is a story behind that. Hazrat Sufi Hamiduddin Khui, was a non-vegetarian like most Muslims. One day an injured cow fell on his feet, the cow apparently had escaped being slaughtered. Hazrat Sufi realised that the cow was pregnant. He felt very guilty, and from that day on he gave up on eating meat and forbade anyone coming to visit him to consume meat and visit him.

We left Ajmer at about 12.30 p.m. It was a late start because Riyasat Bhai had asked his wife to pack a picnic lunch for us, specifically a sookhi daal preparation which I was told was a must have. Nagaur Sharif is a 165 kms from Ajmer. Usually, one crosses Pushkar to go to Nagaur, but since the Pushkar fair was on, we took a detour through some narrow village roads. After about 20 odd kilometres the road becomes amazing. Two lane road, but super quality. Exactly half way to Nagaur, once you cross Merta City, you get to see a lot of spotted deer, neelgaay, blackbucks etc. We only saw a few in the fields, but if you are lucky, they flock the roads too. We also had some amazing pyaz ki kachoris that Riyasat Bhai had gotten packed for the way. They were delicious.

We reached Nagaur Sharif around 3 p.m. We entered from the back entrance and it was not what I was expecting. The mazaar was out in the open under a tree. Hazrat Sufi Hamiduddin Nagori did not like closed spaces and that is the reason his mazaar is out in the open. In fact, it constitutes his, his wife's and his son's mazaar all together in one place. The tree that covers the mazaar is not a very dense tree, but I am told that even when it rains very heavily, the water does not reach the chaadar covering the mazaar. Also, Riyasat Bhai told me that the leaves of this tree have magical powers. If the leaves of this tree are eaten in a certain manner, for 3 months by a childless couple, it is guaranteed that they will have a child. Faith is a indeed a big healer.

After we had done the ziyarat, we sat under a covered space and had our picnic lunch. Amazingly soft, melt in the mouth parathas, with a delicious pumpkin sabzi and the most delicious sookhi daal with green chilli pickle - the perfect picnic lunch. A hot cuppa tea would have just taken it to another level.

Though I would have loved to just curl up in a quilt and go off to sleep, we had to leave and I had to drive. There was a yummy dinner also waiting. We reached back by about 9.30 pm. Freshened up and went to the Dargah Sharif for the last time during this visit. The doors had closed, and it was very quiet, and not too many people around. Nawazish, offered prayers on my behalf and did my rukhsati for which I was given a bandhini dupatta. (I have quite a collection of those now from all my visits to Ajmer Sharif).

In a strange way, I was sad that this trip was over. The last 3 days had been amazing in terms of what I was exploring, in terms of the stories I heard, in terms of the people I was with and in terms of the food that I ate. I had dinner that night with Riyasat Bhai's family. His wife had made Laal Maas and his sister had made Dungar maas (mutton smoked with charcoal, ghee, and cloves) and fruit custard. How much I ate that night. I licked my plate clean. We chatted over lemon tea for quite some time. Riyasat Bhai extended an invitation for me to visit during Ramzan and the month of Muharram which I will, for all the ambience and the food these times have to offer. Those I am sure, will be 2 very interesting experiences though very different in their moods.

I left the next morning, loaded with goodies, yummy chicken curry for my kids, pyaaz ki kachoris and gulab jamuns, with the promise to try and return in April during the month of Ramzan. What an amazing family I spent these 3 days with. Rarely does one get to meet people who have so much love to give, people who are so giving in every sense of the word. I truly feel very blessed to have met them and to know them.

Punjab - The Land of Spirituality (November 2021)

It had been a crazy year and a half, nearly two years for all of us during the pandemic. It seemed like a never-ending phase. For the longest time, travel seemed like a distant dream. With Covid settling down and the things starting to look up in the last few months of 2021, the gypsy in me was naturally wanting to just step out and go. I planned one road trip to Western MP which got cancelled 2 days before I was to leave. A month later planned a trip to Banaras. A dream trip which has been eluding me for a long time. I left for it and had to return on day 2 itself because of a family emergency. Things were not working out in terms of travel and I was, to say the least, very dejected.

While I was trying to figure out how to make things work, *the Husband* decided to take a break from his corporate career and go on a sabbatical. And suddenly there was a window that came up. He had been wanting to go on a road trip for a long time but his work schedule did not give him the time. Now he had all the time. His wish list was Punjab and for me all that mattered was a road trip and one with *the Husband* was like a cherry on the cake. So, Punjab it was. A little bit of a research was done, a broad itinerary made, places of stays firmed up and we left. Bookings, we decided we would do on the go as we were not sure on how much time we would need in each place of stay. Surprisingly, not much in terms of travelogues is available to base that bit of planning on.

Day 1

We left Gurgaon early morning, had our customary breakfast of parathas at Amrik Sukhdev Murthal, and our first stop was Gurdwara Fatehgarh Sahib at Sirhind. Fatehgarh Sahib is the location where the two sons of Guru Gobind Singh ji, Fateh Singh (9 years) and Zorawar Singh (7 years) were bricked-up alive on orders of Wazir Khan, the then Governor of Sirhind in Dec 1705. Betrayed by their cook and servant Gangu to the Mughal army, they were kept in immensely inhuman conditions, tortured and asked to convert to Islam. And when they resisted and refused, they were bricked up alive. Under this gurudwara in the basement is the Gurudwara Bhora Sahib (Blessed Basement) where the boys were bricked up. Although the wall does not exist now, the bricks have been preserved and the throne of the Guru Granth Sahib blesses this place.

Gurdwaras are always very peaceful and calm places. The vibe in Gurdwara Fatehgarh Sahib is that and more. It is sombre. I would not describe what I felt as sad, but there was a strange sense of quiet. I am usually one for clicking photos of every possible place, but something held me back. I just wanted to sit quietly. It was difficult imagining the pain the boys must have gone through, the courage it must have taken. Somewhere deep inside the heart was heavy. Such experiences are always humbling. *The Husband* and I sat there for a while and then we left.

We left Sirhind and moved towards Ludhiana. This was to be our first place of stay. Ludhiana for me was going to be only food. Of course, the city is known for Chawla's Cream Chicken, and Aman's

Tandoori dishes and Baba's Butter Chicken, but this time around when I was researching, I found some interesting street food dishes. So, the first stop according to my research was a cart owned by a guy called Vijay right opposite the Guru Nanak Stadium that sells what he calls the Kulcha Pizza. According to Vijay, he is the second generation into this business. His father set this up some 50 years ago. It is a kulcha layered with chhole, topped generously with OTC as they call it - onion, tomato, capsicum and then finally garnished with mayonnaise, a tangy tomato sauce and grated cottage cheese. All for Rs. 30 per Kulcha Pizza. Was it worth it? Oh, absolutely. It was delicious. He also sells simple Kulcha chana. The kulcha is served like a stuffed Pita. But the pizza version is a must have.

One of these is enough to fill you up but when you have limited time and so much more to eat, you stretch yourself, quite literally. The next stop was Khalsa College for Aunty ji's Pav Maska. Pav maska is basically pav bhaji. The pav is toasted with butter on the tawa. Then layered with OTC (the same as above) and a thin layer of bhaji with some more butter. It is covered with another layer of butter toasted pav, topped with some more bhaji and a plop of butter and served hot. For me, it was a little high on salt. The thing with pav bhaji is that the bhaji is cooked in salted butter. You cannot substitute the salted butter with anything else if you really want the taste. One needs to keep in mind the salt in the butter when seasoning the bhaji. Had that been done in this and the salt was less this would have been one super amazing plate of food. But for now, at Rs 130/-, it was some expensive calories consumed.

One thing was sure, now my dinner seemed like a goner. But lassi is a liquid and liquids are known to make space for themselves. With that logic in mind the next stop was Haqiqat Sweets. Rs. 30/- for a glass of this heavenly lassi. The reason I avoid lassi is that once I consume it, I go into a drugged slumber. And well, that is what happened to me. With a promise to the self to skip dinner we headed back to the hotel to check in and crash. Of course, 4 hours later dinner did happen. How could I miss Baba's. We do have an outlet in Gurgaon now, but the original is the original. Baba's butter chicken is very different from the usual butter chicken and of course their lemon chicken is worth a try. It was only day 1 and I was already dreading the weighing scale.

Day 2

Day 2 was taking us to 3 gurdwaras. We left Ludhiana at 7 am and a drive of about 175 kms through NH, SH and interior roads, through fields of burning stubble, post a hearty breakfast of parathas at Haveli Jallandhar, we reached the first destination of the day, Dera Baba Nanak.

Gurdwara Sri Darbar Sahib is situated in the town of Dera Baba Nanak in Gurdaspur District. Recently, it has come much into limelight during celebration of the 550th birth anniversary of Guru Nanak Dev ji when the Kartarpur Corridor was opened and pilgrims were allowed to visit Sri Kartarpur Sahib in Pakistan. Legend has it that Guru Nanak ji visited this place in 1515 after his first Udasi (missionary tour). Guru Nanak's wife and two children used to stay here with his father-in-law Lala Mulraj ji who was a Patwari in the village Pakho-ke-Randhawa. There is a well in the form of a baoli in this premises called Ajite Randhawe da Khoo. Guru Nanak used to sit here and meditate and preach to his followers.

During the latter part of his life Guru Nanak settled down in Kartarpur (now Pakistan) and lived there for 18 years. In 1539, Guru Nanak left for his heavenly abode along with his physical form. All that was left behind and cremated were his clothes. This is where the Gurdwara Sri Kartarpur Sahib was built. The gaggar which contained the ashes of Guru Nanak's clothes was buried there. Much later Baba Sri Chand Ji dug this gaggar out and brought it to Dera Baba Nanak and the same is now placed under the Thada Sahib or the Palki Sahib. A 1660-page handwritten copy of the Guru Granth Sahib is also preserved in this Gurdwara.

Had Covid not happened, we were scheduled and all set to visit Kartapur Sahib on the 27th of March 2020. And as luck would have it, we were at Dera Baba Nanak just a couple of days before it was reopened for pilgrims. Hopefully soon I will be able to. But for now, we went up till the Kartarpur Corridor at the border and could see Kartarpur Sahib at a distance like a spec.

One thing that we missed, and I so regret missing it, is visiting Gurdwara Sri Chola Sahib, a small gurdwara a few hundred meters away from the Darbar Sahib. I wish I had done more research before my trip. This gurdwara is looked after by the 16th generation of Guru Nanak's descendants. The legend has it that the Chola Sahib belonged to Guru Nanak and it is said that it was no ordinary chola, it was given to him by God Almighty. It has 30 verses from the Quran Sharief written on it. There is a rumal that was embroidered by Bebe Nanki ji, Guru Nanak's sister and was gifted to him on his wedding. It is said that this is the chola that Guru Nanak wore when he went to Mecca and Medina. Within the premises there is also an octagonal well the water from which is supposed to have healing powers. Well, we missed it but I guess we will get another chance, because I will be going to Kartarpur Sahib soon. After this we went to the Kartarpur Corridor. The place from where pilgrims go to Sri Kartarpur Sahib.

About 75 kms away was our next stop, the town of Tarn Taran. The foundation of Gurdwara Sri Darbar Sahib was laid in 1590 by Guru Arjan Dev ji. It is made on the similar lines of the Golden Temple and the sarovar is apparently the largest in the world. The name Tarn Taran originally belonged to the sarovar. It literally means "the boat that takes one across the ocean of existence." According to the legend, the water from the sarovar had medicinal properties and was specifically effective in curing leprosy. Guru Arjan Das ji also established India's first home for lepers in Tarn Taran.

We walked the entire periphery of the sarovar and it measured about 1.6 kms. Well honestly, I walked the whole distance because I was hoping that all the calories, I had eaten in the previous days would miraculously get burnt and I could start with clean slate. Alas, such miracles do not happen.

The 3rd and final stop for the day was Amritsar. It is a drive of about 25 kms. By the time we reached Amritsar it was 6 pm. We checked into the hotel, it was a pretty bungalow converted into a boutique hotel bang on the Mall Road. As per our original plan, Amritsar was not on the itinerary. After Kapurthala we were to go for the Retreat Ceremony at Hussainiwala and then were to stay the night at Faridkot. But we got to know that the retreat ceremony for the public had not been restarted since after Covid. There was a whole load of juggling and re-juggling and we figured the best would be to stay a night in Amritsar. The thing with Punjab is there are not very many towns where you get good places to stay in.

A quick shower and change and we were on our way to the Golden Temple. As we stepped into the Golden Temple premises, we were hit by a massive crowd. To be honest, the last 2 years had made us weary of crowds. I am not one who is overly cautious, but I did refrain from crowded places. Initial hesitation gave way soon. I decided that if it has to happen, it will happen. With that mindset, we stepped in and within minutes we were all part of the crowd.

It took us about an hour to come out of the Harmandir Sahib. Obviously, there were two things on my mind - Jutti shopping and food. The lane leading to the Golden Temple has shops on either side. There is only one shop that I visit for my jutti shopping. And I do that for two reasons - one is of course that the juttis are amazing, they are expensive but good. The second reason is compassion they show towards the stray dogs that roam the street. In winters especially they put mattresses inside the store for the dogs to snuggle in. It is the peaceful co-existence that always works for me.

We finished shopping and headed to Bhrawan da Dhaba for dinner. On my previous two visits we went to Kesar da Dhaba which honestly, I found very over hyped. On both my visits I was kind of disappointed on the food. The fun part probably would be the auto ride into the narrow lanes to reach Kesar da Dhaba, but the food failed to catch my fancy. When we reached Bhrawan da Dhaba, it was packed. It took us about 15 minutes to find a table and order food. I was focused on sarson ka saag and makki ki roti. Of course, when in Punjab what else would be on the wish list and that is what we ordered. Sarson ka saag is made in many ways. Different recipes have different things added to the dish and each preparation has its own taste. This one was delicious. The only thing that I found missing was a nice blob of butter on the saag, that would have been heavenly.

Honestly speaking, after having visited three gurdwaras and having all the Kadha Prashad that had been eaten, dessert should have been the last thing on my mind. It would have been but for my friend suggesting I must try the Kulfa (Kulfa is a mix of kulfi and rabri) at A-One Kulfa. So naturally, the last stop for the day was A-One Kulfa. I was also curious because I have had kulfa in Lucknow (remember Laddoo Chanakya?) and that is an amazing dish and I wanted to know how this one compared to that one. The kulfa here was disappointing. Simply put, it is kulfi falooda topped with rabri. I have had better kulfi and better rabri. The Lucknowi Kulfa wins hands down and there is no dessert that can come anywhere near it.

Period.

It had been a long day, and I was tired. It just made me realise that I no longer had the same travel stamina that I had during the pre-covid days. I need to work on rebuilding the same else these kinds of trips will only become a pain. With that thought I hit the pillow and next thing I realise is that my morning alarm was ringing.

Day 3

The plan was to have a lighter day. We had a somewhat leisurely breakfast. As I entered the reception to pay up and check-out, I saw two lovely golden retrievers sitting there. They were as excited to see me as I was to see them. Me being me, naturally I just had to sit with them and spend some time. They were brought here about 5 months back from Bikaner. Since they had come from Bikaner their names were Bika and Neri. Very creative I must say. While there was a lot of ruckus and commotion that we created, I heard another dog barking. Apparently, there was another one, a much older one. When his distant barking did not quieten us, he came to see what it was all about. It was the cutest dachshund I had ever seen. Small little fellow and well his name was also one hell of a creative one - Choocha (meaning very tiny). He was actually just that - choocha! He was mighty disgusted that we disturbed his slumber, barked at us showing his discontent at our behaviour and just walked out of the room with much attitude. Much as I wanted to spend more time with the dogs, we had a destination to reach.

Our first stop was Khem Karan. About 70 kms from Amritsar, Khem Karan is a border town in the Tarn Taran District. It was the site of a major tank battle in 1965. The Battle of Asal Uttar was the second largest tank battle since World War II. A few kilometres before the border post are the Shaheed Abdul Hamid Smarak. On

10th December 1965 Company Quarter Master Havildar Abdul Hamid, single handedly destroyed 3 Pakistani Patton tanks with an outdated gun. He was martyred when his jeep got a direct hit and was blown apart. He received the Param Vir Chakra posthumously. A captured Pakistani Patton tank stands on site with its turret down as a reminder of all the sacrifices made by our troops.

Right next to the Shaheed Samark, there are fields where farmers were working. What was amusing was that the tractors are fitted with huge big speakers and I just loved the way music was blaring out of them.

You drive straight ahead on NH 354 for a few kilometres and you reach the Border post. For security reasons I took no photographs. Also, the BSF officer gave us some interesting stories, none of which, unfortunately, I can write about. Some stories are just meant to be kept to yourself.

About a two-hour drive from here was our next destination. Gurdwara Ber Sahib, Sultanpur Lodhi. All through the drive until now, one thing that was very noticeable was the stubble burning. Big and small, one after the other. There seemed to be smoke everywhere. It is strange how the authorities just turn a blind eye over these farm fires and continue to make us believe they do not happen.

Sultanpur Lodhi is named after its founder Behlul Lodhi who was a general in Mahmud of Ghazni's army in 1103 AD. But before this, Sultanpur Lodhi was called Sarwmanpur and it was a great empire of Hinduism and Buddhism. When Mahmud of Ghazni invaded this area, Sarwmanpur was burnt to ashes and a new city was born - Sultanpur Lodhi. This city was also the central point of the trade route between Delhi and Lahore.

Guru Nanak ji's sister Bibi Nanki was married to a Shri Jai Ram in Sultanpur Lodhi. In 1483 Guru Nanak's father sent him to work with Jai Ram. This is where he got married and had his two sons. Guru Nanak spent 14 years, 9 months and 13 days meditating under a Ber tree on the banks of Kali Bien, a rivulet that flows into the confluence of Beas and Satluj at Harike. In 1497, he disappeared into the rivulet for 3 days and when he reappeared, he had attained enlightenment or "sach khand" - the union with God. This is when Sikhism was born. Gurdwara Shri Ber Sahib was built on this site. The Ber tree here is from that time. If legend is to be believed, Guru Nanak ji appeared from the river wearing the Chola that is kept in Sri Chola Sahib, Dera Baba Nanak. This is when he received the "mool mantra" - "Ik Onkar." He received 6 items of the "Udasi libaas. Chola sahib, seli, topi, mala, pothi, khandwa. Wearing these he did his Udasi tours (spiritual tours).

Ber Sahib, is a beautiful, pristine white structure. There was a lot of hustle bustle with all the preparation for Gurpurab in a week's time. Pandals being set up, tonnes and tonnes wood for the langar, cleaning and painting being done. Below the Gurdwara is the Bhora Sahib, the place next to the Ber tree where Guru Nanak sat for his meditation. The ber tree is supposed to be from the same time, close to 600 years. It is humongous.

It was lunch time, although I had had a hearty breakfast, I was ravenously hungry. So, we decided to have the langar. Not many people were there. But from the looks of all the preparations that were going on, millions were expected to visit. Langar was a simple black daal, rajma aloo and roti. Simple, yes, but the most delicious and satiating meal I have had in a long time. Langars are always delicious, but this one was another level. Post the langar I went back for my second helping of kadha prashad, dessert is a must after such a satisfying meal. By now I had realised that when I go back the needle on the weighing scale will most definitely be tipping on the wrong side.

Our stop for the next two nights was Kapurthala. Kapurthala is about 30 odd kms from Sultanpur Lodhi. Kapurthala is about palaces and royalty. In fact, it is said to be the Mini Paris of Punjab. It has palaces and gardens worth seeing. But unfortunately, one cannot visit them. The Jagatjit Palace has been converted into Sainik School. Even if one gets permission to get into the campus, one can only see it from outside. The Elysee Palace is also, I think, part of the campus of another school. Unfortunately, when you google Kapurthala, these pop up as places to visit, one comes here with all eagerness only to not be allowed inside because it is no longer possible. No doubt from the photographs, the Jagatjit Palace looks like a beautiful one. Kapurthala is also known for its rail coach factory.

The one place we could visit and did visit was the Moorish Mosque. Moorish mosque is to be made on the lines of the Grand Qutubiya Mosque of Marrakesh, Morocco by Maharaja Jagatjit Singh, the last ruler of Kapurthala, in 1930. Serene and stately is the only way one can describe it. What looks plain and simple on the outside, is intricate from inside. It is artistically painted and intricately carved with a wooded roof dome. It was made at a cost of about Rs 4 Lakhs. Even though it is not an active mosque any more, it is amazingly maintained on the inside. Worth a visit when in Kapurthala.

I was a little disappointed that one could not visit the palaces I was so looking forward to. We checked into the hotel and settled in. Here I need to mention, the food that we had at the hotel was the best we had in this entire trip. Honestly the dinners we ordered on both the nights were sans any expectation of being well prepared and tasty, but we were pleasantly surprised. The rooms were clean to a fault and the staff was as courteous as can be.

I was now looking forward to the next day. There were no

gurdwaras on the plan, but food was part of the day. It was going to be a reasonably early start for a round trip of about 300 kms - just for food.

Day 4

Post an early breakfast we tanked up on fuel and were off on our day's drive. First stop was Hussainiwala Border in Ferozepur. A drive of about 110 kms. Now the thing is, Bollywood has been instrumental in creating an image of Punjab. I would like to blame it on Yash Chopra for showing all the "hare-bhare sarson ke khet." I am a diehard DDLJ (Dilwale Dulhaniya Le Jayenge) fan. I watched that movie 7 times in the movie theatre and each time I bought the tickets in black at double the amount. Obviously, I was expecting a scene out of the movie. But no such luck. What I found throughout my drive through Punjab is stubble burnt fields. In all fairness, my timing was wrong. The fields were being prepared for sowing hence the barren lands. Probably 2 months down the line one would witness a Punjab straight out of a Yashraj Film. One more thing I noticed about Punjab, and I was quite surprised about it. There was not much in terms of dhabas on the highways. The only time I saw them was on the highway towards Patiala.

Situated on the banks of the Sutluj, Hussainiwala Border served as a major road crossing between India and Pakistan till 1970. There was a proposal to open the border for trade again in 2005, but nothing has happened on the proposal. It is the 2nd of the 3 borders in Punjab where the Retreat Ceremony happens. The first being Atari in Amritsar, and the other being Fazilka. Unfortunately, since Covid this ceremony has remained a restricted ceremony and had not been opened to the public. Through a friend who knew someone in the BSF, we got the permission to visit the place where the ceremony takes place. The venue is like how it is at Atari but on a smaller scale. The Indians and Pakistanis practically sit opposite each other during the ceremony. The person in charge at the border gave us a guided tour of the museum on site. The pistol used by Bhagat Singh used to be on display at the museum. Since Covid it has been removed. Hussainiwala has been part of the Indo-Pak war in 1956, 1965 and 1971.

Hussainiwala is also home to the National Martyr's Memorial famous as the cremation place for our freedom fighters, Bhagat Singh, Rajguru, and Sukhdev. After they were awarded the death sentence on 23rd March 1931, their mortal remains were brought and cremated in haste by the British. This was under Pakistani control till 1961. On Jan 17th 1961, it was received back after India gave back 12 villages in Fazilka to Pakistan. A very solemn atmosphere indeed.

Fun fact - Hussainiwala railway station is the end point of the Northern Railway. Another fun fact - My phone caught both the Doha time zone (on manual search) and Islamabad time zone (on automatic search) while we were at the border.

It was 1 pm by the time we got free from Hussainiwala. Food was on our mind and the destination was Faridkot, about an hour's drive from Hussainiwala. Named after Baba Farid, Faridkot was a princely state during the British rule. My reason for visiting Faridkot was food, more specifically sandwiches. Raju Coffee Corner is a food cart owned by Raju who makes amazing grilled sandwiches and serves hot and cold coffee. Each sandwich is made of three slices of bread with fillings between them. He serves potato, malai, corn and veg, and pasta stuffed sandwiches. We had Malai, corn, cheese and veg, and pasta sandwiches. And the most amazing cold coffee I have ever had. It was indeed a class apart. Even though we split the sandwiches between us we were stuffed. But we still had another stop before we headed back to Kapurthala. Kotkapura for the famous atta chicken and Dhodha.

Kotkapura is the birthplace of Dhodha. Royal Dhodha is where you get the original Dhodha. Honestly, I felt the dhodha that you get at Om Sweets Gurgaon is way better than any other dhodha. The one at Kotkapura was a big no for me at the first bite because it had cardamom in it and the only way I can eat cardamom is in Kisme toffees and gajar ka halwa.

Atta chicken is the exclusive recipe of Kanwaljit Singh who learnt it from his father who was an army officer in the Northwest Frontier Province bordering Afghanistan in the pre-partition days. The family migrated from Pakistan and settled in Kotkapura. Kanwaljit Singh introduced the atta chicken to the people in 1972. The chicken is marinated in spices, stuffed with almonds, wrapped in muslin, and again wrapped in wheat flour dough and cooked in the oven. I was told that the chicken if kept unopened can last upto 3 weeks in the fridge. First, we thought we would eat it there, but then decided against it as we were super stuffed with the sandwiches. We had the chicken packed to carry back for dinner.

Back at the hotel in Kapurthala, I sat down with a knife to open the atta chicken. I did not know what to expect. I split open the baked dough and I found the chicken wrapped in muslin cloth. The sight was honestly a tad bit unappetising. I struggled a bit and was able to get to the chicken. My review of the famous atta chicken - had it been opened and served to me I would have enjoyed it more. The sight of the muslin wrapped chicken just kind of ruined it a bit for me. Nonetheless, yes, it is something that was worth a try.

It had been quite a day. We practically did a 300 km drive only for food. With little energy left in us, we crashed early for the night.

Day 5

The next morning, we were on our way to the last leg of the road trip. The day took us to Sri Damdama Sahib and ended at Patiala. Gurudwara Sri Damdama Sahib is situated in Talwandi Sabo in Distt Bhatinda. It is the 4th Takht of the Khalsa Panth. In 1705, After fighting the cruel rulers, Guru Gobind Singh ji took rest by untying his waist band at this place and since then it has been called Damdama Sahib. This was also the place where Guru Gobind Singh ji got the holy Beed of Aadi Guru Granth Sahib ji written by Bhai Mani Singh ji. It was here that Baba Deep Singh ji got the 4 copies of the Beed Sahib (Guru Granth Sahib) written and sent it to the other 4 Takhts (Anandpur Sahib, Harmandir Sahib, Patna Sahib and Hazur Sahib).

The main gurudwara in the complex has an interesting architecture. Very different from what I have seen so far. It has fortress-like structures. Inside the sanctum sanctorum the Guru Granth Sahib is placed on a high platform which is beautifully decorated. There are a few more gurdwaras within the complex and an interesting one is Gurdwara Sri Likhansar Sahib. As the legend goes, after Guru Gobind Singh ji dictated the guru Granth Sahib to Bhai Mani Singh Ji, he threw all the ink and the kalams (pens) into the sarovar of the gurdwara and gave it a blessing that whoever would write the 35 letters of the Gurmukhi alphabet here would have a very sharp mind. He also named it Guru Ki Kashi. Along the sarovar there is black stone on which one can see people writing the alphabet with chalk. It is amusing how one can see people struggling to write (no judgements or disrespect here).

There is Gurdwara Jandsar Sahib, Gurdwara Gurusar Sahib, Gurdwara Burj Baba Deep Singh are all part of this complex. By the end of our visit I must have had at least half a kilo of kadha prashad.

I know that is a lot of it, but what to do - it is my weakness. However well I may be making it myself, there is something about the one that you get in a gurdwara. I sometimes wonder whether I go to a gurdwara for spiritual reasons or simply for the kadha-prashad.

Talwandi Sabo to Patiala is a two-and-a-half-hour drive. A highway which seemed well populated with good dhabas enroute. We had had a heavy breakfast so skipped on lunch. Checked in into the hotel, a regal Neemrana Property. Huge bungalow called the Baradari Palace. The room was big enough to fit in a small apartment and I am not even kidding on that. I have, as a kid, lived in high ceilinged bungalows, but this took high ceiling to another level. I am not complaining though.

It was late afternoon so we decided to just drive around the city and see if one could do some shopping. We all know Patiala is famous for juttis and phulkari work. Adalat Bazar is the place to shop for phulkari and just adjacent to it is an entire lane of wholesalers of juttis. One can go crazy buying both. And when one compares the rates at which one gets it in Delhi, its literally at throw away prices. There was madness in the market, but I picked up some very amazing stuff.

Happy with my shopping adventure, we headed back to the hotel. Just adjacent to the Baradari Palace is a huge park. It seems like a place where the entire city comes for a walk. The trip was coming to an end, and the day before only I had kind of calculated how much kadha-prashad I had eaten, and well also gave a thought to what effects it would show on the weighing scale. The thought greatly motivated me to go for a walk. And walk I did for whatever it was worth. Walk done, guilt thrown out of the window, we ordered a hearty dinner. Nothing comes between me and food, not even guilt.

Next morning we first headed to the last gurdwara on the list.

Gurdwara Dukhniwaran Sahib. A beautiful gurdwara that is said to have been visited by Guru Tegh Bahadur. It is said that the sarovar has healing properties and a person who pays obeisance here is rid of all his sufferings. This was one of the most peaceful, beautiful, sanctum sanctorum of a gurdwara that I have seen.

My research on food in Patiala took me to Prem Chat for golgappas. I never associated Punjab with golgappas but believe me when I say they were one of the most amazing golgappas I have had. There were 4 types of water, a solid filling of potatoes and chana and the last one was with curd. Delicious. More than worth the effort we made to find the place. Mind you, in Patiala it is better to park your car someplace and then take the e-rickshaws to wherever you wish to go. The next place we went to was Lahori gate for Mahinder ke Chhole Bhature. If you are a cleanliness freak, this place is not for you. It is a small shop with tables and benches literally stuffed into it. You just find a place and sit, yes, share the tables with whoever is already sitting. It also has a certificate of Heritage People's Choice Food Award 2020 hanging on the wall. They also serve stuffed kulchas but chhola bhatura is what you must eat here. Bhaturas are exactly how I love them. The chhole are tasty too. I would say when in Patiala, you must eat here. It is one of the iconic places to visit.

There is more in Punjab. There is more food to be had. There are more places to be visited. But for us this was it for now. We did 17 of the 23 districts. It was time to head back home. At least a road trip happened after a whole lot of plans getting cancelled. Like I said in the beginning, there is not much in terms of travelogues on Punjab, and I find it strange. I am glad I did it.

Kuchh Din To Guzaro Gujarat Mein (January - 2022)

One Monday morning while having our morning cuppa, *the Husband* and I were discussing that ever since he took a sabbatical from work, we had not been able to really travel like we had planned we would. Covid had played spoilt sport. After the 2nd wave the previous year, the onset of the 3rd wave brought along with it crazy apprehensions. Now, I have never been paranoid and have been extremely level headed about this, but travelling in these times was a crazy thought. Different states brought in different rules and regulations and one really did not want to get stuck in all this while being on the road. But the discussion stayed with me through the day. By evening, Gujarat was already flowing through my mind. I had been to Kutch two years back and the rest of Gujarat had been on my mind. It was growing on me by the hour. By late night *the Husband* and I regrouped on this and a decision was taken. A little juggle here and there and we left on Wednesday morning. I am known to be impulsive, but this must be my first impulsive road trip.

Part 1

We left early morning. It was a long drive day of about 850 kms. Gurgaon - Jaipur - Ajmer - Beawar - Barr - Pali - Sanderao - Sirohi -

Abu Road - Palanpur - Mehsana. Once we turned right from Beawar towards Barr, the roads were beautiful and the drive scenic. I could imagine how awesome it would be to drive here post the monsoons.

We reached Mehsana at around 7 pm. Enroute, I searched the internet and zeroed in on the hotel we were proposing to stay in. That went well, we did not land up with any surprises there. I have a pilot friend who lives in Ahmedabad and he arranged a joyride in a 4-seater plane in Mehsana the next morning. It sounded like a whole lot of fun. Originally, we were to leave early morning for Patan, Modhera and then on to Rajkot. When this flight plan happened, we pushed the plan to make time for the flight. As luck would have it, we woke up next morning to clouds. The airport in Mehsana is without any navigational aids and is only a training centre. And because there are no navigational aids, they need to have visibility without clouds. The choice was to wait till about noon and see or shelve the plan. Much as I was looking forward to flying, we shelved the plan and continued with the original plan and post breakfast headed towards Modhera.

Both Modhera and Patan are usually done while going to Little Rann of Kutch. If you remember my Kutch trip, we missed it then because we got delayed enroute, and we needed to be in Zainabad in time for the last safari to the wild ass sanctuary. Modhera is about 25 kms from Mehsana situated on the banks of the Pushpawati River. It is a lovely drive through the fields. The Sun Temple was built during the times of King Bhima of the Chalukya Dynasty. It dates to the 11th century. It is built on 23.6° latitude, approximately on the Tropic of Cancer. It has the Gudha mandap or the shrine hall, the sabha mandap or the assembly hall and the kund or the reservoir. The halls have intricate carvings on the pillars, roof domes and the walls on the inside and on the exterior. The reservoir has steps going down and there are 108 shrines made on different levels going down the steps. There are 3 main shrines on 3 sides, one of each dedicated to Ganesha, Vishnu, and Shiv. the 4th side is the temple. The Sabha Mandap is made on 52 pillars signifying the 52 weeks of the year.

The carved murals give you an insight into the society that existed. Intricate detailing speak volumes about their costumes, jewellery, lifestyle, depictions about their performing arts, erotica, intense lovemaking, all etched in stone. And that again brings me back to the hypocrisy we follow. Erotica is etched in stone in our temples - homosexuality, bestiality, orgies, you name it and it is there. These are not restricted to only temples in Khajurao. I have seen them in Konark and here in Modhera too. And in the so called "modern times" we live in, sex is a taboo topic. Parents cringe when talking about it to their kids, most don't want to talk about it. Let me not even get into how judgemental we are about the sexual orientations. Were we regressive then or are we regressive now. I can go on and on but let me not digress.

The statue of the Sun God no longer exists in the temple. It is said that the temple is designed in such a way that every equinox, the first rays of the rising sun fell on a diamond that was placed on the crown of the Sun God. This would light up the entire shrine. Mahmud of Ghazni plundered the temple in 1024-25 AD. No worship is now offered in this temple.

The next stop for us was Patan, a drive of about 40 kms. Have you closely seen the new 100 rupee note? The monument in the picture is Rani ki Vav and that is what we visited in Patan. Listed in UNESCO's list of world heritage sites, Rani Ki Vav was built in 1063 by Rani Udaimati of the Chalukya Dynasty to commemorate her husband, King Bhimdev. It took 20 years to build the step well. It goes 7 levels down, is lined with carved pillars and is said to have more than 800 sculptures, mostly of Vishnu and his various avatars. Historically there are 4 types of step wells - Nanda - with one entrance, Bhadra - with two entrances, Jaya - with three entrances, Vijaya - with four entrances. Rani ki Vav is the Nanda vav. When you enter the compound, you do not expect what you see. With every level that you go down, the "awe" factor doubles and triples. It does leave you awestruck. The workmanship is so amazing. No level of technical advancements and modernisation of today can match up to the craftsmanship of those times. I am glad I did not fit in these two places in my Kutch itinerary. Had I visited them then, I would have rushed through the places as I was short on time then and would not have done justice to any.

Rani ki Vav is not the only thing Patan is known for. Patan is also the home of Patola. Patola is a double ikat woven saree, usually made from silk. Like all the traditional weaves like Kanjeevaram and Banarasi, Patola too is a dying art. It is said that there are only 4-5 families in Patan that make these now. It used to be a closely guarded technique taught only to the sons. A handwoven saree takes about 6 months to a year to make. We visited a patola workshop and were given a tour of what all goes into making a patola saree. So much intricacy, so time consuming, so much detailing. Right from opening the raw silk, to combining the threads, to bleaching the raw silk, to twisting of the silk, to making the warp, to making the weft, to tying of warp and weft, to making grids, to tying threads as per design, to dying the threads, to opening and retying for the next colour to be dyed and so on till all of it is done then put on the looms to weave the saree. One mistake and everything needs to be redone. The price? Well, a handmade patola silk saree starts at 1.5 lakhs. And then something dawned on me. Amongst the other sarees that I had inherited from my mom, there is a handmade silk patola saree. My dad had gifted her one way back in the 80's. It was always one of my favourites of her sarees, but now it just became more special.

Part 2

By the time we got done from Patan, it was 1 pm and we were hungry. We had no clue where to eat so we decided to move towards our next destination - Jamnagar and stop at whatever place looked decent enough to eat at. We were supposed to head to Rajkot, but that was the previous day's plan. That is the fun of an unplanned trip. While the original plan was to drive till Rajkot and then the next day leave for Jamnagar, it began to make no sense. In Jamnagar there is a Marine National Park which was on the to-do list. When I spoke to the guide there, he asked us to be at the park latest by 8 am. It would take at least two-and-a-half-hours at the park and as the sun would come up and the temperatures rise, the marine life would start going deeper into the water. The drive from Jamnagar to the Park was about an hour plus. So, it made all the sense to be in Jamnagar a night before. Hence the Rajkot plan got shelved and we headed towards Jamnagar.

As we drove along, we saw an eating place with straw shacks and it had a couple cars parked outside. Looked okay, in fact looked pretty fancy. When we asked the guy what was there to eat, promptly his answer was Punjabi thali and he rattled out a whole list of Punjabi dishes. Now, this is what I have noticed in Gujarat. They are obsessed with Punjabi food. The waiter was a little taken aback when I said I want Kathiawadi food. They had no Kathiawadi thali on their menu only à la carte. With 2 people, it does not make sense to order à la carte. I did not want to order multiple dishes and then end up having to waste the left overs. I somehow sweet talked him into customising a thali for us. My stomach was growling away and I was hoping the food was good to justify the entire exercise.

The food arrived and it looked good. There was lahsuni bateka nu shak (garlic potato sabzi), sev tamatar nu shak, and ringan no oro (baingan bharta), daal, bajra rotla, chapati, rice, chhaas and a very delicious garlic chutney. Was it worth it? Absolutely, yes. It was superlative. INR. 170 for a thali and we could take a second helping too. It was spicy and delicious. Contrary to what people think, everything in Gujarati food is not sweet. The Kathiawadi food has an amazing spice punch. And even the sweetness that is there in some dishes, just balances out so beautifully in every bite that you take.

We absolutely enjoyed our lunch post which we were on our way to Jamnagar. The drive throughout Gujarat is mostly a very scenic drive. You either have mustard and cotton fields around you (this time of the year) or you drive along the salt pans. The state highways are mostly superb while the national highways are a mix of both good patches and bad. But one thing is common almost throughout - unfortunately the washrooms enroute are filthy. This I noticed when I was on my Kutch trip too. Rajasthan still tops my list in cleanliness.

While we were chatting along, *the Husband* popped a question whether I had ever done "hotel hopping". Is that even a thing? Well, apparently when you go from one hotel to the other looking for a room for reasons that may be either because you did not like it or that there was no availability it is called hotel hopping. It had never happened to me and honestly the thought of such a possibility had never crept in. Jamnagar was a big city. The "Oil City." There were so many hotels, there would never be any issue. We reached the hotel we had zeroed in on. It was a big chain in Gujarat. I went in and was told they were sold out. Stunned at what just happened I walked out not sure whether to laugh or get worried. Sat in the car and called the next hotel on our list and guess what? - that was also sold out too. I was not worried because I was not alone. I was amused. I called the third one on our list and there they had a room against a no-show. The reason for all of this was apparently the wedding season.

It was 9.15 pm by the time we checked in and settled in. I was not interested in eating in the hotel restaurant. I was more interested in the Gujarati street food. The issue was we could not go far because there was the night curfew to be kept in mind. The front office manager at the hotel was a very nice and helpful guy. He told us we could step out and eat from any of the food carts that were around the hotel. They were all good. Our first try was dahi golgappa. Then we had dahi papdi. They were both tasty but I had a problem with the curd and that I found throughout Gujarat, even in the high-end restaurants, they do not beat the curd well. It just kind of does not look very appealing and appetising. Then we had the vada pav. That was indeed delicious. Talking about hygiene of these carts - they were clean. Expecting total sanitisation is a little too much. More than what we ate that night, I would like to talk about what we drank. In Jamnagar there is a drink that people have. It is called Kawa. No, it is not a Gujarati take on the Kashmiri Kehwa, it is nowhere close to it. Only similarity perhaps is the huge kettle it is served out of. It is a piping hot concoction of some ayurvedic churan like stuff. The taste grew on me as I sipped along. It is quite nice and worth a try.

The plan for next morning was to visit the Marine National Park. The park was about one and a half hours from where we were, which meant we would have had to leave at 6.30 am. Which meant the wake-up time was 5 am. Suddenly it did not sound very appealing, more so because the last few days had been very early mornings and the following day would also be an early start towards Dwarka. It was just kind of a silent consensus that we not do the Marine Park. Yes, it would have been a very different experience, but the need for sleep and rest took the upper hand. I know we missed something unique but well I guess it was not meant to be.

The next day felt like a lazy morning. We had a hearty breakfast and stepped out. There was shopping to do and there was food to explore. It was a totally relaxed day. Jamnagar is famous for bandhej and silver. It is also famous for dry kachoris. And I shopped all of these. For farsaan the place to go is Jain Vijay. They have some brilliant stuff. There is Chandi Bazaar for silver. Not the usual jewellery, though I did find some pretty stuff in jewellery. If you are looking for silver utensils and artefacts, it is the place to go. Good quality of silver and much cheaper in terms of labour rates compared to Delhi. I usually do not shop on my trips, but the sarees were amazing. If I had my way, I would have shopped a suitcase full. I must say, *the Husband* is a very patient man.

For lunch we were suggested this restaurant in Hotel Aram. Delicious unlimited Gujarati and Punjabi thalis. Of course we went for the Gujarati thali. First came the Chhaas then on the plate was veg cutlet, sandwich dhokla, bateka nu shak (aloo sabzi), something called lilva tuvar. It looked like peas, turiya patra nu shak (language barrier made it impossible to understand what the guy said but of what I can make out it was ridge gourd), paneer butter masala (I told you they are obsessed with punjabi food), daal and kadhi, rice and roti. For dessert they had the most delicious dry fruit basundi which is a kind of a chilled condensed milk and piping hot pooran poli dunked in ghee. The food was great but the dessert was out of this world. I had had pooran poli with shrikhand in Gwalior a couple of years back and thought nothing could be better. But this one just took it to another level. The only thing that one could do next was sleep. And it was like a drug induced sleep. All this food should come with a disclaimer because once you have had it, you become completely inept to do anything.

There is a small lake in Jamnagar with a small fort in the middle of it. People go for walks around the lake. Inside the fort there is a museum. Naturally after the meal we had, a walk was a great thought to burn off the calories consumed. We reached there at around 6 pm. We were a tad bit late and hence could not enter the fort but walked around the manmade lake. And suddenly there was a swarm of starlings that went flying by. A few minutes later the swarm got bigger. And there were what seemed like thousands of starlings flying. It seemed like they were putting on a show and enjoying it. Swooping from one end to the other smaller swarms going in and then flying together and then separating out, circling around, and coming back together. All this carried on for good about 30-40 minutes. It was so amazing to watch them. It was like meditation. So full of grace. I have never seen anything like this ever in my life. Just being there at that moment made my entire 4,000 km journey worth the effort. I could have just sat there forever and ever. This is apparently an everyday thing at that lake.

Once the birds settled down on the trees for the night we left. Our next stop was a small outlet called Kutchi Dabeli. Yes, that is also what you get there. It opens at 4 pm and only serves Kutchi dabeli and what is called bread katka. The dabeli was the best one I have had till date. The spice punch was exceptional. The bread katka was a first. It is a pav topped with green chutney, garlic chutney, peanuts with the dabeli masala and sev. The first bite was okay, I did not think much of it. But with every consecutive bite the flavours just started to hit the palette. What a snack! It tasted absolutely amazing. All for Rs. 30 each - this was too good to be true, both the taste and the price.

During the course of the day, we had had multiple interactions with the front office manager and the helpful guy that he was, he helped get us a booking in Dwarka, our next destination. The same chain of hotels. Not only did he help get a booking in Dwarka and then later in Junagadh and Surat, he also got us upgrades.

Part 3

Our next destination was Beyt Dwarka and the day was to end in Dwarka. The roads were lined with mustard and cotton fields. It was a pretty scenery, to say the least. I have been always curious about what kind of a plant is the cotton plant and what part of it makes the cotton. We stopped at one of the fields in which the plants were close enough to the fence. I was quite fascinated with the plant. The cotton is the flower. It is amazing how the cotton is naturally bound to the plant – as if sewn with a thread. It just looks like you could break the flower and use it as a cotton ball. Nature is truly fascinating.

Beyt Dwarka or Shankhodar is an island in the Gulf of Kutch. It is off the coast of Okha. Mithapur and Okha are home to fishing and salt processing industries. Tata Chemicals is in Mithapur. You need to park your car at Okha and walk upto the jetty from where you get the boat to go to Beyt Dwarka. These boats ply every 15-20 minutes. The water was an emerald green. It looked gorgeous. The colourful boats bobbing in the sea added to the landscape. As I walked up to the jetty, I saw these two guys standing and a whole swarm of seagulls hovering over them picking up something off their hands. I went closer and saw they were selling biscuits that you put on your palm, raise it up and the gulls swoop down and pick it up. Of course I had to do it too. What an experience it was. The way the gulls flap their wings vigorously to stay stable in the wind and the way they swoop down to pick up the biscuit, water dripping from their beaks. You throw the biscuit in the air and they just snatch it up in mid-air. I could spend hours doing this.

Here we got to know that since the last 6 days both the temples, Dwarkadheesh in Dwarka and the one in Beyt Dwarka were closed due to Corona restrictions. There was a meeting scheduled for the next day to review the situation and decide whether they would reopen the day after. We could not even go onto the island. But the seagulls more than made it up.

Beyt Dwarka gets its name from the word Bhaint or gift. It is said that Lord Krishna received a gift from his friend Sudama in this place. It is believed that a part of the city of Dwarka has gone underwater due to years and years of coastal erosion. There is a mythical claim that this place was the original house of Lord Krishna during his ruling years at Dwarka. It is also believed that the idol in this temple was placed by Devi Rukmani herself. Well, beyt also means island.

From Beyt Dwarka we proceeded towards Dwarka. About 35 kms. Just short of Dwarka is a beautiful beach by the name of Shivrajpur Beach. In non-covid times it must have been a very busy beach with a lot of action happening but when we went it was absolutely deserted. What was very noticeable was the clean white sand beach. What was missing was the blue water of the sea. It would have made such a pretty picture. It was not mucky or dirty but brown nonetheless.

We knew that the Dwarkadheesh temple was closed but post lunch we went to the area. There is the Sudama Setu and the Gomti Sangam. Sudama Setu is a recently built suspension bridge for pedestrian passage across the Gomti river. This is the point where the Gomti meets the Arabian Sea. On a clear sunny day, I am sure it would look way more scenic. The day we went it was extremely overcast.

The Dwarkadheesh Temple is believed to have been built by Lord Krishna's grandson, Vajranabha over Lord Krishna's residential palace. It is apparently 2,200 years old. It was destroyed by Mahmud Begada in 1472 and subsequently rebuilt in the 15th-16th century. If legend is to be believed, Meera merged with the deity at this temple. It is also one of the 4 peeths established by Adi Shankracharya.

While on the beach at the Gomti Sangam, I noticed an area where small stones were stacked up. There were many such stacks. Curiosity got the better of me and I asked a couple sitting there about it. Apparently, people who do not have a house of their own and married couples wishing eternal togetherness stack these stones up. They did not however know, how and why this started here. I always get fascinated by these beliefs. They may be completely illogical and baseless, but they give so much hope to people.

About 17 kms from the Dwarkadheesh temple is the Nageshwar Jyotirlinga temple. This is one of the 12 jyotirlingas in India. As per the legend, a demon called Daruk imprisoned a Shiva devotee called Supriya. The "om namah shivaya" chanted by her invoked Lord Shiva who came and vanquished the demon. A self-manifested shivalinga appeared here. There is big sitting Shiva statue also at this site.

Covid seems to have quietened this city big time. Even though it was tourist season, it seemed dead. This city seems to essentially survive on tourism and it made me wonder how the it was coping. We had a quiet evening at the hotel that day. Next morning post a hearty breakfast we left for our next stop - Porbandar.

Porbandar is famous as the city where Mahatma Gandhi was born. Little known fact is that it is also believed to be the birthplace of Lord Krishna's devotee and friend Sudama. The city was also a prosperous trading centre conducting business with the Arabian and Gulf countries and East Africa under the Mughals, Marathas and the British.

Our first visit was Kirti Mandir, the memorial that was built adjacent to the humble house where Mahatma Gandhi was born.

There is a photo gallery which showcases Mahatma Gandhi's life. There are also artefacts displayed that were used by him. As you enter the Kirti Mandir, on your left is the entrance to Mahatma Gandhi's house. Built by his grandfather, it was originally a three-storey building. In one of the rooms a swastik sign marks the place where he was born. There were these steep, rickety wooded stairs take you up to the first floor. There is nothing displayed in these rooms, the stone of the floor shines with all the wear and tear they have gone through over the years. There is something so calm and peaceful about the place. The silence just engulfs you. The street outside was all hustle-bustle and noisy as there were numerous shops lining the lane coming up to it, and there was so much peace and quiet inside. It was amazing.

It way past 11 when we left the Kirti Mandir and the city showed no signs of opening to the day. The shops were still closed. This is how life should be. No hurry, no running after anything, just so laid-back and relaxed.

Our next stop was the Sudama Temple. This is a new temple, built way back in 1902 to commemorate the friendship between Lord Krishna and Sudama. There is also a maze in the temple complex called the Lakhchaurasi Parikrama. They say that a life must go through 84 lakh rebirths before you attain nirvana. If you go through this maze, you avoid the cycle of rebirths and attain nirvana. I saw an old lady, bent with age, walking through the maze. Like I said earlier - I love these beliefs only because they give so much hope to people who believe in them. Sometimes hope is all they have.

Next on our map was Somnath. Somnath Temple is of great importance for Shiva devotees. It is one of the 12 Jyotirlingas in India. There is an interesting story here. Chandra dev (the moon) was married to the 27 daughters of Sage Daksh who was the son of Brahma. In Vedic astrology Daksh's 27 daughters are the Nakshatras or the constellations. When Chandra Dev got married, Daksh made him promise that he would treat all his daughters equally with love and care. But Chandradev was fonder of his fourth wife Rohini. The other 26 wives were very unhappy and they complained to their father. In his anger, he cursed Chandra Dev that he would lose his shine and reduce in size with every passing day till he becomes invisible. Lord Brahma told Chandra Dev that he should pray to Lord Shiva and that he is the only one who can get him out of his curse. Chandra Dev meditated and prayed to Shiva who in turn gave him the boon that he will grow back to his size. When Shiva appeared, he sympathised with Chandra Dev and told him he could not reverse the curse but he could work around it to some extent. He told the moon that he would increase in brightness (waxing moon) for 14 days and decrease in size (waning moon) for the next 14 days fill the world with brightness on full moon days (Poornima) and disappear on new moon day (Amavasya) This way the moon passes through each Nakshatra approximately each day and goes full circle in one month thereby spending equal time with each of the nakshatras. The place Chandra worshipped Shiva is called Somnath, the Lord of the Moon. It is also believed that the moon shines the brightest at Somnath. Mythology does have interesting tales to tell.

The temple history goes back to 649 A.D when it was built. Ever since it was first built it has been destroyed and rebuilt numerous times. They say it has been demolished 17 times. The temple as it stands today was rebuilt in 1995. If legend is to be believed, in the originally built temple the shivalinga was a levitating one hanging in mid-air. They say the shivalinga was made of iron and the loadstone of the canopy made of magnetite. The whole thing was architecturally planned in a such a way that the magnetic force was equal upwards and downwards because of which the lingam floated in mid-air. It is mind-boggling how advanced we were back then.

When you go towards the seaside, you notice a pillar with a globe on top which has an arrow going through it. The arrow points to the sea. This arrow indicates the unobstructed path across the ocean to the South Pole. Imagine the expanse of water here. The next piece of land is Antarctica.

We walked out of the temple and saw a lady selling a very strange fruit. Strange because I had never seen anything like that. Curious, I bought one to try it. Will come to what it was later. For now, we were on our way to Junagadh, our stay for the night. When you go from Somnath to Junagadh you cross a small town called Keshod. This town is famous for tender coconut halwa. You do not have to go anywhere off the highway to get these. There are a number of kiosks by the highway selling them. It is an interesting halwa, people who like coconut will love it. There is also a mango pulp/juice sold in bottles that is a must buy. I bought only one bottle to try it and having tried it regret not buying more. It is like having freshly puréed mango. Delicious and fresh.

Oh! are you wondering what happened to our lunch? No gujarati food? Naaa ... we had nothing exciting for lunch. But, while you are in this part of Gujarat, do try their local ice-cream brand Sheetal.

Part 4

I first heard of Junagadh as a little kid of 5 may be 6 years of age. My uncle used to work there. For some strange reason that name always fascinated me. It kind of stuck around in my mind. In recent times I have been following a brilliant photographer by the name of Aman Channa on Instagram. He posted some pictures of this amazing piece of architecture from Junagadh. I just had to visit this place. For old time's sake and new. So, my Gujarat itinerary had to give a prominent place to Junagadh. Junagadh is the base town for Sasan Gir, home to the Gir National Park. No, we did not to go Gir. After having visited Masai Mara, national parks in India do not excite me. Watching animals in the wild there is a different experience. I now quietly give it a skip here.

The main attraction for me in Junagadh was Mahabbat Maqbara. Right in the heart of the busy city, there lies one the lesser-known monuments of India. A unique blend of Indo-Islamic and Gothic architecture with elaborate stone carvings, finely designed arches and domes and winding staircases, the Mahabbat Maqbara and the Mausoleum of Bahadudin Hussain Bhar are India's most unsung monuments. These house the tombs of Mahabbat Khan II, the Nawab of Junagadh State and his minister Bahaduddin Bhar. The monument was undergoing restoration and was closed to the public but I managed to "bhaiyaji" my way through and see it, at least from the outside. While the restored monument looks very pretty - painted and fresh, I personally feel that they have lost their character. The photographs I saw from earlier were somehow more amazing. But nonetheless, at least they are being taken care of and are not in neglect.

From here we went to the Junagadh Museum. The Junagadh Museum preserves the possessions of the Junagadh Maharajas. It exhibits nearly 3000 artefacts in its picture gallery, palanquin room, textile and costumes gallery, weapons gallery, sparkling chandeliers, silver, carpets woven with gold and silver, jewellery and more. The Uparkot Fort was also closed for restoration. Just to clarify, The Junagadh fort is not to be confused with the fort in Junagadh. Junagadh fort is in Bikaner. Remember my Bikaner story?

There is one thing you cannot miss in Junagadh and that is a visit to Chamunda Lassi. A shop which has a variety of lassis. Mango, pineapple, maava, vanilla, chocolate chip, and a whole load more.

Every time I passed the shop I tried one flavour. But my favourite was mango lassi. You get interesting Bhelpuri at Narayan Bhai Bhelwala. The golgappas at Subhash Panipuri is supposed to be very good, but I have had better golgappas so I would say its avoidable. For lunch we had the Gujarati Thali at The Grand Patel Restaurant. Great food. Unlimited thali and the preparation was delicious. I highly recommend it.

If you remember I had mentioned that Gujarat was obsessed with Punjabi food. What they are also obsessed with is Chinese food. So that night we decided to try out the Gujarati version of Chinese food. We took the risk because the hotel we were staying in was fancy as fancy can be. It was a five star property. I just imagined they would have chefs to back it up especially because Junagadh is the base for Gir National Park and there is a huge amount of foreign tourist inflow to cater to. It was ummm .... errr .... interesting, for a lack of better word. I would like to leave it at that.

Now let me tell you about the interesting fruit that I bought outside the Somnath Temple. On the outside it was big and hard-shelled and red in colour. Open it and it had several smaller seed like things, black in colour and looked like jamuns. These black things had two skins. One soft and one hard. When you take these off, you come to a white part. That is what you eat. It tastes just like an almond. I asked around and got to know that it is something called a Kath-badam.

Next day we left for Bhavnagar from where we were to take the RORO (Roll on Roll Off) Ferry for Surat. The previous night I had booked the tickets for both of us and the car from their online portal. It is simpler to pre-book. The ferry plies once a day from each side. 10 am from Surat to Bhavnagar and 4 pm from Bhavnagar to Surat. As we were approaching Bhavnagar, we saw these hawkers selling guavas that were red in colour. My first reaction was that they were injected with colour because what we get here is pink, I have never seen such red ones. When we saw that almost all had the same shade of red, we thought of trying out one. I have never tasted such guavas in my life. They were delicious. And the Bhavnagari guavas are that unbelievable shade of red.

When I called up the DG Sea Connect people to find out what time we needed to reach the jetty, I was told to be there before 3 pm. We barely had time to have a quick lunch and buy the famous Bhavnagari Gathia. Das Penda is one of the best places to buy these. The whole check-in process is very organised. Once they announce your loading, you drive in your cars towards the jetty. At one point they check your tickets and give you a wrist band which has the classification colour of which class of seat you have booked - Executive, Business or Cambay Lounge. Then you drive to the ferry ship and they guide you into it and help you park. I was impressed at how organised they were. Once you park and lock your car, you go upto the deck where you are supposed to sit and then you are confined to that space till you sail.

The ferry ship was big. The ferries I had taken on the coastal route from Goa to Mumbai were much smaller, more like boats, but then the distance to be covered was also 15 - 30 minutes. This ship had a capacity to take about 150 trucks and cars in its belly. I had booked the Cambay lounge. Well, that is supposed to be the First Class. It had space for about 12 people, sofas around the walls. It was pretty comfortable but not fancy as the name would suggest. Although if one had to sit there for 4 hours it would get claustrophobic. There was a half an hour delay in sailing and we left at 4.30 pm and by 5 pm we were allowed to go to the top deck. The deck was huge and they had chair benches along the railings for people to sit around facing the water. The rush that came out of the respective lounges seemed like the wildebeest water crossing in Masai

Mara. The first thing I did was get hold of one of the bench chairs for the both of us. I had no intentions of being cooped up in the room down below and was sure I was spending my 4 hours up at the top deck. With garba music blaring on the sound system, I was just waiting for someone to break into garba right there. Nothing of that sort happened though.

People went crazy clicking photographs. I was one of the "people" too, might I add. Then there were families that just plonked on the floor and brought out their picnic baskets. Gujaratis and their love for "nashta" is pretty well known. Some were playing games while sitting on the floor. And in all the din there was the garba music playing in the background, blaring is more like it. With no offence meant I was secretly wishing they were playing softer music. That would have taken the experience to another level for sure. After about an hour or so, people started going back to their respective lounges and it became quieter but for the still blaring music. As the sun went down it started to become nippier. We did have our jackets but had left them in the car and one is not allowed to wander off to the parking deck while the ship is at sea. Slowly it started to become colder and the light jackets that we were carrying did not seem enough so we decided to go down to the lounge.

What was supposed to be a four-hour ride turned out to be six and a half hours. We reached Hazira Port at about 10.30 pm. Disembarking took about half-an-hour and we were on our way to our hotel. It had been a tiring day although we did nothing much. It was a room service dinner. After nearly a week in Gujarat, finally there was nonvegetarian food. Crashed out instantly for the night.

The next day we checked out of the hotel and went in search of typical Surati breakfast, something called a Surati Lochho. We searched the net and found this place that took us across the Rander Causeway over the River Tapi. What a lovely drive it made with seagulls all around. Locho is made of gram flour by steaming it. It is soft in consistency, does not really have a shape like khaman and is served with green coriander chutney. It is now made in different versions, Italian, Mexican and what have you. It is an interesting dish. I am still not sure how much I liked it, so I will leave it at "interesting."

Our destination was the Statue of Unity and then onwards to Baroda.

Part 5

The last leg of our journey. Our morning drive took us to the Statue of Unity.

There were a few things which I was told I must eat while in Surat. Lochho, Oondhio and ponkh. Loccho was ticked off at breakfast. While driving to the Statue of Unity we crossed some fields and right beside those fields were several hawkers selling something green in colour. We stopped and asked and yes, they were selling ponkh. Ponkh is tender jowar and is a winter speciality. They are small like daal, soft in texture and these hawkers were selling it as a mixture of ponkh and palak sev. I asked for a little to taste what it was and I loved it. I bought a little each of both ponkh and the sev separately to eat later.

At 182 metres, the statue of Sardar Vallabhbhai Patel at the Sardar Sarovar Dam is the highest statue in the world. The second highest being the Spring Temple Buddha in China at 153 metres. It is made of reinforced concrete and bronze. The sheer size of the statue is intimidating. There is a viewing gallery from inside the statue at a height of 135 metres. If you look from outside, it is at the level of the first button of the kurta from the top. It gives a spectacular view of the Sardar Sarovar Dam. This statue is indeed a marvel.

There are restaurants within the complex, there is a cactus garden, a butterfly park, and a flower park. All beautifully maintained. There is a zoo too. All tickets can be booked through the Statue of Unity App. Across the river on the way to the Butterfly Park and Cactus Garden, there is a selfie point from where you get the best view of the whole statue if you want to photograph it. In the evenings there is a sound and light show after which the shuttle buses take you for the Narmada Arti. We had no idea of all this and we had to get to Baroda so we left after we visited the statue. But you can easily spend a whole day there. There are a number of hotels suiting all budgets in case you wish to spend the night there.

Baroda is often called the cultural capital of Gujarat. It was ruled by the Gaekwad Dynasty from its formation in 1721 till its accession to the Republic of India in 1949. The present-day Maharaja still lives in the Lakshmi Vilas Palace, a part of which is open to public viewing.

The Gaekwad rule began in 1721 when the Maratha General, Pilaji Rao Gaekwad conquered the city and defeated the Mughals. When their ruler Malhar Rao Gaekwad passed away, he left no male heir to the throne. His wife Jamnabai then adopted this 12-year-old boy, Gopalrao Gaekwad. Known as Sayajirao Gaekwad III, he ascended the throne in 1875, but was given full powers only in 1881 when he turned 19. Call it kismet, call it destiny - I truly believe it is a thing. Sayajirao went on to become a connoisseur and a noted patron of arts.

Baroda (for some reason I can never call it Vadodara so pardon me) for me has always been synonymous with the Lakshmi Vilas Palace. It is a must visit. In all my travels thus far, I have visited a few palaces, the Lakshmi Niwas Palace in Bikaner (I thought it was an architectural marvel), the Jai Vilas Palace in Gwalior better known as the Scindia palace (I thought it was one of the most opulent palaces ever), the City Palace in Udaipur (the crystal collection is amazing) are palaces that are tops in my mind. But the Laksmi Vilas Palace in Baroda out shadows each one of these.

The palace was built in the 19th century in Indo-Saracenic (also called the Indo-Gothic style) at a cost of 180,000 Pounds. Built over 500 acres, this fairytale palace is the largest private home built till date and is supposedly four times the size of the Buckingham Palace. It has around 170 rooms. The premises also houses the Fateh Singh Museum building and the Baroda Cricket Ground. It was built by Maharaja Sayaji Rao III and named after his 3rd wife Rani Lakshmibai.

Coming back to the exterior of the palace - it is one straight out of a fairytale. Beautifully carved domes, arches, and walls. There is a 11 ft mosaic artwork on one of the exterior walls. It is an amazing piece of art. It looks more like a painting than mosaic art. The sunken garden up front has beautiful sculptures by the renowned artist Fellici.

You enter the palace and every part of it leaves you awestruck. There is a room with armoury on display, the coronation room has a simple gaddi. It is minimalistic but for the paintings by Raja Ravi Verma. The one part that I cannot get out of my head is the Darbar hall. It has stained glass windows and intricately carved jharokas made of rose and sandal wood. The floor is an amazing mosaic for which 12 artists were brought in from Italy. The roof is even more beautiful. I could not make out if it was mosaic or paint. The grandeur of the Darbar hall took my breath away. In a corner there is a big wooden doll house which was used by the princess. No photography is allowed inside and you get an audio guide. The pace of the commentary is such that you will necessarily go through the place slowly and thereby take it in as it should be. Beautifully done and maintained.

Within the premises of the Palace is the Maharaja Fateh Singh Museum. This houses the art collection of the Gaekwad family. Once the school for the children of the royal family, the building was converted into a museum in 1961. The museum showcases art pieces from the collection owned by the Maratha Family. Collection of portraits by Raja Ravi Verma, European Renaissance paintings, sculptures by renowned European artists can be seen here. I do not understand art and I will not even attempt to discuss the paintings. But I have to say this, I was overawed by the portraits done by Raja Ravi Verma. Mindbogglingly amazing. They look like photographs. The detailing in the paintings is amazing. Raja Ravi Verma was commissioned by the Maharaja to make 43 paintings for the palace. Those portraits are a sight to cherish. I have never seen such life like paintings ever.

The Baroda Museum, unfortunately, was closed as Thursday is a weekly off. But by what I read now, we missed something. Constructed in 1894, designed by the famous architect R. F Chisholm, the museum is one of the most famous museums of the country. The Picture Gallery was added in 1910. I am told it is a treasure trove. Some pieces displayed in the museum date back to the 5th century A.D. It, I believe, also houses an Egyptian mummy and the skeleton of a blue whale.

I was very dejected to not be able to visit the Baroda Museum. I had read of a lesser-known place in Baroda called Tambekarwada. Tambekarwada is a typical Maratha house in the midst of the crowded city. Finding parking around it is a big issue. It was the residence of Bhau Tambekar Vitthal Khanderao, The Diwan of Baroda from 1849 to 1854. It is clean but dilapidated. Has painted walls like you have in the Shekhawati region and pretty jali work on windows.

The next day we were to head back home. It was going to be long drive day. At the last minute we added Chamapner to our plan. It was a slight detour and we thought we would take about an hour at the maximum in Champaner and we would be on our way. Well, it took us 3 and a half hours in Champaner.

Champaner - Pavagadh Archelogical Park is a UNESCO World Heritage Site. Champaner was founded in the 8th century by Vanraj Chavda, the most prominent king of the Chavda Dynasty. Champaner has a long history with the Solankis, Khichis, the Chauhan Rajputs, Mughals and the British who came to the town in 1803 when it had only 500 people residing here. They re-funded the town and it became a great exporter of silk with facilities of washing and preparing raw silk. A cholera epidemic in 1812 nearly wiped out the population. Pavagadh is home to a Kali Temple on top of the hill which was under renovation then. Champaner is dotted with a number of mosques. Jami Masjid, Sehar ki masjid, Kamati Masjid, Kevda Masjid, Nagina Masjid to name a few. There is a Kabootar Khana which housed the messenger pigeons. All the mosques are mostly similar in the way they have been made, the pillars, the arches, the carvings - beautiful, intricate, very indo-islamic. Some of the carvings on stone are absolutely jaw droppingly amazing. It is a photographer's delight. All thanks to Aman Channa, the photographer I mentioned earlier, I get to explore these places. Park your car, take a guide and explore. In recent times, Chamapner came into the limelight during the Godhra Riots.

We left Champaner at 1 pm. A straight shoot drive to Gurgaon. Practically an all-nighter, a first for me. Reached home at 4 a.m. I was tired and exhausted but I felt totally rejuvenated, if that even makes any sense. There is still so much left to explore in Gujarat. Unlike Rajasthan where I just get up and go, Gujarat needs planning. But I will explore what is left of it. That is for sure. The food is to die for. Kathiawadi food remains one of my top favourites. Oondhio finally found its way on my plate a year later. What an interesting dish it is. Flavour bombs bursting in the mouth - sweet and spicy. Delicious!

Meandering Through Peninsular India (June - 2022)

The one thing that has always limited my travel plans is time. I have never been able to take out more than 8-10 days for any of my road trips. Family responsibilities I guess, do tie you down. This time around things were different. Both my kids had finished their respective courses and were home. *The Husband* was on a break from work and had all the time on his hands. And the kids, for our 25th anniversary, gifted us a month off from home and everything related to home. They thought this was the most meaningful gift they could have given us and well, I could not agree more.

With the house and the dog taken care of, *the Husband* and I started planning our road trip. There were a lot of apprehensions around it but slowly and steadily we dealt with each one and made a broad outline of an itinerary. There were a few places I have been wanting to visit for a long time - Ajanta and Ellora, Bijapur, Hampi, Rameshwaram and Dhanushkodi to name a few. The plan was to do these places for sure and generally plan the rest of the trip around them and explore the places that come enroute. Prepping for a month-long trip also took some extra care and thinking. There was one apprehension that lingered in our minds all along. Two people, couped up in one 8x6 ft space for 12-14 hrs a day, day in and day out for a whole month. That is a tough one. It can get to you big time.

Will we be able to do it? Finally, we just decided that we will go ahead with the plan and at any point in the trip if we feel it is getting too much we will turn back. And that is the reason we did not plan for more than 3-4 days at a time. The itinerary probably turned out to be a tad bit haphazard in terms of routing and the criss-cross therein, but that is okay. We had fun and we accomplished a lot.

Part 1: Chittorgarh - Indore

Indore has been on my must-visit list for some time. In fact, I was to do the Indore-Mandu-Ujjain-Maheshwar-Omkareshwar circuit but that did not happen. Southward bound, Indore is enroute, so naturally it turned out to be the first stop. The iconic food of Indore and the fort town of Mandu being the 2 points to be touched upon. There was a lot of going back and forth on whether to drive straight to Indore, which is doable, or take a break in either Gwalior or Chittorgarh. Finally, we just decided to break journey at Chittorgarh.

Chittorgarh, on its own merit, deserves time. The fort is a place that is steeped in history. Our focus was to hit the south as soon as we can and then explore that area. Chittorgarh could be visited even in a 3-4 days' time frame. Since we had reached early, we decided to just drive around the town and explore a bit. What we noticed was that the entire town was shrouded in a ghostly silence. There were hardly any people on the streets and the shops were closed too. At least most of them were. It was midweek so it could not even be a weekly off. It felt very strange. On our way to the fort, we saw a few cops standing by the road side. Curiosity was getting to us so we stopped and asked them why it was so quiet. Apparently, the previous night there was a fight between people from two sects and it resulted in a murder. A lot of tension followed post that and that was the reason for the ghostly silence. The cops advised us to not roam the streets aimlessly lest we come in the crossfire. So, we headed back to the hotel, had a quiet dinner, and retired for the day.

We reached Indore late afternoon next day, checked in and freshened up. There was no point wasting time. There was a lot to eat. Indore has two iconic food streets. Chhappan Dukan and Sarafa Bazaar. While Chhappan Dukan is open during the day, Sarafa Bazaar is a jewellery market by day and the food stalls come to life only by 9 pm at night. During pre-covid days, Sarafa bazar stalls used to be open till 4 AM now they are, I am told, open till midnight but goes on till about 2 in morning.

The issue with these places is that there is a major parking issue. We were lucky we found one right next to Chhappan. A teeny-weeny tip to a guard bhaiya ensured us a parking space which was reserved for customers of the store he was working at. Chhappan is a 100-150 meters long street food lane. It has everything from poha jalebi to sabudana khichdi to chicken tikkas to bun tikki (they call it hot dog) to tandoori chai to a whole load of things. Poha jalebi is essentially a breakfast item so that we did not get. It was honestly a bit disappointing. I was looking forward to tasting it since I had heard so much about Indori poha. We had golgappa from Vijay Chat, Kulfi falooda at Neema, mutton hot dog and veg hot dog at Johnny hot Dog. We also had Dabeli from Young Tarang. The dabeli was super nice, the mutton hotdog was better than veg ones. Kulfi falooda was nice. Do not get me wrong. I am sure people who find these amazing, genuinely find them so. The thing is, when you have had chaat and kulfi in Delhi, it is a little difficult to find something that appeals the tastebuds anywhere else. It is a fact that you cannot find better kulfi and chaat anywhere other than in Delhi. Another thing that is famous in Indore is the namkeen. Naturally a visit to the store was a must. We were recommended Om Namkeen by a friend and it also worked out great as it was next to the place we had parked our car.

We bought what was nearly a truckload of stuff. Sev, mixtures of various kinds and what have you.

Part 2: Mandu

The next morning was an early start. When is it not when you are on a road trip?! Mandu is about 100 kms from Indore in Dhar District. It is a 2-hour drive from Indore. One thing about Madhya Pradesh is that the roads are amazing and it is a very clean state. In fact, Indore is said to be the cleanest city in India. We reached Mandu by about 9 am. And the first thing we did was find a place for breakfast. The locals guided us to one dhaba kind of place in the market called Relax Point. Basic, but a clean place. No prizes for guessing what we ate. Yes, we had poha. Indori poha is very different from how we make it, or even how I have had it in Bombay or Bhopal. Indori poha is poha that is washed and lightly tossed with simple seasoning and then topped with chopped onions, a little sweetness, chopped green chillies, and a light tempering of peanuts and curry leaves. Absolutely light and fresh. What we had that morning was brilliant stuff. Left Relax Point with a very happy and satiated tummy.

Just as we were parking our car outside Relax Point, we were approached by a guide Md Qureshi. He seemed to have a good vibe, so we requested him to give us time for breakfast and we would come back to him. As we were leaving the dhaba, the owner saw him and said we could not have found a better guide than him to show us around.

Mandu or Mandav is a fort town. It was originally founded by Raja Bhoj in the 10th century. It was later conquered by the Muslim rulers of Delhi. Dilawar Khan, the Governor of Malwa region, built his own kingdom in Mandu. His son Hoshang Shah was the first formally appointed Islamic ruler of the Malwa region. In its time it was one of the largest fort towns in India with a perimeter of 82 kms. The guide told us that once he and his friends tried walking the perimeter and it took them three and a half days to walk the entire round. If one has the time and the inclination, it can take almost 3 days to explore each part of Mandu. There are that many monuments. But we had only one day so covered all the touristy monuments. I do have to comeback for the circuit I mentioned before. I will keep enough time for the rest of it then. Also, the best time to visit necessarily is the monsoons to see Mandu in all its splendour.

We first visited the Jahaz Mahal. The Jahaz Mahal was built by Ghiyas-ud-din Khilji in the 15th century. It is said that he had 15000 women from all over the world as his consorts and it is believed that this was the biggest harem of its time. It is built between 2 artificial lakes, the Munj Talao and the Kapur Talao and is designed to appear like a ship floating in water. This is one of the reasons why one should visit Mandu in the monsoons or just after.

The Hindola Mahal or the Swinging palace is a T-shaped roofless building, said to be built during Hoshang Shah's reign in 1425 AD and may have been completed to what it is now by Ghiyas-ud-din Khilji by the end of the 15th century. The uniqueness of this building is that it has been built without a foundation. It has 5 ogee arches (an arch with two curves meeting at the apex). The 3 meters thick walls (in architectural language these are called buttresses) are made at the massive incline of 77 degrees. The resultant slant shape is how it got the name Hindola (swing) Mahal. This seems to have been used as an audience hall.

Close to the Hindola Mahal is the Champa Baodi a circular step well which is believed to have sweet water that smelled like the Champa flower.

Next to Champa Baodi is the Royal Palace which is built about 6 floors - 3 above the ground and 3 underground. The 2nd and 3rd floors have fallen off over time. We went down the first basement. Apparently, the floors below were open to public till about 2 years back (I find it hard to believe since there is no provision of electricity). But the guide said he had been down there with the ASI officials and it is beautifully made. There is a Turkish Hamam which had provisions for steam, hot and cold water and the works. There is an open-air theatre structure with some superb acoustic properties. The buildings are made in a manner that the cross-ventilation winds get cooled by the water bodies around. The water management system looked very scientific and advanced for the times. Since there was major dependency on rainwater, they had rainwater harvesting systems in place which can be seen even today. They apparently used charcoal to purify water. Just makes you wonder in amazement at their advancement and thought process.

The next stop was Jami Masjid. Said to be inspired by the Great Mosque of Damascus, it was built in the reign of Hoshang Shah and is believed to have been completed in the reign of Mahmud Khilji in 1454 AD. It has 3 large domes and 58 small domes. The interior of the Jami Masjid is a classic example of Indo-Saracenic (or Indo-Islamic) architecture. Mirhabs have intricate Hindu patterns. The main mihrab is decorated with an epigraph band with verses from the Holi Quran written on it. The minbar is a Hindu chhatri with s-shaped brackets.

Behind the Jami Masjid is Hoshang Shah's Tomb. It is apparently the oldest marble mausoleum in India. Built in the 1440s, they say it is the first monument to be built in marble. The tomb has some intricate engravings and lattice work on its facade. Lining the boundary of the tomb complex are small room structure with a pillared verandah. This may have been a dharamshala. The pillars have carvings that resemble a trishul, again showing the Hindu influence.

During a brief period of about 150 years between the 1300s-1500s Mandu covered itself in glory and came to be known as Shadiabad or the City of Joy. One can see the synthesis of Hindu and Islamic craftsmanship in the Indo-islamic architecture which came to be known as the Malwa Style of architecture. High platforms on which buildings were constructed, much like the Hindu temple style and the use of colour as an architectural scheme like the Persian traditions.

There is another side to Mandu and its monuments. That is the love story of Baz Bahadur and Rani Roopmati. Baz Bahadur was the last Sultan of the Malwa Sultanate and he reigned from 1555 to 1562. As the story goes, once on a hunting trip he met a shepherdess named Roopmati who was singing in a very melodious voice. Baz bahadur himself loved music and he befriended her and begged Roopmati to accompany him to the palace. She agreed but on the condition that she would live separately in a palace of her own near the Narmada River, a river that she revered and worshipped. He agreed to it and built her a pavilion near his palace. Since the Narmada was very far from the pavilion, he constructed the Rewa Kund, the water for which came from the Narmada. Whether they were romantically involved is anybody's guess, but they shared an extremely deep love for music and that was always the basis of their relationship. When Akbar decided to invade Mandu, he sent Adam Khan to capture Mandu. Baz Bahadur with his small army was no match and he was killed. Sensing her fate at the hands of Adam Khan, Roopmati took poison and killed herself to avoid capture. Fact or fiction, this story has been part of many a folklore since then.

One cannot go inside Rani Roopmati's pavilion, but only upto a point on the outside. Baz Bahadur's palace is very tranquil boasting of courtyards, pillars, pools, and breathtaking views of the Malwa region. While we were going through the place, our guide took us to one of the jharokas that was overlooking the valley. There was this child working on his small farm and he would have been at least 300 meters away. The guide called out to him in a tone which was lower than the tone we were talking in and believe me, the kid heard him loud and clear. He had a conversation with the kid. Then he had us speak to the kid lest we think this was all rehearsed. It is a wonder how the wind carried the voice.

Outside all these places one can find people selling a very strange looking fruit. It is an oblong looking hard exterior fruit. They call it the Mandu imli. You break it open and the inside is white with a marshmallow like texture. And its sour to taste. Well honestly why would anyone eat this I do not know. Our guide told us this is actually the Baobab fruit which is native to Africa. It is also called the Khurasaani Imli, from the Khurasaan region in Persia. He also told us that this fruit has thirst quenching properties. It is apparently a natural preservative and has immense medicinal values. Well, I guess when you put it that way, I can understand why people consume this fruit.

By the time we finished with Baz Bahadur's palace, and I speak for myself, I was melting in the heat. The sun was sapping me out. We were mostly done with the 'touristy' monuments. For the rest I will have to make time on another visit. Actually, and this I realised for some of the other places we visited, the searches on Google do not give you a complete picture on what to expect and how much time one would need. Mandu clearly needed more than the one day I had kept aside for it. But yes, I will be coming back for the Ujjain-Maheshwar circuit, so will ensure I spend more time here then. Maybe I will plan that post monsoons and see Mandu at it is beautiful best.

Back at the hotel it was time for a shower and some rest and we were eagerly waiting for 9 pm when we would head to Sarafa Bazar. Sarafa Bazar is in the old city, parking of course is an issue. We were yet again lucky to get parking at the Chhatris. It is about a half kilometre walk from there. When we reached there, stalls were still being set up. We had the famed Dahi Bhalle and Bhutte ki Kees at Joshi Dahi Bada. Bhutte ki kees was interesting, it was quite nice. Grated corn with some masalas. The dahi bada on the other hand was quite a let-down. Delhi has better dahi bhallas and nobody can deny it. We had an interesting kesar shikanji, a coconut shake (coconut water and the malai churned together) – delicious, Sabudana Khichdi - was too sweet for me, Malpua – it was alright, some kachori, a pizza and garadu (yam) - was honestly bad.

By the time it was 10.30 there was a stampede like situation. Okay, that is an exaggeration. But the thing is we had not seen crowds for the last 2 years and were no longer used to being in crowded places. It felt so claustrophobic. We had had enough and we exited. We were just so relieved to be out of that crowd. If you really ask me, food at the Sarafa bazar was quite a hype - overrated even. Yes, it is an experience going there, but the taste is average. Let us just say that was a point on the bucket list that has been ticked.

Part 3: Ajanta Caves - Aurangabad - Ellora

I had, for the longest time, thought that Ajanta and Ellora were twin cities of sorts. It is only when I started planning this trip that I realised they were more than a 100 kms apart. These, along with Aurangabad were next on our list.

Ajanta Caves are about 30 rock cut Buddhist caves dating from about the 2nd century BCE to about 480 CE. Universally acclaimed as masterpieces of Buddhist religious art, the paintings, and sculptures are the finest examples of ancient Indian art. The caves lay buried in the jungle clad mountains till they were accidentally discovered in 1819. Some of the 30 caves are unfinished and negligible. Five of the caves are Chaitya halls and the rest are viharas. Chaitya halls were places of worship and assembly of monks. They consist of a stupa within the structure. The viharas are monasteries where the monks used to live.

Now the thing is, visiting the Ajanta Caves is no less than a trekking expedition. There are some 300-400 (maybe more) steps to be climbed. And when it is as hot as it was when we went, it feels like ten times more. By the time we reached the base, it was well past 10.30 and the Sun was already very strong. I could manage walking up until cave 10 and then I was ready to collapse in the heat. The water that I was carrying had also finished by then. I knew if I stayed in that heat any further, I was sure to come down with a heat stroke. At cave 10 there was a shaded area where I plonked myself and I asked *the Husband* to go on ahead since he seemed fine. Of what the guards were saying, cave 26 was one that was not to be missed. It had the finest sculptures. Even if I missed it at least *the Husband* would have seen it. The rest in the shade helped me cool down. When I saw the photographs, I felt bad not pushing myself because the cave 26 was indeed worth it. In all the caves that I did see, the sculptures no doubt were amazing, but the paintings that have survived centuries were really what blew my mind.

The drive from Ajanta to Aurangabad is about a 100 kms. The most miserable roads we have ever driven on. Probably not the Batal-Gramphoo (remember from the Lahaul & Spiti story?) level, but close. Took us close to 3 hours to reach Aurangabad. It had us wondering if we would have to come back part of the way on our way to Ellora the next day. We mutually agreed that we were not going to drive our car back on this route. We planned to ask the hotel to organise a cab for us. Why put the car through the misery. Thankfully there was another route from Aurangabad, and that was a super road.

Aurangabad to Ellora caves is about 30 kms. Roads are good but it still takes about an hour to reach. The biggest relief was that there were no steps like there were in Ajanta. Ellora has 34 caves. Going through each cave would take at least 2 days. The touristy thing is to the 7-8 main caves - 10, 12, 14, 15, 16 and the 32, 33 and 34. The heat will probably not allow you to do more. Pro tip: if you really want to enjoy the Ajanta and Ellora caves, go into the history and really soak it all in, then the best time is to go post monsoons. Not only is the weather on your side, it is also the post monsoon green landscape and the numerous waterfalls that are said to sprout in these places.

Like Ajanta, we did the "touristy" thing. As I mentioned above, there are 34 caves in Ellora. They constitute three religions - Caves 1-12 are Buddhist caves, Caves 13-31 are Brahmanism and Caves 30-34 are Jainism.

As you enter the cave complex, the first cave is cave 16. The most amazing of all the caves. The Kailasa Temple. It is a marvel. I really wonder why it does not find mention in the Wonders of the World. Dating back to the 8th century, it is a rock cut structure that is the epitome of technical skill. Regarded as the greatest monolithic structure in the world, built by King Krishna-1 of the Rashtrakutta Dynasty, dedicated to Lord Shiva, the Kailasa Temple is an example of pure genius. Usually the monolithic caves are sculpted 'front in'. The Kailasa Temple has been sculpted 'top down'. It is a brilliant piece of art! The sculptures, the ornamentation, the sheer size. Truly mindboggling. It is a multi-level structure, said to be twice the size of the Parthenon in Athens. It is estimated that the artists sculpted out 3 million cubic feet of stones weighing about 2 lakh tonnes. I, honestly, cannot imagine the level of advancement that existed in those times for them to deliver this kind of art. You have to see it to believe it. If you ask me the highlight of my 28-days trip, I would say it was hands down the Kailasa Temple and the temples of Belur and Halabeedu. These are places that have left me spellbound and speechless.

We did not take a guide here. I usually always do, but for some reason we did not. While we were going into the Kailasa Temple, a man selling his wares came upto us and started walking alongside. He started telling us about the place as a guide would do. He told us that we should walk up little and start with cave 10 and then see 12, 14 and 15 before taking the bus to caves 31-34. We realised he was not a guide but decided that once were done we would buy something off him. He did have some very prettily sculpted elephants that I liked. He walked alongside and waited for us when we went inside a cave. A very simple and decent guy.

They say cave 10 is the only proper Chaitya Hall in Ellora. The façade is richly decorated with sculptures. The roof inside looks like a number of wooden arches but it is all done in stone. On the pillars are figures in bas-relief. And what is bas-relief might you ask? Well, it is a sculpting technique in which the figures or the designs are a bit more prominent than the background. And High-relief is when the half or more of the circumference of the figure or the design project out. Some parts may also be disconnected from the background. Yes, that was my learning about the art of sculpting. At the far end of the cave is a 15 ft. sculpture of Buddha sitting in a preaching pose. As we were stepping out the security guard came upto us and asked us if we wanted to go to the gallery upstairs. Of course we did. He told us to quietly follow him. We went up the stairs. And he opened the door to the upstairs gallery for us. This is usually locked. From the gallery we got a super view of the Buddha sitting down below. The guard then started chanting the Buddhist prayer mantra and the echo was as if there was a harmonium playing. It was the most peaceful sound. It just engulfed the noise that the visitors were making downstairs and transported us to another level of peace and quiet. I do not think we were up there for more than a few minutes, but it felt like forever. Why he picked us out from the crowd to get us up here, I do not know. But I am glad he did.

Known as the "Teen taal," Cave 12 is by far the most important in this group of caves. It is a 3 storeyed structure. While we were inside looking around, yet again a security guard came to us and asked us to follow him to the floors upstairs. Not many people go up, he said. The 3rd floor was amazing. It is a sculptural gallery. The side walls are decorated with huge figures of Buddha flanked by Boddhisatvas. Inside the ante-chamber are also Buddhist goddesses sitting on the lotus flower. On each side of the front wall are 7 sitting Buddhas in different mudras. These are idols and mandalas carved into the walls, and numerous goddesses, and Bodhisattva-related iconography, belonging to Vajrayana Buddhism. Vajrayana practices are connected to specific lineages in Buddhism. They are also referred to as Buddhist Tantras. It includes practices that make use of mantras, dharanis, mudras, mandalas, and the visualisation of deities and Buddhas.

Cave 14 is known as "Ravan ki Khai" because of the sculpture depicting Ravana shaking the Kailasa Mountain where Shiva and Parvati are sitting. Cave 15 is called the "Dasavatara Cave" because of the various incarnations of Vishnu depicted here. In this trip I got quite an insight into the Hindu Mythology. Here is where I first learnt about the 10 avatars of Vishnu - Matsya (fish), Kurma (turtle), Varaha (boar), Narasimha (man-lion), Vaman (dwarf god), Parashuram (Brahmin warrior), Rama, Krishna and Kalki (Kalki is yet to come and prophesied to end the Kali-yug, the present times which are full of conflict and sin). The upper floor is dedicated to

Shiva. There is a huge big Nandi sitting majestically in the centre of the hall.

From here we took a bus to the caves 30-34. It is a ride of about a kilometre plus. These are temples belonging to the Digambar Sect. Cave 30 is also called the Chhota Kailasa because of the similarity to the Kailasa Temple. Cave 31 has images of the Tirthankars. Cave 32 is called the Indra Sabha; Cave 33 is called the Jagannath Sabha.

A tiring day, more so because of the heat and the piercing sun. But an enriching day. Despite the heat, it was worth the while. By the time we finished with Ellora, it was 4 O'clock. The plan earlier was to come back to the hotel, rest a bit and then visit the Bibi ka Maqbara. But then we realised it was a Sunday and maybe it would get even more crowded in the evening. Also, once we went back, we may not feel like getting out in the heat again. So, we headed straight to the Bibi ka Maqbara.

Bibi ka Maqbara is the mausoleum built by Aurangzeb's son Azam Shah in memory of his mother Dilras Banu Begum between 1651-1661. It is inspired by the Taj Mahal and even though it is a very poor imitation of the Taj Mahal, it still has its own grace. The only sad part is that the surroundings are not well maintained.

Aurangabad is also known its sarees - Himroo and Paithani. Himroo is a fabric made of silk and cotton grown locally in Aurangabad. Brought in during the reign of Muhammed Tughlaq when he shifted the capital from Delhi to Daulatabad, Himroo weave is basically a jacquard weave. It is a replication of Kinkhwab which was woven with pure gold and silver in those times. Originally in Paithani fabric, silk was used in the weft designs and in borders and cotton was used in the body. Today Pathani is made only in silk. Did I shop? Ofcourse I did. I may not wear them often, but I am a big fan of traditional weaves in sarees.

Later that night we went looking for Nan-Khaliya, a popular dish in Aurangabad. Apparently, no wedding food menu is complete until you have this on the menu. Nan-Khaliya is a mutton dish. The restaurant that came in the google search seemed to have shut down all thanks to covid. We asked around and we were told there was a street which had vendors dedicated to selling this dish but these were not places where you could sit and eat. It was all about getting it 'parcelled' and eating it in your 'room'. And to top that hygiene was a question mark. Now it is not that one has not eaten from unhygienic places. It is just that we were on a road trip and we were a little sceptical about eating at such places. We could not afford to fall ill and get a fever for any reason in these times of Covid. One just had to be careful. So, we gave up on Nan-Khaliya.

Part 4: Lonar lake and Nanded

Next morning we headed towards our next stop, Nanded. We drove through much of rural Maharashtra. This whole belt was grape farming. And the roads were lined with vendors selling raisins. We bought some and honestly, they were good quality but at half the price of what you get back home. Although the roads need a lot of attention, it was still a great drive. I planned the route such that we visit the Lonar Lake too. Lonar Lake is a National Geo-Heritage Monument. It is one of the four known hyper-velocity impact craters in basaltic rock anywhere on Earth, the other 3 being in Brazil. This meteorite impact is estimated to have been between 35,000-50,000 years ago. The water in the lake is extremely saline with a ph value of 10.5. There are a number of temples around the lake base. Some dating centuries old. But to reach them is a walk through the dense growth around. There are a number of look-out points from where you can take pictures from a height. At one such point we met these 2 guys who had given up their respective jobs and were now full time into exploring and photography. They were here in search of rare migratory birds that specifically only come to this area. Their enthusiasm as they showed us pictures of the rare sitings was infectious and amusing.

There is a temple on the rim of the lake called the Gomukh Dhaar temple. There is a stream or dhaar that flows out of the temple into a kund. According to the locals the underground spring that provides water flow all throughout the year, owes its genesis to the meteorite impact that created the lake. That is the only explanation they have since the source of this water is still unknown even after so many years. There are supposedly some 14 temples within the Lonar crater most of which have fallen to ruins. We saw one from the lookout point. It is just that the dense growth and the trek down through it deterred me.

Next, we headed to Nanded. Nanded is famous for Gurudwara Sachkhand Saheb which is one of the 5 takhts of Sikhism. Built by Maharaja Ranjit Singh, this Gurudwara houses the mortal remains of Guru Gobind Singh ji. A number of weapons used by the Guru are also exhibited here.

Nanded has very basic hotels, nothing fancy. We found one on the highway on the outskirts of the town. Checked in, freshened up and timed going to the Gurudwara at such a time that we would have the langar for dinner. As we entered there was a long queue to enter the sanctum. A separate line for women and men. We entered the sanctum and we were one of the last to enter before the ardaas started. It was a different feeling. One could feel a very different energy flowing through the sanctum. After the ardaas was over they opened the doors to where the weapons were kept. There was loud chanting as the doors were opened. An experience beyond words. The flow of energy was palpable. We were in there for about 20-25 minutes and despite the loud chanting and the pushing around, it was a very peaceful 20-25 minutes that I spent. We came out and headed straight for the prasad counter for the kada-prasad. The first helping was a small one. I of course went for seconds. With a big smile the bhaiji gave me a huge big helping of kada-prasad. I enjoyed it like a kid enjoys a treat. After that we headed straight for the langar hall. Langars are not what they used to be. They used to be a lot more elaborate. Nonetheless a langar is a langar and it is a very satiating meal and so was this one. We spent some more time sitting in the Gurudwara complex before we headed back to the hotel, more like a lodge. With this visit I have visited 4 out of the 5 takhts. *The Husband* has done all 5. There is a Museum of Sikh History which we visited, but I just felt if they had had an audio guide or something it could have been a little more interesting to go through.

Part 5: Bijapur

The good thing about places in the south is that restaurants open early for breakfast. We went looking for a restaurant we had searched for on the internet, but somewhere enroute we saw this one that had a lot of people sitting inside and it also looked clean and nice. Gokul Restaurant. We had our breakfast here. Pretty decent fare. Of course it was the usual idlis, dosa, vada but it was delicious. With our tummies happily stuffed, we were on our way to our next destination - Bijapur.

Bijapur or Vijayapura is a relatively lesser-known destination. Although the Gol Gumbaz is not. Many of the destinations I choose are inspired choices. Ofcourse, Bijapur was yet again a destination inspired by Aman's photographs. Bijapur was also the entry point into Karnataka for us. Historically, it finds mention from The Chalukya period till the Muslim invasion - Chalukyas to Rashtrakuttas to Hoysalas to Yadavas to the Muslim conquest. It was Yusuf Adil Shah who founded Bijapur as an independent state and

Bijapur owes much of its greatness to him.

The drive from Nanded to Bijapur was about 8 hours. We took it easy leaving in the morning, I was very focused on that I wanted to see in Bijapur and had the whole of the next day to do that. Dinner that night was at a local restaurant. The one dish that I just had to have was Gobi Manchurian. It is such a "South" dish and I do not mean any offence here. It just amuses me that is all. I have had better versions of it, but it was nice. We were pleasantly surprised to find a very hip and happening ice cream parlour. Polar Bear is a chain of ice cream parlours down south. They serve some amazing sundaes. I had an All-American Banana Split after like some 3 decades. Reminded me of my college days and our Nirula's visits. The same boat shaped bowl. It had the same look and taste. It truly took me back in time, thank you Polar Bear.

The next morning our first of the two stops was Ibrahim Rouza. While driving through the city we noticed that at every traffic crossing, on the left side of the road a good length of the road was covered by a green pandal of sorts. We realised later that it was to provide shade to the people stopping at the red-light signal. Indeed, it was thoughtful I must say. I have not seen that anywhere else.

Ibrahim Rouza is a set of two buildings - one is a tomb of Ibrahim Adil Shah and the other a mosque. The construction began in 1580 and was completed in 1627. It has fine filigree and decorative work and is adorned by elegant minarets. Ibrahim Rouza is said to be one of the most beautifully proportioned Islamic monuments in India and the finest example of Islamic decoration. There is so much character in the buildings. One needs take off one's shoes before entering and I must say, they have maintained the area very well.

Lucky for us there was no one else visiting the monument at that time. I spent a good amount of time clicking pictures. There are verses in Urdu carved along the doorway, I assume they are from the Quran, Even the arch on the window has Urdu calligraphy in the form of a grill. The arches in the mosque have some very intricate filigree work. There are 6 graves inside the tomb, Ibrahim Adil Shah, his wife Chand Sultana, his two sons, his mother and Malik Sandal, the architect of the buildings. The mosque and the tomb lie side by side separated by a large pond which is now empty. The basements had a granary and an ammunition depot. The peace and quiet of the monument transport you to another era. It is aptly called the Taj Mahal of the South.

After this we went to the second of the 2 monuments that I wanted to visit -the Gol Gumbaz. Soon after his ascent to the throne in 1626, Mohammad Adil Shah began work on the Gol Gumbaz which he wished to make his final resting place. He wanted his mausoleum to equal or surpass the beauty of his father's tomb - Ibrahim Rouza. It took some 30 years to make this remarkable structure which has one of the largest domes in the world. Built in the Deccan Indo Islamic style, it is second in size to St. Peter's Basilica in Rome. The tomb has graves of Mohammad Adil Shah, his 2 wives, his mistress, his daughter, and grandson. Square building with a semicircular dome that is 144 feet in diameter. The acoustics are so amazing that even a whisper in the gallery at the base of the dome gets carried to the other end crisp and clear. One can reach this gallery which is 7 storeys up through a narrow winding staircase. It goes without saying the heat was draining. How I climbed the 7 storeys I only know. Not only was the stairway narrow and spiral, the stairs were uneven and high. *The Husband's* stamina was way better than mine. While it was a piece of cake for him, I went up huffing and puffing. At the base of the dome is what they call the whispering gallery where one could test out a whisper that echoes. To be very hones,t people were shouting and the echoes were hurting the ears. One can step out in the open. There is a gallery that goes around the dome. On the 4 corners of the base square are 4 minarets. The view of the city from here was amazing. Coming down the 7 storeys was precarious too, keeping the balance while not wanting to touch the walls (for hygienic reasons) was a task.

There is a museum too in a separate building which is claimed to be one of the oldest museums in India. Located before the main entrance to the Gol Gumbaz, this building is called the Naqar Khana or the house of drum. This was built to offer a grand royal reception to the king's visitors by beating the drums as was the custom. It was later converted into a museum and houses the rare objects that the British found while shifting the district headquarters Kaladagi to Bijapur. It includes stone inscriptions of Arabic, Persian, Kannada, and Sanskrit languages in different scripts. It also has Brahmanical and Jain sculptures, hero stones, manuscripts, coins, miniature paintings, Bidriware and household items dating between 6th to the 18th century.

By the time we finished with both these monuments, the heat had gotten to me and all I wanted to was go back to the hotel and relax. Dinner that evening was at place called Qaswa Hills. It is a great place for non-vegetarian fare. Highly recommended.

Part 6: Aihole, Pattadakal and Badami

When you do an internet search for Badami caves, Aihole and Pattadakal also crop up as places to visit. Aihole is stated to have 120 temples and one just wonders how it is going to pan out. How much time is required to explore so many temples. That ambiguity always stays. That is where the advantage of booking hotels practically on-the-go helps. Anyhow, the next day we reached Aihole by about 9 am. As we were parking the car we were approached by a guide which is how it usually works. He seemed a pleasant guy, so we decided to go with him. His name was Basavaraj. As we went through the complex at Aihole, we were quite taken in by Basavaraj's mannerisms and his knowledge. He told us he had a Bachelor's degree in Ancient Indian History and one could really see he was passionate about his subject. We had taken him to be our guide for Aihole, but he continued with us to Pattadakal and Badami. He has been the best guide I have ever had in all my travels. Well, to be fair there is one more guide that I can add to the list and that was in the guide at Junagadh Fort in Bikaner. Heard stories about the Vishnu Avatars, learnt how and why Shiva became Ardhnareshwar, the story of Vishnu in his Vaman Avatar and so much more. It has made me start looking for some nice books I can read for more on this. Honestly did not realise how interesting Hindu mythology is.

Aihole dates back to 5th - 8th centuries during the reign of the Chalukyas and Rashtrakuttas. It was originally called Aryapura. The legend has it that a kshatriya kin, Kartivirya Arjuna (he is said to have had a thousand arms) visited Jamadagni Rishi in his ashram. Jamadagni was one of the Saptrishis or the seven great sages and the father of Parasuram. Kartivirya was served a feast using the divine magical cow, Kamadhenu. Kartivirya was so impressed by Kamadhenu that he wanted it for himself. For this he offered Jamadagni wealth which he refused. Kartivirya forcibly took away the cow. Parasuram, killed Kartivirya and brought back Kamadhenu. To avenge the death of their father, Kartivirya's three sons stabbed Jamadagni 21 times and sliced his head. This enraged Parshuram and he killed the 3 sons and got back his father's head for the last rites and then ensued onto a genocide of sorts on the Kshatriyas throughout the world for the next 21 generations. After avenging the death of his father, Parasuram came down to the Malaprabha

River and washed his bloodied axe. This resulted in the colour of the water turning red because of all the blood. A woman who walked by saw this and screamed "Aye Holé!" Which meant "Oh no blood" in Kannada. Since then, Aryapura became Aihole.

Aihole used to be a meeting point for experimentation of the Hindu temple arts especially the temple architecture. Students studied the art of temple making and made small prototypes of different temple styles. Notable bigger temple is the Durga Temple. Originally a Surya temple, it later became a Shiva temple. It is called Durga Temple due to its proximity to the Durg (fort) and not because it is dedicated to Goddess Durga. The other notable temple is the Lad Khan Temple, said to have got the name from the person who used to reside here. This temple has 2 garbh grihs or sanctums. One on the ground floor (Shiva) and the other on the first floor (Surya). So, what I learnt is that a temple consists of a garbh grih (sanctum), Sabha mandap (meeting hall) and Mukh mandap (the entrance). The garbh grih has no carvings, the sabha mandap has some carvings and the mukh mandap is beautifully carved and decorated. Essentially, this cluster of Aihole, Pattadakal and Badami were important sites of architectural learning practice in those times. While Aihole had temples dedicated to Vaishnavism or to Vishnu, Pattadakal has temples dedicated to Shivaism or Shiva.

Pattadakal meaning 'place of coronation' was essentially used for coronation of the Chalukya kings from the 7th to the 9th centuries. It was also called Kisuvolal – "valley of red soil" and Raktapura - "city of red." Pattadakal-Kisuvolal - red soil valley for coronation"

Pattadakal is a complex which has a collection of temples dedicated to Shiva. While most temples are not active temples, the Virupakshi Temple is one where prayers are still offered. One can see both the north Indian and south Indian temple styles here. The Galaganath temple is a classic example of north Indian style - Nagara style and the Sangameshwar temple is a classic example of the south Indian style - Dravidian style. "Every stone tells a story" - Basavaraj's favourite line. He pointed out numerous sculptures - one showing a happy couple, one showing an intoxicated couple, showed a panel which had women with different hairstyles - buns, bouffants, fringes, long hair, braids. There were panels which showed women wearing shorts, bikinis, camisoles and what have you. All showing the level of fashion consciousness of those times. Pattadakal temples have sculptured panels that depict stories from Mahabharata, Ramayana, and the Panchatantra. Truly - every stone told a story.

Badami, earlier called Vatapipuram was the capital of the Badami Chalukyas for 3 centuries. There is a story behind the name Vatapi. It got its name Badami from the almond-coloured rock that the caves are cut out of. As the legend goes, a demon called Ilvala lived here with his brother Vatapi. Vatapi would disguise himself as an animal, and Ilvala would offer his meat to weary, unsuspecting travellers. Vatapi had the power to come back to life after he had been eaten. Ilvala would call out to Vatapi, and he would burst out of the guest's stomach, killing him in the process. This went on until the great sage Agastya visited them. He ate the food that Ilvala offered him, but immediately said "Vatapi, jeerno bhava," and before the demon could spring back to life he was digested by Rishi Agastya. And that was the end of Vatapi, and the menace he and his brother were causing in the region.

Badami Cave temples are 4 rock cut caves that represent the rock-cut architecture of the Chalukya dynasty. They date back to the 6th century. These caves have been carved out one massive stone. The statues have been also cut of the same stone. The first cave is dedicated to Shiva, the second and third dedicated to Vishnu and the fourth cave is dedicated to Lord Mahavira.

There is a very beautiful sculpture of Ardhnari Nateshwar. Or

Shiva in the form of half man and half woman. According to Shiva Purana, this form of Shiva is one of the 63 forms of Shiva. According to mythology, Bhringi was a rishi who was a devotee of Shiva and he worshiped only Shiva unlike the others who worshipped both Shiva and Shakti. One day he visited Mount Kailash and wanted to go around Shiva, but Shakti (Shiva's consort) insisted he go around both. To ensure this Shakti sat on Shiva's lap. Bhringi took the form of a bee to slide in between Shiva and Shakti. This amused Shiva and he made Shakti one half of his body - the Ardhnareshwar. Bhringi then took the form of a rat to gnaw his way through them. This annoyed Shakti so much that she cursed him that he would lose all the parts that come from the mother. According to Tantric Science, it is believed that the rigid and tough parts of the body like the bones and nerves come from the father and the soft and fluid parts like flesh and blood come from the mother. As he was cursed, he lost all flesh and blood and became only skeletal structure of bones and he collapsed. He realised his mistake that Shiva and Shakti together make a whole and one cannot exist without the other. He apologised but he had already lost all his flesh and blood. He was then given third leg that acted like a tripod support.

Indian mythology is intriguing. All thanks to Basavaraj for piquing my interest in the subject.

There is another 5 ft. tall relief of Shiva in the Nataraj pose. The uniqueness of this sculpture is that Shiva has 18 arms. Nataraja is the depiction of Shiva as the cosmic dancer. The 18 arms depict the natya mudras (symbolic hand gestures) some holding objects such as drums, a flame torch, a serpent, a trishul and an axe.

The biggest sculpture in cave 2 is that of Vishnu in his Trivikrama form. Taking one of the three steps. Vishnu's 5th avatar Vaman - the dwarf like brahmin takes the form of Trivikrama - the lord of Three Strides. The demon king Bali was a very powerful Asura king and was going to take on reign of all the 3 realms. In the Vaman avatar, Vishnu visits the court of the demon king Bali and begs him for land that he can cover in 3 strides. Bali found it very amusing seeing the size of the dwarf brahmin and granted him his request. Assuming the Trivikrama form, Vaman took the first step and covered the whole Earth, with the second step whatever was there between the Earth and Heaven. When there was no other space left to cover in the 3rd step, Bali lowered his head for Vaman to take his 3rd step. Vaman stepped on his head and pushed him down to the Pataal Lok. And there by ensured that Bali and the demons do not rule the world. Impressed by Bali's devotion, Lord Vishnu allowed him to come back to earth once a year. This day is celebrated as Onam.

Cave 4 is the smallest and is dedicated to the Jainism. There are sculptures of Bahubali, Parsavnath and Mahavir amongst other Tirthankars. Facing the caves is a lake - Agastya Lake. And besides the lake is the Bhoothnath Temple dedicated to Shiva. It is indeed a very peaceful place.

We finished with Badami and was time to bid farewell to Basavaraj. What an amazing guide he was. I thoroughly enjoyed my day with him.

Part 7: Hampi and Chitradurga

Situated on the banks of the Tungabhadra River, Hampi was the capital of the last Hindu Kingdom of Vijayanagar before it was destroyed by the Deccan Sultans in the 1560s. Krishnadevaraya, the greatest king of the Vijayanagar Empire, built most of the temples at Hampi.

When one enters Hampi, the best thing to do is park your car in one of the parking lots and take an auto from there. The auto drivers charge you INR. 1000-1500 and take you around all the sites in Hampi. It can easily take a whole day to go through the complex. The Vitthalla Temple (the famous chariot temple) is on one end and the Virupakshi temple (the only functional temple in the complex) is on the other end. Amongst the other structures are the Zanana complex, the elephant stables, Hazarrama Temple, a beautiful step well, Lakshmi Narasimha Temple, Badaviling Temple.

The most famous temple at Hampi is the Vijaya Vitthal Temple, dedicated to Lord Vishnu. It was built in the 15th century during the rule of King Devaraya II. Within the temple complex is a stone chariot which is the same one that is printed on the INR. 50 notes. The pillars in the sabha mandapa are supposedly musical pillars. When struck they emit sounds like the musical notes. When we visited, the sabha mandap was cordoned off for restoration work, thus we did not experience the sounds of the pillars. The sad part yet again is, that the restoration work being done is taking away the character of the places. Maybe this the best way to do it, but I just feel it that way. Within the temple complex there is Champa tree that is said to be 150 years old. The trunk and the visible roots make for a very beautiful sight. It is like an amazing driftwood art.

The Badavalinga Temple is the largest monolithic shivalinga in Hampi. It is 3 meters high and is made of black stone. Next to it is the Lakshmi Narasimha Temple. It is the largest statue in Hampi. Ugra Narasimha is sitting on the coil of Shesha, the seven headed snake. Narasimha is half man, half lion and is the incarnation of Vishnu who killed Prahlad's demonic father Hiranyakshipu.

We were done going through the complex by evening apart from the Virupakshi Temple. I had connected with Aman on some photographs that I had seen on his page. He had told me that there is a beautiful trek route from behind the Virupakshi Temple along banks of the Tungabhadra River to the Vitthala Temple. And one place specifically was a must visit - Koti Lingam. Shivalinga reliefs sculpted on the rock face. One is a relief of 108 shivalingas and one is of 1008 shivalingas. Both, *the Husband* and I, left the hotel at 5.30 am to beat the heat. Reached the Virupakshi Temple and parked the car and started walking towards the river. Lush green surroundings welcomed us. We walked about 200 meters and saw the headstone that said Koti Lingam was 300 meters ahead. We went looking for it, went in all directions but never found it. We almost walked till Vitthala Temple, but no sign of the Koti Lingam. We walked back and were quite dejected and almost gave up. And just as we were about to give up, we see this man in a guard's uniform riding a bike over the big rock face. Where he came from, I do not know, but the direction led to the river, no other place. If that was not strange, the fact that he was riding over the steep and smooth rock face was stranger. We stopped him and asked him where Koti Lingam was. He promptly asked us to wait for a bit. He rode up to the walking path, parked his bike and came back. He led us down a narrow path which came to a rocky area. He took off his shoes, told us it was okay for us to keep ours on and then started to climb the rocks. We followed him. It was a treacherous climb by my standards. He helped us on the steeper rocks. And there it was. In between the rocky area sculpted on the rock face. One Pentagonal shape with 108 shivalingas and one rectangular shape with 1008 shivalingas. It was very simple, very plain, but there was palpable energy in that place. All I could do was stare at it for some time. Then the guard asked us to follow him a little ahead. The rocks were a little lose and the step needed to be very long to jump over. I did not go but *the Husband* managed. On the other side was a relief of Vishnu in a lying down position. Beautiful surroundings, beautiful sculptures, and amazing energy. There was something in the air. The uncanniness in the whole story does not end with where he came from and how he came. We asked him his name; he said it was Manjunath, that is another name for Shiva. I am not a believer, but what happened next makes it difficult not to get goosebumps. Once we came down to where Manjunath had left his shoes, *the Husband* just turned around to discuss how much to tip him, and it was less than half a minute when he took out the money from his wallet and turned to give it to him. And there was no one there. No sight of him. The place where he had parked his bike was at least 100-150 meters away from where we were. No way could he have reached there in less than a minute. And even if he did, there was no way we would not have heard or seen the bike go. I am still getting the goosebumps as I write this. Sometimes one experiences things that one cannot explain, and they remain with you forever.

I checked on my walking app and it showed we had walked 8 kms. And it was the most amazing trek. Peaceful, invigorating, exhilarating. We walked to the Virupakshi Temple. Built during the 7th century by the Chalukyas, the Virupakshi Temple is a shiva temple where the ritual worship is done even today. The mysterious thing about the temple is that on the first floor, there is a hole through which sunlight comes in. The shadow of the Raj Gopuram (which is 300 ft away) falls on a wall in the Mandapa. What is amazing is that the shadow is inverted as if it is coming through a pinhole camera. Fascinating!

We got back to the hotel, had our breakfast, booked the spa and took the day off to rest. After 12 days of being on the road, we deserved it. In the evening, we went to the sunset point at the Malyavantha Raghunatha Temple. This a temple dedicated to Lord Rama. According to Mythology, Lord Rama and Lakshman waited here till the monsoon was over and then marched towards Lanka with Hanuman's army. Behind the temple is a Shiva Temple which is also the vantage point to the sunset. There are Nandis and shivalingas carved on the stone. There is a gap in the floor which it is said that Lakshman made by his arrow. We spent some time there waiting for the sun to set, it was peaceful till a minibus load of noisy people came in and spoilt the whole vibe of the place. We left shortly after. There was no way I would have enjoyed the sunset in that noise.

Well rested, the next morning we were on our way to Chikmagalur. On one of the signboards, I saw Chitradurga. Strangely, it pulled at me. We decided since it was enroute, we would stop and visit the fort. To be honest there is nothing much in that fort. And in that sense, I was kind of disappointed. I will admit I was a little angry at the guide for leading me on to believing otherwise. A whole flight of stairs takes you to this small temple - Hidimba Temple. That area also has a vantage point from where one gets a bird's eye view of the Chitradurga town. The guide was rattling out something and I was barely listening. Suddenly I heard him say something and pointing to a man down below. I saw a lot of people gathering around. The curious cat that I am, suddenly I was all ears. So, there is this guy by the name of Jyotiraj. His talent is that he can climb straight walls and steep rocky surfaces without harnesses, skimming his hands over the surface like monkeys do. He is called the Monkey Man. I was intrigued. Jyotiraj showcases his art on the weekends and he was prepping for it as I watched from above. We rushed down. In the fort there is a structure that was the royal swing. Must be some 30 ft high at the least. And the man just climbed it like a monkey. He was deft and sure of himself. As he reached the top bar, he fixed himself with his legs and just hung himself upside down with his hands flaying. I was spellbound looking at him. Then he went on to the other side almost prancing the bar and came down. The collective gasp of the people watching was so audible. When he came down people crowded around him tipping him and getting selfies clicked with him.

The guide then told me his story. Jyotiraj got lost and was

separated from his biological family when he was 3-4 years of age. He was adopted by a family but he ran away at the age of 13 as he was tortured by them. He grew up with another family and since he was unhappy there too, he tried to commit suicide at the Fort. He was climbing rocky hill to jump off it and saw people watching the way he was climbing in sheer amazement. This just gave him a new lease of life. He started climbing the fort falls and the surrounding hills for entertaining people and earning tips. Slowly, he started taking in kids from around and training them. He is a bachelor, but he considers his students his children and provides for the needs of the underprivileged kids from the tips he earns. His aim is to get the district administration to lease land to him where he can construct a wall as per the Olympic standards and train youngsters to compete in national and Olympic levels. I was obviously curious to meet him. I waited till he had finished with the crowds. I could see how proud he was of his craft and how much passion he had for it. We had a long chat about how he started, what his dreams were and where he was getting stuck. It is sad how in our country these lesser-known sports are totally neglected. Jyotiraj told me that he had climbed the Jog falls some 22 times. His ultimate dream is to climb the Angel Falls Venezuela - the highest uninterrupted waterfall in the world with a plunge of 807 meters, Whoa!! That would be insane. An Australian film maker, Stanley Joseph is making a biopic on the monkey man. The only part that is left for completion before the worldwide release is the scaling of the Angel Falls.

I was so awed by what I had seen and then meeting this guy who had gone through so much in life. Even though he did not have enough for himself he was taking care of so many underprivileged children. The humility of the guy was salute worthy. Of course I got a picture clicked with him. It was an absolute honour meeting him.

As I was bidding him adieu, he pointed towards my guide and

said that he was also a national level wrestler. Sorry, what?!

So, Narain was a national level wrestler from Karnataka State in 2010-12. Sports politics got him out of the game. He has a degree in Finance and Accounting. Now that he was married, he needed money to run his house, so wrestling took a back seat and he started working 5 days a week at a friend's shop looking after the accounts. Over the weekend he works as a guide. There are 25 guides and they have worked out a roster system so that everyone gets equal opportunity to earn. Apparently as a guide, they do not get a salary. It is only the money that they get from the people. Don't national level players get a govt. job, I asked him. They do, but one must pay to get one, he tells me. He also tried for the Sub Inspector exam but did not get through. Apparently the "asking" amount for that was an obscene amount. He says if he had that kind of money he would start his own business. But he is happy. He is managing and that is all that matters to him.

I may not have been impressed by the fort, to be very honest, meeting Jyotiraj and Narain made my day. I'm glad that my travels not only take me places, I get to meet interesting people. People who give a different perspective to life, through their struggles, dreams and achievements.

Part 8: Chikmagalur and Belur

Our stay at Chikmagalur was with no other agenda but to relax and chill out. Of course, *the Husband*, is a coffee connoisseur in his own right so for him it was coffee haven. The first day and a half were spent doing nothing. The highlight of the stay for me was the Malanad thali that I had for a dinner. Malanad is the region covering Uttara Kannada, Chikmagalur, Chamrajnagar, Udupi, Belgaum, Dakshina Kannada, Hassan, Kodagu and Shimoga. Amazingly finger-licking-good is how I would describe the food. Sorry, sometimes one needs to do away with being grammatically correct to be able to get the right emotion. What was on the thali - Chicken ghee roast (it is an ancestral recipe of the people who run the Shetty Lunch Home in Kundapura), Keema curry in palak, Mushroom korma, Bandekai gojju (okra curry), Chicken Chettinad, Akki roti, (rice flour roti), neer dosa, Broken wheat payasam and coconut laddu. Quite a plate of food it was and it was delicious food, no doubt.

There is a coffee museum in Chikmagalur which we visited. They show you a 10 odd minute audio-video and there are 2 rooms that you go around which have information on various coffees and have coffee machines on display. Interesting story behind how coffee came to India. Coffee was first grown in India in 1670 AD in Baba Budan Giri Hills in Chikmagalur. Baba Budan was a Sufi saint. On his way back from his Haj, he happened to travel through Mokha in Yemen. This is where he discovered coffee and liked it so much that he wanted to bring it back to India. It was, at that time, illegal to take out green coffee beans out of Arabia. The only form it could be taken out was either roasted or boiled to prevent any germination. The Arabs were very strict about it. So, Baba Budan carried 7 green coffee beans wrapped around his belly and smuggled them to India. When he reached home, he planted the seeds in the Chandragiri Hills in Chikmagalur. These hills are now called Baba Budangiri Hills in his honour.

It goes without saying that *the Husband* bought his stock of coffee and I bought my year's stock of spices. The best place for coffee in Chikmagalur is Pandurang. The task was now to pack the coffee and spices in such a manner that the car doesn't end up smelling of either. *The Husband* managed to do that well I must say.

The next day was going to be a long one. Not in terms of distance but in terms of visiting places. We were visiting Belur and Halabeedu before reaching Mysore. We set off after an early breakfast. Belur is about a 45 min drive from Chikmagalur. It is famous for the Chennakeshava Temple.

So far, the temple architecture that we saw and admired and raved about in terms of sculptural beauty belonged to the Chalukyas and the Rashtrakuttas. I thought these were pieces of art that could not be surpassed. And how wrong was I. What we saw in Belur and Halabeedu was beyond amazing. The temples in these places belong to the Hoysalas.

The origin of Hoysalas is said to be from the Yadavas in North India, some claim they came from the hill tribes of Malanad in the Western Ghats and some say they belonged to the Halumantha community, but there are apparently no firm records of it. They ruled between the 11th to the 14th centuries covering most of modern-day Karnataka and parts of Tamil Nadu and Andhra Pradesh.

The Hoysalas were great patrons of art and architecture. They built a number of temples in their 300-year rule. The Chennakeshava Temple is one of the finest examples of Hoysala architecture. The Hoysala temples are usually set on a platform in a typical star shaped plan. The temple is carved out of soap stone quarried from Tumkur. The stone is extremely easy to chisel but attains iron like firmness once it is exposed to the atmosphere. That explains the intricateness in the work.

The Chennakeshava Temple was built to commemorate the victory of King Vishnuvardhan over the Cholas. It is said that up until the 11th century the Hoysalas were followers of Jainism. It is in the 11th century they converted to Vaishnavism. According to a local lore, this temple was made to mark the conversion of King Vishnuvardhan from Jainism to Vaishnavism. Whatever the reason, the fact is that it took 103 years by 3 generations of the royal family to complete this marvel.

Each inch of this temple is intricately carved. The outer walls are carved with elephants, lions, female figures, larger figures from the Vishnu avatars, figures from the Hindu mythology, stories from Ramayana and Mahabharata, ornamental niches. At the bottom of the exterior walls is a row of 650 carved elephants going all around the periphery. The uniqueness of this is that each of these 650 elephants show a different mood. And even in the carvings above, no two sections or friezes are similar. On the outside, angled between the upper wall and the overhanging eaves are 38 free standing bracket figures. These figures are of voluptuous women known as Madanikas in ritual and dancing postures. Mind blowing is an understatement. To me the most beautiful figurine is that of Darpan Sundari. The entrance has the finely sculpted Makkara Toran and it depicts the 10 avatars of Vishnu. On both sides of the entrance is the royal Hoysala emblem - a tiger being killed by Sala. As a folklore goes, a young tribal Chieftain named Sala and his teacher, a Jain saint were in a temple in Angadi when a tiger attacked them. The teacher handed Sala an iron rod and said "Hoy Sala" which in Kannada translates to "strike Sala". Sala took the rod and killed the tiger in a single blow. In another interpretation, it represents the victory of King Vishnuvardhan over the Cholas as the tiger was the emblem of the Chola Dynasty.

Inside the temple there are 42 pillars, each carved differently. The ceiling is carved so amazingly intricately. I am sorry my limited vocabulary cannot put it any other way. The 4 central pillars are joined with the ceilings with bracketed figurines - Shuka Bhashini (a lady in conversation with her pet parrot), Queen Shantaladev, Gandharva dance and Mesh Shringara (a lady wringing her hair after a bath). The ceiling is mind-blowingly intricate. The central part is an inverted Linga and it has Narasimha carved on it. The entrance to the inner sanctum is flanked by Vishnu's dwarapalas - Jai and Vijay. Inside the sanctum is a 6 ft. statue of Vishnu in his Chatturbhuj or 4-armed mudra. Vishnu is flanked on either side by his consorts Bhudevi and Sridevi.

In a big glass box, there is a pair of slippers made from deer skin. It is said that these were Lord Vishnu's slippers. According to the folklore, Lord Vishnu came in Vishnuvardhan's dream and asked him to build a temple for him in Belur. It is believed that Chenna Keshava (Vishnu) walks frequently to the hills of Baba Budan to meet his consort who lives there. (I am assuming it was Chandagiri at that time because Baba Budan came only in the 1670s). This is why the cobblers offer footwear at the temple and these mysteriously vanish in the night. Apparently, every pair offered has vanished. Beliefs do make strange stories. Who knows what the truth is behind this.

Within the temple complex, there is a 42 ft. pillar called the deepastambh carved out of a single stone. It is also called the anti-gravity pillar. It is practically standing on its own weight on a raised platform. If one looks at the base only one side of the square base touches the ground the other three sides do not. There is a gap. Although one is not allowed to go upto the pillar, one can see that there is ample space for a paper or a muslin cloth to pass through. It is mind-blowing how the pillar is balancing on only one side. There are smaller temples also within the complex each one as exquisite.

Honestly while I was in school, History was not a subject that I enjoyed. In fact, I hated it. But now when I am visiting these places I wonder why. Maybe seeing is believing. The Hoysala art and architecture is of a level that words fall short describing. Basavaraj was right. Every stone tells a story, and here at Belur, each story etched in stone is more beautiful than the other.

Part 9: Halabeedu and Mysore

Halabeedu was the capital of the Hoysalas. It is about 17 kms from Belur. Belur, Halabeedu and Shravanabelagola make the Golden Triangle of Karnataka. We did not go to Shravanabelagola. There are always some regrets that happen when you travel ... this is one of them. A little bit of a push and we would witness another marvel - the 57ft statue of Bahubali. Well, no point fretting now - what is done is done.

While Belur temples were dedicated to Lord Vishnu, Halabeedu temples were dedicated to Lord Shiva. As you enter the temple complex there is Hoysalas emblem of Sala killing the tiger on one side and a Ganesha idol on the other. On either side just before you enter are 2 Nandi Mantapas. The monolithic Nandis are huge and beautifully carved out. One is in Black and one in white.

As you enter the door has the intricately carved Makara Toran on the top and the door is flanked by Dwarpalaks on either side. For the life of me, I cannot remember their names. The flip side of not writing on the go and then delaying writing for so long. Age catching up on the memory, I guess. Makara is a mystical animal composed of peacock, lion, pig, crocodile, and elephant. The sanctum has the statue of Shantaleshwara in the form of a shivalinga. The Navarang is intricately carved. Navranga is a unique element of the Hoysala architecture where a rectangular area is divided into nine rectangular blocks using a simple geometrical principal. The ceiling of the dancing area in the centre is intricately carved with the Ashta Dikpalas. Ashta means eight, Dik means quarters or directions and Palas mean the rulers. So Ashta Dikpalas are the rulers of the eight directions. Symbolically Ashta Dikpalas mean God is in all directions and whichever way you go you will ultimately find him. The Ashta Dikpalas according to Hinduism are:- Kuber (God of Fortune) -

North, Yama (God of Justice and Death) - South, Indra (God of Weather) - East, Varuna (God of the Seas) - West, Sadashiv (God of Birth, Death, Resurrection and time) - Northeast, Agni (God of Fire) - Southeast, Vayu (God of Wind) - Northwest, Nirriti (Demigod of Death, Sorrow, and Decay) - Southwest.

As in the Chenna Keshava Temple in Belur, the exterior is exquisitely carved. The lowest rung is elephants, the second is the mystical lion, the third rung is men and horses dressed in war attire, above that is a row of Makara, and above that, swans. And then there are sculptures of Ganesha, Vishnu Avtar, Shiva, Parvati, Lakshmi, Brahma, and Saraswati. Also, there are images from Ramayana, Mahabharata and Bhagavat Gita. The carvings were so intricate and detailed. The minutest of details have been carved with such great intricacy. Each stone was telling a story, and how I missed Basavaraj here. It would have been a very different experience with him explaining each frieze.

Once we were done with the Hoysaleshwara Temple, we drove up just around the bend to a Jain Temple. As I mentioned earlier, up until the 11th century, the Hoysalas followed Jainism and it is only during the 11th century that they converted to Vaishnavism. Vishnuvardhan was considered the greatest Hoysala ruler and he considered Jainism at par with Vaishnavism. His wife Shantala Devi remained a follower of Jainism.

Parshavnathanatha Basadi is a temple built in 1133 AD dedicated to Lord Parsavanath, the 23rd Jain Tirthankara. It was built during the rule of Vishnuvardhan. The interior is adorned with elaborate carvings and there are 12 pillars which finely polished to a mirror finish. The central ceiling is again exquisitely carved with minute detailing. The sanctum has an 18 ft. black granite stone image of Lord Parsavnath with a seven headed serpent above it. Shantinath Basadi is devoted to Lord Shantinathswami, the 16th

Jain Tirthankar. It was built in 1192 AD. This too has an 18 ft. statue of the deity. The Adinatha Basadi is one with fewer carvings. There is a sanctum sanctorum, a mandala hall, and a porch. There is an image of Adinath and Saraswati in the temple. There is an 18 ft. manastambh outside the temple.

While the Jain Basadis were nowhere close to the elaborate temples that we had seen, what really made them stand apart was the landscape. The clear blue sky dotted with clouds, the lush green surroundings, and red roofed houses in the back drop made a pretty picture. The cleanliness of the temples in this area was remarkable.

It was evening by the time we reached Mysore. The heat had kind of sapped us out so the plan was to freshen up, eat something and just chill. I was desperate to have a South Indian meal. No not the dosas and idlis. But the more elaborate stuff. Strangely I could not come up with one decent place which served it for dinner. During lunch, you can get any number of meals but not for dinner. Well, it was not meant to be so after roaming the streets for some time, we just headed back to the hotel and had dinner there. It was quite strange that in a place like Mysore, no good restaurants came up on the google search. Anyhow, the good part was that that evening it rained hard. It was much needed. The agenda in Mysore was very clear, the palace, the Brindavan Garden, and some shopping. And of course, how could I forget - Mysore Pak.

The Palace grounds are huge. It is bang in the middle of the city. They say it is one of the largest palaces in India also that it is one of the most visited monuments In India. On the outside it is quite an imposing building. I particularly loved the colour scheme. The domes, a dark rich maroon and gold, look totally amazing. The arched hallways inside are quite nice. The octagonal sloping-stained glass roof in the central hall with its chandelier is quite a sight. The floor tiling is beautiful. In fact, the central hall is quite a grand and opulent space. There are some gorgeous silver items on display. The painted ceilings are quite a pretty sight. But there was something missing.

I had heard a lot about the beauty of the Mysore Palace and no doubt it is pretty, but if I must be honest, I felt quite let down. Two years back I had been to the Scindia Palace and I was taken in by the opulence inside although the exterior was not that pretty. In January, we had gone to the Baroda Palace. Believe me in terms of grandeur and opulence no other palace that I have seen in India comes even close. And in that sense, all that I heard, read, and seen of the Mysore Palace just fell short by a big margin. I should not be comparing, but I cannot help it.

Another thing I noticed - and that I will say for even places like Belur and Halabeedu, the guides that are available are extremely impersonal and it is as if they must just rattle out what they know in precisely half an hour irrespective of whether you want to take in what you are seeing and spend a little bit more time or just want to know more. The guides in Belur and Halabeedu were a waste of time. The one at the Palace was more interested in taking in a group of people and I of course wanted a personal guide. When that did not happen, we just went around by ourselves. The guide scene here on onwards was quite dismal and disappointing.

After the Palace we headed straight for some saree shopping. The musical fountain show was to be in the evening so we decided to finish the shopping first. Mysore has a huge parking problem. We had to park our car at one place and took and auto-rickshaw back to where the saree shops were. We walked into a couple and I just did not get the vibe so we stepped out as soon. We went into a 3rd one and as we entered, the first thing I noticed a whole shelf of interesting antiques. There was something about this place that was hypnotic. Yes ... that is the word I would use. The salesman came, asked me what I wanted and led us to the basement. I was looking for something and he insisted on showing me something entirely different. Disappointed I got up in a huff and walked up the stairs. As we were about to leave the store, one gentleman walked up and asked us what we were looking for exactly. He seemed like a man of action and authority, and in the next 5 minutes we were settled in our chairs and he had taken out a whole load of stuff of the kind I was looking for. I ended up buying more than I had thought of. We got chatting and it turned out he was an ardent biker. It was quite an interesting chat talking about common places that we had visited, and the stories from our respective travels. He told us about his love for collecting antique collectibles. In all this banter, he treated us to some amazing filter coffee. And when I mentioned Mysore Pak, he quickly sent his guy to get us some. Believe me when I say it was the best Mysore Pak I have ever had. For me, the standard is Sri Krishna Sweets in Chennai. This was better than that. The thing is when we asked around earlier where we could get the best Mysore Pak in Mysore, only one name came up as a recommendation - Guru. When we were parking the car, we saw the shop and had decided would buy once we were done from here. Now when we had the Mysore pak at this shop we just assumed it was from Guru. Guru was just about 100 meters from the place. So, we had some here and did not bother to ask where it was from. On our way back I picked up more than what I was originally going to. I had loved it so much. You cannot imagine our disappointment. This one was horrible. The one we had at the store was from somewhere else. Maybe it was destiny's way of saving me from consuming all those calories.

Right after this we made a straight shoot to Brindavan Gardens. It was getting dark so we headed straight to the arena where the musical fountain show happens. I personally was here only for the fountain show. I had heard so much about it. There is an amphitheatre that slowly got packed to capacity and then some more. Sharp at 7 pm the music began playing, and the show started amidst a lot of cheering from the crowd. It started with a song from the south film industry, I couldn't identify with it because I had not heard it before and I did not understand the lyrics - for obvious reasons. The music and the fountain went in sync in some places others they were not. The next song was from Bollywood, one I had heard of but well, the syncing was still not happening. And the third song was Sare Jahan se Achha. And that was it. End of show. So much hype for a 15 minutes show. Pretty disappointing to say the least. And as we walked back to the parking, the lake was nicely lit, the reflection was looking nice, the weather was nice and breezy. We just took a stroll in the garden, which was clean and well lit. I am sure a drone view would have been quite nice.

At the end of the day, when I sat back in bed to mull over the day, honestly, I just felt very let down in Mysore. The hype created around it really did not live upto it. Maybe I did not go to the right places. Anyhow, the next day was a new destination, and I was looking forward to it.

Part 10: Madurai and Rameshwaram

Madurai. That was our next destination. And the drive was amazing. At Chamarajanagar one enters a Wildlife Sanctuary. Green and serene, no traffic - just meandering roads and great weather. As you enter Tamil Nadu and drive a bit you hit the Dhimbam Ghat. This is a 14 km stretch consisting of 27 hair pin bends. Frankly, I have not been on such close to each other sharp hairpin bends. I was secretly happy we were going downhill. Dense forest on the hill slope. When you look down the valley all you see is the treetops. I can only imagine the wildlife that must be living in these forests. And fun fact, this forest and this ghat was part of the Veerappan territory.

Here I would take a moment and write about something that left me totally impressed. We stopped at one of the small dhaba kind of places. Tamil Nadu has very different kind of highway eating joints. More on these later, but this was more like a café with sandwiches and shakes on the menu. I ordered a sandwich and while it was being prepared, *the Husband* stepped out for a call. He was going to sit in the car and take the call. Must have been just a minute when I heard a loud thud. Everyone rushed out and so did I. I rushed out because I thought *the Husband* must have started the car to switch on the AC and the car may have been in reverse, and the car hit something at the back. Of course, *the Husband* is a great driver, and more than that a very observant one. He would never be that careless, but it was a was a thought nonetheless. I stepped out and my heart skipped a million beats. It sank. There was a man lying right behind our car. I stepped a little further to figure out what happened. And I heaved a sigh of relief. What had happened was, a commercial-goods' auto guy came and hit the guy walking by. People collected around, so did the guy who hit him. The guy who was hit seemed okay; he was just in shock. The guy who hit him got a bottle of water from his auto gave it to the people around and drove off. The people picked him up and took him to the side. And we heard an ambulance coming. It came, it stopped, put this guy in and was off. And all of this did not take more that 5-7 minutes. No crowding around, no blame games, no bashing anyone, no videos, and selfies, nothing. The guy who was hit was okay, so all the other drama was unnecessary. What was important was to get him to the hospital to check if all was fine and that was it. The civilised handling of the accident and the speed at which the ambulance arrived impressed me.

Madurai was our first pitstop in Tamil Nadu. Interestingly, Tamil is known to be the oldest language in the world. The Pandiyan

Kingdom is said to be the oldest democratic kingdom in the world and Madurai is said to be the oldest living city in the world. Our stay in Madurai was 3 nights. The original plan was to stay in Madurai, do a day trip to Rameshwaram and then move to Thanjavur. While planning on the go, we decided having come so far, we may as well do Kanyakumari. So, Thanjavur was cut out and Kanyakumari was added to the itinerary. The day we reached Madurai, we went to the Meenakshi Temple.

Meenakshi Amman temple is one of the most important temples in India. It is a temple of great mythological importance. It is believed that Lord Shiva assumed the form of Sundereshwar (the handsome one) and married Meenakshi (Parvati) at the place where the temple is today. My newfound love for mythology led me to another story related to the Meenakshi Temple.

The royal couple King Maayadwaja Pandya and his wife Kanchanamalai were a childless couple. They performed a yajna and prayed to Lord Shiva for a son. What emerged from the fire was, to their dismay, a triple-breasted girl. Seeing them concerned over the girl's deformity, a divine voice told them not worry as the girl's 3rd breast would disappear once she meets her future husband. They parents named her Meenakshi and the King crowned her his successor. She ruled over the ancient city of Madurai. Legend has it that along with capturing the neighbouring kingdoms, she also captured Indralok. She was well on her way to capturing Kailash, Shiva's abode. When Shiva appeared before her, her 3rd breast vanished and she knew she had met her better half. Shiva and Meenakshi returned to Madurai where the wedding took place. It was Parvati who had taken the form of Meenakshi. Till this date the wedding of Shiva and Parvati is celebrated every year. The temple, they say was built by Kulashekharar Pandian on instructions given by Shiva in his dreams. It went through the process of rebuilding several times to come to what it is today as it was plundered multiple times by the Muslim invaders.

It was pouring like crazy that evening. We decided to take an auto since there was as usual an issue finding parking near the temple. The auto guy got us to the temple from another side, not the main entrance. We had no say in it, as we were both clueless. Also, unfortunately no cameras or phones were allowed so no photographs. None of the exterior too as it was raining. The temple was naturally mucky with all the rain muck coming in. As we entered, we saw a board showing us where to buy the Darshana tickets from. It mentioned Rs. 10 as normal and Rs. 50 as the VIP ticket. We took the VIP tickets to get into a shorter line. Even in that line it took us about 20 odd minutes to get to the sanctum. It also gave us time to take in the interiors of the temple. The temple is built over 14 acres and is enclosed in high walls which were built in response to the invasions. The two main shrines are dedicated to Sundereshwar and Meenakshi. There are other shrines that are dedicated to deities like Ganesha, Murugan, Lakshmi, Rukmini, and Saraswati. One thing very noticeable was that it was well aired inside. One was not feeling stuffy or suffocated. The prashad was a ladoo which was quite delicious.

Right in the middle is a pond called Ponthamarai Kulam which literally meaning a "pond with a golden lotus." Legend has it that Lord Shiva blessed the pond and no marine life ever grows in it.

It was pouring so bad that one could not see anything clearly. The gopurams, the pond, nothing. But the energy that one could feel inside the temple was another level. I always say this, I am agnostic, and am more inclined towards spirituality than religion. And that, I think, helps me take in the positive energies for what they are. Just pure positivity.

The next day we had planned a day trip to Rameshwaram. Rameshwaram is about 175 kms from Madurai. Remember I wrote about the highway dhabas in Tamil Nadu. These are basically Coffee-tea places which have a very limited menu. My favourite was the breakfast menu - chana daal vada and tea. All through our drive in Tamil Nadu whenever we had an early start to the day, we would carry hot water in our flask, pick up chana daal vadas at these joints and then make our own tea and that would be our breakfast. Delicious stuff. This day was no different. We picked up the vadas and made our tea and had our breakfast by the roadside. Things are always nice when they are kept simple.

Rameshwaram is a sacred town on the Pamban Island. It is believed to be the place from where Rama started his journey for getting back Sita from Ravana. The bridge to Lanka called the 'Ram Setu" was about 30 kms long and is believed to have been passable on foot till about the 15th century when it was destroyed in a storm.

Built in the 12th century, Ramanathswamy Temple is the southern most of the 12 Jyotirlingas. The temple has ornate corridors with huge sculpted pillars. The innermost sanctum has the main deity. The second corridor has 108 shivalingas and a statue of Ganesha. The 3rd corridor is the famous pillared corridor. It is beautifully painted in bright colours. They say it has 1212 pillars and it is the largest pillared corridor in the world. Now I did not know of this fact when I was at the temple. When I think back, I don't remember the corridor being long enough to have that many pillars but then, if they say so I am sure it is so. Here too there were long but well managed queues for the darshan. There is a separate queue where you officially pay Rs. 200 and cut across the line and get a quick darshan.

According to the legend, there is a story linked to Ramayana, while returning to Ayodhya after killing Ravana who was a devotee of Lord Shiva, Rama wanted to worship Lord Shiva to ask forgiveness as he had killed a brahmin during the war. For this, he asked hanuman to get the shivalinga from Mount Kailash. When Hanuman got delayed, Sita made a shivalinga using sand and Rama did the Pooja using it. This lingam is the Ramanathswamy Lingam or the Rama Lingam. When Hanuman returned with the shivalinga, he was very disappointed that Rama had not waited for him to return. To appease him, Rama instructed that the shivalinga be installed next to the one made of sand and called it the Vishwalingam. The devotees were instructed to pray to the Vishwalingam before the Ramalingam.

Language is a big barrier in the south. We did not speak Tamil or any of the south Indian languages and hence found it very difficult to ask for directions or guidance on what to see where. We did find a couple of people (claimed to be guides) that spoke broken English, but honestly, it felt as if they wanted a free ride in the car and make a quick buck. Somehow the vibe was not very comfortable so we just avoided asking them anything. We drove along and came to the road which took us to a small temple - Kothandaramar Temple. The drive was quite nice with the sea on both the sides. This was the place where Rama did the Pattabhishekam of Vibheeshan as the King of Lanka after Ravana's death.

Then we figured out that there was a temple about 3 kms from the Rameshwaram Temple, Rama Tirtham. This is a temple where Lord Rama's feet can be found on a chakra. Legend has it that Lord Rama rested here while on his search for Sita. Legend also has it that this is where Vibheeshana came and met Lord Rama and extended his support against Ravana. What is nice about the temple is the that because it is on a hillock, the view from the roof is amazing.

The whole trip to Rameshwaram was planned because I wanted to visit Dhanushkodi. In the last few years of my actively following travellers and their travel stories, I had seen a number of photographs of this long road with the Bay of Bengal on one side and the Arabian Sea on the other. Just a drive to the end point where there is a roundabout with the Ashoka Pillar. The arial pictures are amazing. Dhanushkodi was a small town on the south-eastern tip of Pamban Island. It was destroyed in the 1964 Rameshwaram cyclone and has been an abandoned town ever since. In fact, it is also referred to as a ghost town. This is the place where as per mythology, Lord Rama ordered Hanuman and his monkey army to build the Ram Setu across the Palk Strait to reach Sri Lanka. This point is also the closest point between Sri Lanka and India. Sri Lanka is only about 16 miles from here. One can find several guys there with telescopes who charge Rs. 10 per head, and while you look through the telescope, they describe the scene - meeting point of the Bay of Bengal and the Indian Ocean, the Ram Setu and beyond that Sri Lanka. A great business model I must say.

Finally, we were driving on that road. The sea barely metres away on both the sides. It was a very peaceful and scenic drive. As we came to the end of the road we were in for a rude shock. All the peace and quiet went flying into the sea. It was so crowded. People and vehicles all over. Minibuses being driven by manic drivers. The onus of saving yourself from the minibus hitting you was purely on you. It was craziness of another kind. We somehow managed the customary photo with the Ashoka pillar as the backdrop and got into our car and moved away from that point and headed back. We found a nice spot by the roadside and spent some time just taking in the sight. Looking into the horizon and seeing only the sea for as far as the eyes could see, the sun playing hide and seek with the clouds, listening to the sound of the waves coming in gently and hitting the rocky shore and the wind adding to the sound of the waves creating their own orchestra and the mind was silent, just taking it all in. Could it have been more peaceful? I don't think so. It is only at moments like these one understands the meaning of being "in the moment."

We had probably explored a fraction of what Rameshwaram had to offer but that is okay there is always a next time. I guess this happens when you do not research enough and I feel here I did not. I got to know later there was the Panchmukhi Hanuman Temple which has a statue of Hanuman with five faces. In all the language issues, we could make out something about the floating stones being somewhere, but could not figure out where. And I am still confused where one can go to the Ramsetu. Because the Ramsetu is said to be at Dhanushkodi and well you can't go beyond a point there. There are also some sacred wells too which we asked around but got no useful answer. Anyhow like I said there is always a next time.

As you head back onto the Pamban bridge there is a point where you will find a lot of cars parked and people on the road. Well, that is the point where you get the best view of the Pamban Railway bridge. The railway sea link was built way back in 1914. It was destroyed in the cyclone of 1964 after which it was reconstructed. It was said to be the longest sea bridge (2050 meters) in India up until 2010 when the Worli Sea Link was opened. It is India's first vertical lift bridge where a 63 meters stretch goes up vertically to allow the ships to pass through. Fascinating, isn't it? There is a train that passes on the bridge between 3 and 4 in the afternoon and that is I believe a sight to see.

Part 11: Kanyakumari

The original plan which we made on the go was to head to Thanjavur from Madurai after we had done Rameshwaram. But by now, in all honesty, both *the Husband* and I had had enough of temples. And well, coming this far and not visiting Kanyakumari just seemed like a thing "not done". I had always planned on doing Kanyakumari when I did Kerela. But Kerala continues to elude me. So anyhow, Kanyakumari is where we headed out. Upto a point the route is the same as we took the day before for Rameshwaram. This meant the same coffee place was enroute. We had a hearty breakfast of the delicious chana daal vada and chai. While we were having our breakfast, I saw 5-6 women dressed identically. The same saree, the same orange flowers in the hair. This I had noticed a lot of times during this trip. Curiosity got the better of me and I went up to one of the ladies and asked her why. Well apparently, when they go to their family temple for some pooja, all the sisters wear identical clothes and all the brothers wear identical clothes. How nice was that! I think it just adds to the festive fervour. They were genuinely wearing very pretty sarees and were happy to get complimented. All the sisters came together and so did the brothers. They were quite amused to hear that we had been travelling by road all the way from Delhi. We chatted for a while and then parted ways.

Kanyakumari is about 240 kms from Madurai. Great roads lined with thousands of windmills. The landscape is so amazing. Windmills fascinate me. And I felt like a kid in a toy store. There were tall windmills, short windmills, windmills with solid pillars, windmills with metal pillars, a cluster of windmills all in one direction with one lone windmill in the opposite direction. And the sound of the windmills cutting through the wind was percussion to the ears.

Our first stop was the Vivekananda Rock. Built in 1970, the Vivekananda Rock is located about 500 meters off the mainland. It was a memorial built for Swami Vivekananda. The way to reach it is via boat ferry. Tickets as usual are of 2 types. The normal and the VIP. The VIP ticket of INR 200 (the normal being INR 50) lets you bypass the long queue which can be a wait for as long as a couple of hours.

There was a time, eons ago, when India, South America, Australia, Madagascar, and Antarctica were one supercontinent called Gondwana Land. It was one big Charnockite rock island. 600 million years ago this land started fragmenting into different landmasses and slowly over time, the subcontinent split. Around 160 million years ago, India, Sri Lanka, Madagascar, Australia, and East Antarctica broke away from the rock island under the memorial. Pranay Lal in his book, Indica: A deep Natural History of the Indian Subcontinent writes - "Between 180 to 118 million years ago, when India separated from Antarctica, it left behind this islet, a desolate witness to the merging and breaking of Gondwana landmasses. Geologists call the Vivekananda Memorial 'the Gondwana Junction' because it marks a place where India, Madagascar, Sri Lanka, East Antarctica, and Australia were once joined together."

One part of the Memorial is the Vivekananda Mandapam and the other is the Shripada Mandapam. According to the folklore, Goddess Parvati in one of her incarnations as Kanya did tapasya at this spot to obtain the hand of Lord Shiva. There is a natural projection in the form of a human foot which they say is Goddess Parvati's foot. Around this the Sripada Mandapam is built. In the Vivekananda Mandapam, there is the Sabha Mandala which has a statue of Swami Vivekananda and adjacent to that are the Dhyana mandapa which is a set of meditation rooms. There is also a sunrise calendar etched on the rock floor behind the Vivekananda Mandapa. In the middle courtyard there is a compass etched that shows the direction of the Triveni Sangam where the Arabian Sea, Bay of Bengal, and the Indian Ocean meet. On another island rock is the Thiruvalluvar Statue. This is a 41 meters high statue of the Tamil poet and philosopher Valluvar, who authored Tirukkural an ancient Tamil book on Dharma and Morality. The access to this statue is also via ferry, but because there was construction work happening, we could not go there.

Kanyakumari is also one of the 2 or 3 points in the world from where you can see the sunset and sunrise from the same point. Unfortunately for us, we could not witness either. We were headed back to Madurai the same day. One thing that I noticed while we spent some time at the Triveni sangam is that it was very peaceful. It was crowded but still one felt so at peace. There was no fishy smell which usually one gets on seashores, the air did not feel salty, it in fact, felt very fresh. The sound of the waves seemed to shut off the noise of the crowds and in that moment, it was a feeling of being one with nature. Absolute peace!

We headed back to Madurai happy that we altered our plan and included Kanyakumari in it. Yes, there were things we missed doing, but I do say there is always another time. Will club it with Kerela when I do it as was the original plan always. We reached Madurai by about 4 pm and had time enough to visit the Nayakkar Palace. Located around 2 kms from the Meenakshi Temple, the Thirumalai Nayak Palace was built in 1636 by King Tirumala Nayak. He ruled The Nayaka Dynasty in Madurai from 1623 to 1659.

By the time we reached the palace, it was 4.30 and I was told that I had only half an hour to quickly go around and come out. And really .... I was shunted out at 5 pm. But in that half an hour I did manage to go through the palace. It was very different from the other palaces that I had seen. The palace is a classic fusion of Dravidian and Rajput styles. They say the original palace was about four times bigger than the present structure and, in its time, it was considered to be one of the wonders of South India. As you enter the premises, you walk into a huge courtyard with arched corridors surrounding it. These arches are carved and painted. Some of the roof sections are also painted. These are more present-day paintings. There is one big room which is converted into a museum. Honestly speaking, I wasn't very impressed by the palace or the museum. And the fact that they rudely shunted me out kind of just added to it. The courtyard is where they have a light and sound show every day. We did not see it since we were exhausted from the day trip. The palace really did not make sense in its present-day structure. But if they say it was much bigger in its times then this probably is the left-over structure.

On our way back to the hotel, we drove through the market. Everywhere we saw shops selling something called Jigar-thanda. Naturally I had to figure it out. Jigar-thanda is a milk-based drink quite like rabri-falooda made from milk and almonds. It contains what is called Gond Katira - a natural gum obtained from the dried sap of the almond tree. It is said to have a lot of health benefits. Served chilled, it is a delicious drink, actually more like an ice cream shake of sorts.

With Madurai, we were ideally at the end of the planned "sight-seeing." After this we were headed to Bangalore, Manipal and Bhopal which was purely for chilling and relaxing with friends. Except for Manipal which was basically to explore the city for our son who was joining the culinary school in MAHE.

Part 12: Bangalore, Manipal and Bhopal - The ride back home

We visited Bangalore after some 19 years. We had lived there for a couple years. The Bangalore of that time was so much saner than the Bangalore of today. Well to be honest the traffic was bad then too but My God!! It is a different level of crazy now. The one thing that has not changed over the years is the Bangalore weather. Amazing as ever. If I ever go back to that city to live, it will be only for its weather.

Bangalore to Manipal is quite a beautiful drive through tropical Karnataka. It is a drive through dense coconut forests. Amazing is an understatement. On this very route somewhere in the Shivamogga district the River Tunga meets River Bhadra and becomes Tungabhadra. There is also a dam on this river by the name. About 50 kms short of Manipal is a set of 14 hairpin bends called the Agumbe Ghat. Agumbe is a small village in the Shivamogga District. It is called the Cherrapunji of the South. In fact, it is also called the Cobra Capital of India because of the number of cobras that can be found here. It is registered as a World UNESCO site for its rich biodiversity. The drive through this ghat in the monsoons is a treat in itself. There are some turns where the clouds come down to the level of the road and it is like a scene straight out of a horror movie. There is a sun set point at the top from where, they say, on a clear day you can see the sun setting across the Arabian Sea. But of course, it was cloudy like crazy when we there. There was beauty in that as well. The clouds floating down till the pit of the valley, the trees peeking out of the clouds, roads wet from the mist, moss covered hill sides – Serene and beautiful. Somewhere along the way we stopped at an unused bus stop kiosk and made tea for ourselves. I finally used the butane stove that I had bought years back for my travels which I had used only once thus far. It is a very different feeling to be on the roads in a densely forested landscape and have no other vehicle or soul in sight. But after a while of driving through these roads there came a time when all this green-ness, the forest surroundings, the peace and quiet of the place started to get to us. There was a kind of claustrophobia that was beginning to set in. I just wanted to get back to a concrete landscape.

Manipal is a world in its own right. It is an education city offering some 100 plus courses in the field of engineering, medical and hospitality and may be some more that I do not know of. An extremely self-sufficient city in terms of anything and everything a college student would need, ample recreational stuff for the kids too. Between Udupi and Mangalore there are several very well maintained beaches and also a couple of hanging bridges. We did not visit any because we had only enough time to take a round of the hospitality school. I am sure in the coming three years one will get the opportunity to explore more of the city.

We covered Manipal to Bhopal in two days with a transit stop at Pune. The route from Pune to Bhopal took us through the grape belt of Nasik. Sula is a vineyard they say is worth the visit. Unfortunately, we did not have the luxury of time. But we did stopover in Dindori to pick up a few bottles of the wines from that region. There was miles and miles and acres and acres of grape plantations.

Bhopal has always had a special place in my heart. A city where I made the most beautiful memories and a city that also gave me some ugly, life changing memories. An extremely laid-back city, no one is ever in any hurry and has people with so much warmth in their hearts. And this I am seeing ever since I was a kid. Nothing has changed. Bhopal for me has always been about my childhood. My core friends are still my friends from the 4 years I spent in school. I did not pass out of that school (been through six schools through my school days) but I consider the one in Bhopal as my Alma Mater.

We did Bhopal to Gurgaon in a single day but made two pit stops enroute. One was Narsinghgarh. About a 100 kms from Bhopal, in District Narsinghgarh is a quaint little temple - Shyamji Santa Temple. This temple was built in the memory of King Sangram Singh (Shyam Singh) by his wife, Bhagyawati in the 16th-17th century. Dedicated to Lord Krishna, the temple has some amazing carvings. Truly a gem of a place. I never expected the temple to be so beautiful. It was quaint, clean, and beautiful.

The next stop for us was Shivpuri. Shivpuri is famous for the Scindia cenotaphs or the Scindia Chhatris. As a kid on one of the school trips we had visited the place and for some strange reason I always wanted to go back there. In 2019 when we holidayed in Gwalior, we never ended up going there. This time around I was sure I would visit the place.

The two Scindia Chhatris are set in what would once have been an elaborate Mughal Garden with fountains, and bridges over the water canals. While the chhatris are clean and well maintained, the surroundings unfortunately, are in a state of neglect. On the outer periphery, there are benches to sit on with backs that have fine filigree work. On what seems like one of the entrance doors there is a huge Cooke and Kelvey clock that dates back to 1921. The older Chhatri was made in the memory of Madhavrao Scindia's mother Maharani Sakhya Raje Scindia. And the newer one is in the memory of Madhav Rao Scindia. Both the chhatris are a spectacular fusion of Hindu and Islamic architectural styles. I can only imagine how amazing this whole area would look had the gardens been well maintained. Inside the chhatris is amazing inlay work on marble and stunning filgri work on the windows. There are beautiful carvings on the inside walls. Antique fans and lights hang from the roof. One of the more beautiful cenotaphs that I have seen in my travels, then again, these cenotaphs are still visited on occasions of by the Scindia family so there is a different vibe here. Yes, I think it was totally worth the visit. When we visited Gwalior in 2019, I realised the Scindia family was a lot about tasteful opulence and the same sense of understated elegance can be felt and seen in these cenotaphs too.

We reached home that night tired and exhausted but at the same time there was a strange sense of achievement too. It is not easy to spend almost 13-14 hours a day couped in an enclosed space with the same person day after day. We did that for 28 days. There came a time that we did not want to even listen to music because how much can you listen to the same playlists repeatedly. How much can the same two people talk. We laughed, we fought, we sat in silence, but we loved each moment of the 28 days. There was a lot we experienced enroute, there was a lot we missed out on but that is okay. It indeed turned out to be the most memorable trip I have ever done. This one month off was indeed the best, the most precious and the most meaningful gift the kids could have given us.

Echos and Reflections

Reflecting on my travels, I am reminded that India is both vast and deeply interconnected. I've savoured foods I couldn't pronounce the names of, navigated conversations in unfamiliar languages, and been touched by the kindness of strangers. Every city, town, and village I drove through, offered unique lessons and surprises, enriching my appreciation for the incredible diversity that defines India. These experiences have broadened my perspective - challenging my preconceived notions and fostereing a profound respect for cultures different from my own.

Each mile traveled was a step towards humility and patience, teaching me to embrace the unknown with grace. Through these journeys, I discovered that the road, with all its twists and turns, is not just a path to new destinations, but a journey within, where true healing and growth occur. I have learnt to find beauty in simplicity, strength in adversity, and joy in the small moments that are often overlooked. The kindness of strangers, shared meals, and quiet sunsets taught me that the essence of travel lies in the connections we make and the stories we share. The experiences I had and the people I met didn't just help heal my depression; they revitalized my spirit and deepened my connection to the world around me.

As I move forward, I carry with me the lessons of the road, ready for the next adventure and forever transformed by the magic of travel. The road has been both my teacher and healer, reminding me that life's greatest treasures are often found off the beaten path. This memoir is not just a collection of travel stories but a proof of how resilient the human spirit is and how transformative exploring the world with an open heart and mind can be.

I hope you all enjoyed reading my travel stories as much as I enjoyed living them.

Adios, until the next trip.

www.ingramcontent.com/pod-product-compliance
Lightning Source LLC
LaVergne TN
LVHW041916070526
838199LV00051BA/2631